Asbestos and Cape

A Tale of Three Stakeholders

Peter Gartside

First Published December 2023
J P Gartside M.A.(Cantab.)

Printed in Great Britain by Kingfisher Press,
Bury St Edmonds, Suffolk, England
A Carbon Balanced Printer

Cover Design: Arthur Foulser
Cover Poster by permission British Safety Council.
www.britsafe.org

To my wife, Gillie

In gratitude, reflecting the many absences working for Cape,
and who, when asked, said 'he travels in lagging'

Contents

Preface

I found that nobody wanted me to write this book. Asbestos was a killer and Cape Asbestos was an accomplice. But this made me more determined, as there is a tale to be told, and one which thrust the interest of shareholders, employees and industrial disease claimants into conflict for four decades, and occasioned trade-offs which placed great demands on management.

For most of the period covered by the book, asbestos was history. During these years, Cape people pioneered asbestos-free products and established a world class industrial services business. Through their efforts it was possible for the company to set aside profits approaching £300 million to compensate those who suffered and continue to suffer from asbestos related disease. It is to those Cape people that this book is dedicated.

A disadvantage in not receiving support for the book is that I am denied copyright for some of the illustrations I planned to include. An advantage is that I am not beholden to any influences other than my own modest attempt at an objective interpretation of events.

Peter Gartside
December 2023

TIME LINE

External		Cape
	1953	UK First - *Rocksil* Mineral Wool Insulation
Doll Report Links Cancer and Asbestos	1955	
Pneumoconiosis Act South Africa	1956	
TICA formed	1957	Asbestos Research Council Founder
Pneumoconiosis Conference Jo'burg	1959	Anglo American Seize Control of Shareholder CMIC
Evidence Covering Mesothelioma	1960	Acquires Small & Parkes (Automotive)
	1961	Asbestos Imports UK Peak
	1964	Production of Caposite Asbestos Insulation Ceases
Decision to Revise Regulations	1965	Representative joins Govt. Advisory Panel
	1966	Acquires UAC (Asbestos Cement)
Crocidolite linked to mesothelioma	1967	Asbestos Information Committee set up
First UK Personal Injury Claim		Disposal of Barking Site
Asbestos Industry Regulations	1969	Charter Consolidated Acquires Majority Shareholding
TDN13		Closes Acre Mill, Hebden Bridge.
UK Import of Blue Asbestos Ceases	1970	Forms Cape Contracts
The Dust at Acre Mill, Granada TV	1971	Asbestos free Supalux & Monolux Patents Filed
	1972	First IDC Provisions Declared
UK Health & Safety at Work Act	1974	USA Litigation.
Acre Mill 'Killer Dust'. BBC Horizon	1975	Acquires Newalls Insulation Contracting
Asbestos Production Peaks in S Africa	1976	Establishes Middle East & UK Offshore Presence
World Production of Asbestos peaks	1977	Establishes Contracting Presence Mainland Europe
Advisory Committee on Asbestos	1978	Asbestolux/Marinite Replaced by Superlux etc.
Simpson Report	1979	Cape sells Mines. Cape Scaffolding formed
Recession. Insulation Market collapses	1981	Acquires Cape Durasteel
Alice - 'A Fight for Life'	1982	Commences Industrial Painting
	1984	Disposal of Insulation Division. Leave S Africa
Use of Crocidolite and Amosite Banned	1985	Disposal of Automotive Asbestos Interests
	1986	Re-financing. First LNG Services Contract Australia
USA Litigation fails in UK Courts	1988	Introduce Unicem Asbestos free Cladding
UK Recession	1991	Exits Asbestos Cement. Cape East Singapore Set Up
	1992	First LNG Contracts in Qatar
Charter Disposes of Cape Shareholding	1994	Rutland Trust Invest
	1996	Attempted Flotation of Cape Industrial Services
	1997	South African Litigation Commences
FM/Turner & Newall File for Chapter 11	2001	Montpellier Invest
Gencor Engaged in S.African Litigation	2002	Sale of Cape Calsil. South African Settlement
Rutland and Montpellier Sell Out	2004	Fund Raising & Scheme of Arrangement
	2006	Fund Raising & Australian Acquisitions
	2009	Scheme Review & IDC Provisions Raised
	2010	David Chandler & EL/PL Insurance Litigation
	2016	Scheme Review & IDC Provisions Raised
	2017	Cape Acquired by Altrad

Introduction

'The fellowship of victims gave way to the fellowship of actuaries, lawyers and accountants.'

This book could be looked upon as a sequel to the publication *'Cape Asbestos 1893-1953'*. Whilst it does give an account of the ensuing years, it is neither a company sponsored project nor an attempt to present a self-congratulatory picture of events. The earlier publication does give us an idea of how Cape struggled to emerge as a pioneer in the mining and processing of asbestos, and thereby provides a backdrop to what was to come. Nor is the book an attempt to display any expertise relating to asbestos and its debilitating effects, which has been the subject of a great deal of scholarly research. Hopefully, in being written by someone from within the industry, it does add something to the narrative.

It is perhaps a paradox that a common theme throughout the story of Cape has been the issue of safety, given that it has been associated with an industrial disease that has caused so much suffering. From a period when the mining and processing of asbestos was considered fundamental to safety from fire, Cape re-emerged as a business focused on key elements of safety in the construction industry.

Cape survived; most of its competitors didn't. This book seeks to provide some of the answers as to why - some to its credit, others not so. It exposes some significant management failures, but it also shows the pressures on management in having to deal with the competing interests of three stakeholders – shareholders, employees and claimants.

Once it was perceived to be free of its past, in 2017, the Company lost its independence, and this marks the end of the book. An essential purpose in writing it is to draw attention to the obligation imposed on Cape's successors to satisfy the demands of future industrial disease claimants.

Chapter 1

Entering the Second Sixty Years

'It is our hope that we may remain, like our product, unquenchable.'

Thus, Giles Newton, Managing Director of Cape Asbestos, finished his foreword to *'Cape Asbestos 1893-1953'*[1]. He obviously chose the word 'unquenchable' carefully. It refers to the ability of asbestos to extinguish or quench a fire and derives from the Greek αμίαντο. The publication concludes with the statement: 'During the past sixty years of its existence the Cape Asbestos Company has been successfully engaged in (*these battles*) and will continue the fight with the certain knowledge that the mines and the manufactured products from the factories are indispensable to modern industry.'

The products referred to relied on the mining of the mineral labelled 'blue' or 'brown' asbestos in South Africa, and it's processing into fire protection and thermal insulation products in the UK, Europe and the USA. In 1952 the financials were good, and shareholders were gratified to receive a hike in the dividend, reflecting record trading profits of £1.4 million. The Company's capital base had increased form £589,000 in 1938 to just short of £5 million in 1952, and as a publicly traded company it figured on the UK Stock Market. In 1949 it had abandoned its gloomy offices at Morley House in Holborn for a bright new London Head Office at 114-116 Park Street, in fashionable Mayfair, and as staff numbers approached one hundred, in 1953 acquired No.112 next door. As the company celebrated its diamond jubilee in 1953, a self-congratulatory mood was clearly evident. In this chapter we will seek to understand the factors underpinning this apparent pride in its product and status.

Firstly, the mineral itself, labelled the 'Magic Mineral.' The Greek and Italian names place it on a romantic pedestal of indestructability, purity, and incorruptibility - 'Amianto' (Italian). The French 'Asbeste' and English 'Asbestos' define its fire-fighting properties; the Germans straight-forwardly give it a name that enables us to visualise it – 'Steinflachs' which means 'stone-flax.' It occurred in ironstone deposits and comprised needle-like silken fibres which had to be prised out of the base rock – a process often conducted using hand tools. By 1953, it had transitioned to a process involving crushing and milling equipment.

It was its heat and fire-resistant qualities which defined earlier uses. Insulation was less critical when coal was cheap, so its main application was personnel protection and resistance to fire, a quality that proved difficult to replicate when it was eventually phased out. Ironically, as it transpired, 'safety' was a key attribute ascribed to the product. Fire had been a major hazard in buildings and ships from the beginning of the industrial revolution, and it was only as the 20th century progressed that fire deaths started to come down. In the USA alone fire deaths per 100,000 population more than halved during the peak period of asbestos use.[2]

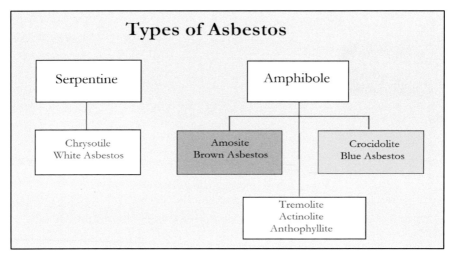

Cape's interest was in amphibole asbestos, the major deposits of which were to be found in South Africa, and it was here that Cape carried out the mining of crocidolite (blue) and amosite (brown) asbestos. The most productive source of blue asbestos was in the north of Cape Province where mining developed alongside the exploitation of De Beers' diamond deposits, in Griqualand West. As the political and economic hub of the region, Kimberley was the administrative centre for Cape Blue Mines Pty. Ltd. The mining of brown asbestos had been a later development and was carried out north-east of Johannesburg in the Transvaal and Limpopo Province. Johannesburg was the centre for the gold industry and for Cape's businesses - Egnep Pty. Ltd. (one of the mines – Penge - spelt backwards) and Amosa Pty. Ltd. ('Asbestos Mines of South Africa'). Of the other types of amphibole asbestos, deposits were rare in South Africa and not within Cape's portfolio. Anthophyllite and tremolite became associated with the cosmetics industry and the production of talcum powder. Competing geographical sources of asbestos fibre in Canada, Russia and Rhodesia supplied the Serpentine or Chrysotile type, which was a softer material, produced in far greater volumes and more widely used.

It is important to place Cape's role in the context of world supply – in 1950, Southern Africa, although the third largest source, produced around 13% of total world supply[3] and Cape's share of supply, at its peak, was no more than 30%. In a global sense it was in fact a minor player. Cape's significance was due to its

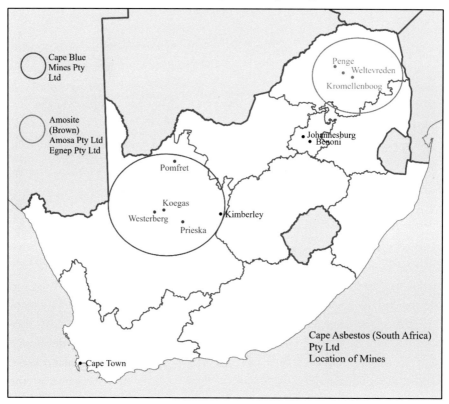

market leading position in the production of the amphibole type of asbestos (crocidolite - blue – and amosite - brown), which was harder and displayed a range of longer fibres. Although more difficult to mine, and the hardness of the material made for difficulties in the crushing and milling process, it offered exceptional qualities of strength and versatility. These qualities made crocidolite, or blue, particularly attractive in the defence industries, where its many applications as an insulation and fire protective packing, made for lucrative trading conditions during both world wars.

The mining of asbestos fibre had been fairly rudimentary until the fifties. Cape had only introduced tungsten carbide drills after the war when a new Mining Manager – Douglas Todd - had improved both output and productivity[4]. By 1953 Cape was remarking, in company reports, on the extent of improvements achieved in the quality and process efficiencies at its mines. The period up to the 1950's had also seen the mines moving on from 'tributor' mining to direct control of the mining process itself. Tributor was the name given to artisan miners from whom Cape could procure feedstock for its mills. The number of mining sites was reduced, access improved, and crushing and milling equipment updated. More than £1 million had been invested in the mines between 1949 and 1952. Whilst figures were not broken out in annual company accounts, it was apparent that the greater proportion of the company's profits was derived from its mines. Their output satisfied the demands of Cape's own processing facilities in the UK and Italy, and agents and outlets in Europe and the USA. The number of employees in the mines was approaching five thousand, although given the nature of the activity, it is doubtful if accurate records were maintained.

Whilst Cape had a highly marketable product, the country of its source played a significant part in its commercial viability and success. Societal conditions in South Africa provided a cheap source of labour and political conditions were supportive of mining activity. As the need for manpower rose, the industry attracted migrant labour. The National Party had come to power in 1948, and with it came the beginnings of apartheid, for which the critical mining industry provided, in some respects, the model. The origin of the discriminatory Pass Laws can be traced to the mining industry, given its dependence on forced oscillating migrant labour. Real wages had not risen in the gold mines for black workers for two generations[5]. White workers were highly privileged, having their own unions, black workers having no right to collective bargaining or union representation. There was a strict segregation of black, mixed race (labelled 'coloured,' many of whom in the Northern Cape were Griquas - mixed white and the non-Bantu indigenous people of the Western Cape), and white workers.

Women and children were widely employed[6]. Migrant workers were beginning to be housed in compounds where control could be better exercised, but their low wages and absence could leave their home territories impoverished. The main driver behind this working structure was the gold and diamond mining industry, and latterly coal. Asbestos mining was a minor activity, but being under the same industry umbrella, had been subject to the same societal factors since its foundation. Without the infrastructure provided in support of diamond and gold extraction, asbestos mining in South Africa might not have taken place. Where it was at a disadvantage was the bulk and weight of the product, which made it particularly dependent on rail access.

Applications

The company had taken full advantage of the opportunity to widen the applications for asbestos and its added value products. The versatility of asbestos is evidenced by the range of applications involving its use – it was claimed it found its way into 18,000 different products[2]. It could be woven into fabrics for protective clothing, safety curtains, paper, and millboard; it was used in gas masks, in firemen's hoses, incorporated into an entire range of building products and in motor vehicle brake and clutch linings. It was widely used in the process industries, given its fire protective and insulation properties. It was endemic in specifications, or prescribed by means of performance parameters not achievable by alternative products, throughout industry and government. Nowhere more than in shipbuilding, where its various applications directed towards fire prevention caused governments to stockpile it during and after the world wars.

The post war period in the UK was one of infrastructure and housing development; in parallel the power generation industry was expanding its steam generating capacity throughout the country. Techniques had developed where asbestos reinforced coatings could be sprayed, commonly used on turbine casings and congested areas of a building. Cape was harnessing many of these applications and, by 1953, and in addition to its range of thermal insulation mattresses and pipe coverings ('Caposite'), manufactured at Barking, Essex, it had a joint venture with the Johns-Manville Corporation of the USA manufacturing a high density insulation board for marine applications ('Marinite') at Germiston in Scotland. At Barking, in 1951, it had commenced manufacture of a new patented building board called 'Asbestolux'; this replaced 'Plutoboard', a fire-resistant board widely used in shipbuilding. Full scale production was subsequently located at Cape's Uxbridge Flint Brick Company and nearby Harefield Lime Company, where a type of white glazed brick for lightwells was produced, the demand for which was in long term decline. In addition, it produced brake and clutch linings ('Capasco'), having acquired the Weaver Manufacturing and Engineering Company in 1939. Cape had pioneered the development of heavy-duty moulded brake liners and clutch friction facings, the main outlet for which was public service and commercial vehicles; it was an original equipment supplier for Scammell. It had a range of textiles, produced at the company's Acre Mill site at Hebden Bridge, Yorkshire, also at Barking. Both sites enjoyed good employee relations - even when faced with the full force of adverse media attention over its activities at Hebden Bridge in later years, it was acknowledged that 'Cape was popular because it paid and treated its employees well, organising parties and outings for families'[7]. This was hardly a tenable trade-off against the outcomes of working conditions later revealed.

The marketing of the output of its mines had received a fillip during the second world war, no more so than in the USA. Both crocidolite (blue) and amosite (brown) fibre had been adopted by the American Navy and processing was undertaken by a number of Stateside factories set up by Union Insulation and Johns-Manville Corporation. No other material could meet the US Navy specifications for lighter weight, fire resistance and insulation value. Glass fibre, which was heavier in weight, was not as dependable at elevated temperatures, particularly in the presence of acid. So the USA was an important market for Cape fibre, and the Company had set up a subsidiary, North American Asbestos Corporation (NAAC), to service the US government and manufacturers. Cape also manufactured plastic based asbestos textiles in Canada under the name of Noramite.

These products offered exceptional fire protection properties and there were few alternatives. Emerging from the old slag wools, mineral wools based on silica (glass fibre) or molten rock (rock fibre), were only just being produced in commercial quantities. Asbestos based insulation products held sway for 'hot' insulation applications and cork for 'cold.' However, Cape's Directors were smart enough to recognise the market potential for mineral wools, and in 1953 the company commenced manufacture of rock fibre insulation at a new facility at Sterling, Scotland, the first plant of its type in the UK. The location reflected the source of raw material and took advantage of grants, but it had the disadvantage of high transport costs to market and distance from the Company's core of insulation expertise at Barking. It relied on a licence from Grunzweig & Hartmann (G&H) of Germany, at the time an important export client for Cape's Asbestolux. Marketing of the product, branded 'Rocksil,' was undertaken by distributor William Kenyon & Sons. The production technology involved represented a major step forward when compared with the messy process of producing Caposite, which was labour intensive and required dust suppression. It is doubtful that Cape, at this time, would have been thinking beyond asbestos and the establishment of the Rocksil business appeared fairly low profile in company publications. This may be due to the fact that there were initial teething problems, but also perhaps due to the Directors being clear in their mind as to where the profits were made. Competing with glass fibre, Rocksil used dolomite rock and fireclay in place of the sand/lime and soda for glass, which made for a limiting temperature of 1400 deg.F against 900 deg.F for glass. This was an important advantage in the industrial sector (power plants, oil, and petrochemical installations) where Cape largely operated. However, it was more expensive to produce than glass fibre. Both rock and glass fibre were considered inferior in performance to asbestos based alternatives when it came to surface spread of flame, so to a degree Caposite and Rocksil were complimentary.

This was a far-seeing move for Cape, and one of the first initiatives amongst asbestos based companies to move away from asbestos containing insulation. At the opening of the factory Sir Alec Douglas Home declared it 'a great and new asset to the country and to the Highlands'[8].

Competitors

In terms of UK competitors, the only fully integrated company engaged in mining, production and distribution of any size was Turner & Newall (T&N), a public company and overall UK market leader with over 60% of the UK trade in asbestos products[9]. T&N had acquired a number of competitors such as Bells and United Asbestos. The company did not have the same commitment to the mining of blue and brown asbestos as Cape, sourcing chrysotile from its mines in Canada and Rhodesia to support its historical presence in asbestos cement products for cladding and piping. It was also a market leader in brake linings

('Ferodo'), which also relied on chrysotile fibre. T&N was particularly identified with the development of sprayed asbestos for fire protection and insulation ('Limpet'), and this had a wide application for turbines and complex configurations within ships and buildings. For this application it purchased Cape crocidolite, given the length of the fibres and light weight. Both Cape and T&N were occasionally pressurised by key clients into providing installation services where the application was complex, but their clear preference was to supply their products to independent installation contractors.

Internationally there were similar vertically integrated asbestos companies like Eternit (Latin derivation 'eternal'), operating out of Belgium, owned by the Emsens family, and in Switzerland, by the Schmidheiny family. In the USA Johns-Manville Corporation and Union Asbestos and Rubber Company (Unarco) bought fibre from Cape as did James Hardie in Australia. Hardie controlled over 70% of the building market in Australia and New Zealand, its Fibrolite board being used widely in housing construction. After the war it could not produce enough to satisfy the market, the main constraint being a shortage of fibre. Whilst there was a low volume Australian mine run by competitor CSR – Australian Blue Asbestos, located at Wittenoom, WA - it was shunned by Hardie in favour of cheaper imports, reflecting the labour cost differential. Cape proved to be the best source and by the mid-fifties Cape was supplying one third of total asbestos fibre imports into Australia. Hardie's dependence on Cape was reflected in their first purchase of Cape shares in 1948 'as a gesture of goodwill'[10]. They continued to build up a holding in the fifties together with purchases by the Reid family who ran James Hardie. By the end of the decade this was approaching 5% of the equity of Cape Asbestos.

In Japan Nippon Asbestos (later Nichias Corporation) and Asahi Asbestos (later A&A Corporation) dominated the Far East market, purchasing fibre in the open market. Their chrysotile was largely sourced from China but for amphibole they looked to Cape. Cape established a close working relationship with Nippon Asbestos, involving the marketing and manufacture of marine board under licence in Japan.

As a miner in South Africa, Cape's main competitor for crocidolite and amosite asbestos was Gefco (The Griqualand Exploration and Finance Company, formerly the South Africa Saltpetre Company). Gefco, like Cape was a long-established London-based Company with offices in the City near the old Cape Head Office. It had its own UK marketing company – Central Asbestos Ltd. and had a factory at Bermondsey. No doubt the Directors would have known each other, and it would be surprising if the conversation did not on occasion turn to the price of fibre! The two companies had a common shareholder in Transvaal Consolidated Land & Exploration, from whom they leased mining rights. A further competitor was Kuraman Cape Asbestos (KCB) a subsidiary of South African Asbestos ('Asbestco'), owned by Swiss entrepreneur Ernst Schmidheiny, of Eternit. There was a limit to the premium that Cape could charge, as chrysotile asbestos sourced from Canada and Russia leant itself to applications where the length and strength of the fibre was less critical and was more easily and cheaply mined. A further difficulty was that the pricing structure of fibre had placed blue and brown at a disadvantage against chrysotile.

There existed a cartel before the war amongst the leading producers and processors of asbestos – Internationale Asbestzement AG, known as SIAIC. In 1929, T&N proudly announced in its annual report 'We have been able to arrange, with the principal manufacturers of ten different countries, an international cartel'[9]. This applied to the production of asbestos cement. It had been set up on the initiative of the Belgian and Swiss Eternit companies[11]. Named as the 'Continental Wenham Scheme,' the agreed market shares for UK & Ireland were 80% to T&N and 20% to Eternit interests. There was also an agreement on the marketing of chrysotile fibre covering Canada, Rhodesia and Russia, again largely involving the producers of asbestos cement. Not being involved in asbestos cement production nor chrysotile, Cape appeared not to be a participant in these arrangements, and it seemed to be left alone to plough its own furrow in the blue and brown asbestos sector. Cape and T &N did not overlap in many areas, and in South Africa, for example, T&N's mines were in Rhodesia and Swaziland and involved chrysotile asbestos, leaving Cape with the blue and brown mines in neighbouring South Africa. They purchased fibre from each other as many products required a mix of both chrysolite and amosite.

Corporate and the Board of Directors

From a motley collection of subsidiaries Cape had by 1953 set-up an orderly structure of companies reflecting their geographical and operational functions. A holding Company was set up in South Africa - Cape Asbestos South Africa

Pty. Ltd (Casap). Hitherto the blue mines had been run from Kimberley which reported administratively to Cape Town, whereas the Transvaal mines reported direct to Cape Town, but in matters of finance each reported to London. Under the new structure, the management of both businesses was centred in Johannesburg. At this stage it can be said that Cape had a cohesive management structure in place. Control was being decentralised - hitherto it was alleged that expenditure above £30 had to have the authority of Head Office in London[9].

Staff tended to stay with Cape for life and the senior managers were all time served. Robert Walker had served as Chairman since 1934 and was a Director of Consolidated Mining and Investment (CMIC), Cape's minor shareholder. Deputy Chairman and Managing Director Giles Newton had been Managing Director since 1933, joining Cape from ICI where he was Head of the Metals Division. He had been the main driver behind the promotion of amosite asbestos and its adoption by the U.S Navy and the trade in fibre through U.S. outlets. A profile in 1961 paid tribute to his skills in putting together a skilled team of experienced and loyal executives[12]. He had a policy of personally appointing all new recruits to the Company at Head Office and senior positions elsewhere. Rupert Riley, Assistant Managing Director, had joined in 1938 and post war spent a number of years in South Africa – 'his task in South Africa completed beyond all bounds and expectations'[1]. He had drawn together the disparate strands of the business to form Casap, and in rationalising operations, had set higher standards of efficiency. Of the other Directors, Claude Cornish-Bowden, whose father was Surveyor General in South Africa, was Casap's Managing Director, having been with the company since 1945, as had Kenneth Gray, who had previously been the Government's Director of Warlike Stores during the war and was a CMIC nominee. A further Director was George Courtauld, of the Courtauld family, of whom more later.

The presence of Lord Elton as a Non-Executive Director on the Main Board for over a decade is interesting. Godfrey Elton was an academic and historian, and a contemporary of Giles Newton at Oxford[13], and cited by George Orwell as a 'Neo Tory' for his nationalist views[14]. He acquired his hereditary title on the recommendation of Ramsey Macdonald, allegedly for having achieved no greater distinction than having tutored his son, Malcolm Macdonald! Malcolm Macdonald subsequently became Secretary of State for the Colonies and then the Dominions. Elton had tried for parliament more than once, unsuccessfully, as a labour candidate. Whilst he remained at the centre of politics, amongst his many roles beyond 1939 was as Secretary of the Rhodes Trust. (Cape appears to have been his only corporate directorship in the fifties). This might suggest he was just a token peer who could lend status to the Board. However, if you look beyond, he was an imperialist with strong connections to the Dominions and in particular South Africa. He had expressed frustration with the Labour party's disinterest in the people of the Dominions. This he believed was based on the fact that the socialists were 'for instantly freeing the African negro from their British oppressors' and that in this 'the wage earners of Great Britain were their loving brothers.' In practice however, in his words a 'British wage-earner took remarkably little interest in African negroes' and 'had no desire whatever in raising their standard of living, if it meant lowering his own'. Because of this dichotomy he argued that the condition of the people of the Dominions, was a no-go area for the Labour party. For Elton it was, and in South Africa he was firmly against the Nationalists, any colour bar and the emergence of apartheid (a view also held by fellow Director George Courtauld and his Rhodesian-based kinsman, Sir Stephen). It may be for Cape he was the Board's moral conscience, but it also may mean the Board shared his views, and the plight of its mine workers was now a matter demanding attention.

The final member of the Board was Thomas (Tom) Hale, an Executive Director with over 30 years' service, having started work at Barking at the age of sixteen. Other senior executives included F Hodgson, Chairman of the South African holding companies and Dr Richard Gaze, later to become Cape's Chief Scientist and Medical Adviser, who had joined Cape in 1943. He had worked alongside Dr. Hubert Wyers, a Physician at Barking who had, in 1946, completed a doctoral thesis on asbestosis amongst the workforce, including incidences of cancer. It is true to say therefore that the executive management of Cape would have been more than aware of both the applicable regulations and the evidence of ill health amongst those involved with the mining and handling of asbestos.

Asbestos Regulations and Employee Health and Safety

In 1928 Dr. E.R.A. Merewether had undertaken an Inquiry on behalf of the Factory Inspectorate relating to an asbestos worker in Glasgow, who was suffering from pulmonary fibrosis. This was becoming known as 'Asbestosis', a chronic disease involving the thickening and scarring of lung tissue. The effect is a debilitating shortness of breath which in severe cases can prove fatal. Because of his findings, Merewether was called upon to carry out a wider-ranging investigation into the health hazards associated with the handling of asbestos within the industry. In 1930 Merewether produced his report, the first half written by himself relating to a clinical and radiological survey of a group of 363 asbestos workers, and the second half, written by Charles Price, covered the processes involving the use of asbestos fibre. Merewether concluded that 'Fibrosis of the lungs is a definite occupational risk amongst asbestos workers'; Price profiled processes which required dust suppression. As a result, the Factory Inspectorate identified a need for regulations under the Factory and Workshop Act of 1891[15]. The industry was consulted and, in cooperating, was considered to have played a proactive part. For Cape's part, James Gow, Works Manager at its Barking factory, performed a key role in establishing methods and equipment for dust suppression, including experiments in ventilation and cleaning at the factories. The sub-committee of three, of which James Gow was a member, was praised by Merewether himself for their valuable contribution to the findings.

This gave rise to a call for a set of regulations for the industry, and The Asbestos Industry Regulations 1931 came into being. In playing its part, Cape's management was fully aware of the perceived safety hazards associated with the handling of asbestos. On publication of the Regulations, Cape and T&N undertook and carried out a number of dust suppression improvements and worker protection procedures in their factories in the UK. Regrettably, during the second world war, procedures were compromised, some disciplines became lax and policing by the Factory Inspectorate less frequent and attentive. But given the long latency period, evidence of disease was still not at a level to cause great alarm. The Chief Inspector for Factories recorded 1,368 deaths from pneumoconiosis (a sub-group of pulmonary fibrosis involving mineral dusts) in 1953 but the number attributable to asbestosis was less than 2% of the total, the major proportion relating to silicosis and coal miner's pneumoconiosis. The number of deaths from byssinosis in the cotton industry in 1953 exceeded those attributable to asbestos[15]. This was regarded as evidence that because of the dust suppression that had taken place, arising from the 1931 Regulations, the incidence of disease was declining. However, the main factor was the latency period that applied between contact and consequential disease. A period of 15-40 years could elapse between exposure and disease manifestation. This latency factor (later described as 'slow violence') could, of course, be used as an excuse for inaction, a charge of which Johns-Manville in the USA was considered guilty[16].

That the Directors of Cape should be aware of the health hazards of asbestos was also implicit given the fact that a consequence of Merewether's 1931 Regulations was the inclusion of asbestos related disease (essentially Asbestosis) as a compensable condition under the old 1897 Workman's Compensation Act. This placed a responsibility on Cape and fellow employers to compensate those suffering from disease from 1931 onwards. After 1946 the Industrial Injuries Act and benefits of the Welfare State reduced the liability on the Employer but only as far as disability benefits. In modern day terms the level of compensation was parsimonious, employers and insurers (where involved) quibblesome, and claimants poorly treated, but the asbestos industry was little different from other industries subjected to pulmonary fibrosis compensation claims at this time. The number too, because of the latency factor, was small. The existence of claims for compensation was therefore not such as to undermine the case for asbestos in the eyes of the Directors of Cape.

Whilst hindsight has thrown some doubt on the thoroughness, independence, and expertise of those involved in drawing up the 1931 regulations, and the zeal with which the Factory Inspectorate policed them, in the context of the time they were considered a major step forward. This was a period when a number of health hazards were being identified in the workplace, with many being on a much larger scale, and some showing evidence of being more dangerous than asbestos. The hazard was still widely perceived as being limited to pulmonary fibrosis, although they must have been aware of the emerging link to lung cancer. At this stage, however, although a subject of research, the link was considered not proven, and again they would have considered the steps taken in dust control were sufficiently preventative. Cape certainly did not consider it necessary to label its products with any warnings as to health hazard, a failing of which it was later criticised[17].

A shortcoming in these regulations was the fact that they were industry specific (i.e. factories producing asbestos-based products); they did not apply to the work situation where men were handling and fabricating these products on a site beyond the factory. As a result, it was this category of workers who later displayed the greater incidence of disease. It was too early for some of the other distinguishing features that were to render asbestos different from other mineral dusts, so these were early days in the understanding of the disease implications of the material.

There were no such regulations in South Africa and the means of dust suppression in the mines had remained largely untouched, as tended to be the case throughout the mining industry there. Miners had been granted relief from some state legislation during the war, and the extent of collusion between government and mining companies had protected the industry from regulation. The greater issue in the mines was the living conditions under which employees worked and the use of women and more particularly children. In 1953, in the face of government workplace legislation, Cape was seeking permission to continue employing children as young as 13 years of age at its largest mine at Koegas. With over two thousand employees at the site Cape was claiming in its advertisements that Koegas was a 'self-sufficient community with its own power station, farm, social club and swimming pool'[18]. Such social facilities no doubt

were only for the use of white staff and workers. Commentators have described conditions for non-white workers at best as 'harsh'[18], at worst 'brutal'[10]. Even so, wages were sufficiently attractive for there to be no shortage of available migrant labour and, in the case of women, the wage and conditions were such as to enable a family to work and live as a unit in one place, an option not readily available elsewhere. The argument that miners were better off than had they not migrated to this workplace might have had some merit if it was not accompanied by the potential to contract a fatal disease. To one at least the evidence of industrial disease was apparent – Dr Andre Pickard, a practicing Doctor in the Prieska District during this period, cited instances of asbestosis and alleged that the post war Manager of Cape's Blue Mines had died of the disease together with his wife and children[19].

Conclusion

For the Directors of Cape, the fire preventative benefits of asbestos remained unquestioned and inculcated in their minds. Given the role of asbestos, its widespread specification and range of applications, it was a great business to be in, if not recession proof, certainly secure. So it is probably true that the Directors thought well of themselves, having cooperated in the setting up of the Regulations and having applied them in Cape's factories. At the time they probably hid behind the 1931 Regulations as the 'bible' dealing with the health and safety issues associated with asbestos, and considered that the precautions therein prescribed, and observed by Cape, enabled it to claim the high ground as to standards of worker protection. Unfortunately, no such consideration could apply to conditions in its South African mines.

There is no evidence to suggest Cape management were willfully suppressing reports they had of more harmful effects of the product, a charge later made against Johns-Manville Corporation in the USA. Amongst the parting words in the '*Cape Asbestos 1893-1953*' publication were 'Successive guiding hands... have seen to it that the first to benefit from prosperity, when it came, were the employees in mine and factory, laboratory and office, at home and abroad'. So the Board believed they had served their people well.

In this year of Cape's Diamond Jubilee, 1953, it is reasonable to assume that the Directors and Management of Cape had cause for optimism and faith in the future and that Spes, the Goddess of Hope, embraced in the Company's logo – Spes Bona – Good Hope - was very much on their side.

Cape Asbestos

The Story of The Cape Asbestos Company Limited

1893 - 1953

PUBLISHED FOR
THE CAPE ASBESTOS COMPANY LIMITED,
112-116 PARK STREET, LONDON, W.1,
BY HARLEY PUBLISHING CO., LTD., LONDON.

Frontispiece 'Cape Asbestos 1893-1953'.

(Reproduction of the frontispiece and illustrations sourced from the book are by kind permission of Christopher Newton)

Amosite (Brown) Asbestos.

Cape Asbestos Advertisements

Caposite. Bags of Amosite Asbestos from Cape's South African mines being offloaded to barge '*Caposite*' for delivery to Barking.

Below: 114 Park Street and Giles Newton.

Chapter 2

The Fifties

'In their zeal to condemn the asbestos industry ….. they overlook the fact that if asbestos was a life-taker, as it clearly was, it was also a life-saver.'

'The Way from Dusty Death'. P W J Bartrip.

'Cape Asbestos 1893-1953' referred to the battles it had fought in the first 60 years. Such battles would pale into relative insignificance within the second sixty years when the life-taking properties of asbestos became apparent. But for the remainder of the 1950's some of Giles Newton's optimism proved justified - the Company prospered.

Mining

The annual report of the Department of Mines in Pretoria recorded that the annual sales of asbestos from sources in South Africa trebled in the 1950-60 decade to a figure of £10.8 million. (Not surprisingly Cape's own sales in the decade trebled to £16.6 million). By 1960 the industry claimed that it employed one thousand European and 20,000 local workers. For Cape, the picture in each of its two mining locations differed. By the end of the decade demand for blue asbestos was beginning to give way to brown asbestos, so it was its Transvaal assets that were beginning to receive more of the investment. Douglas Todd, Formerly Cape's Mining Manager, had joined Gefco as General Manager and together with Kuraman Blue Asbestos, the two companies took market share. Gefco now claimed to be the blue asbestos market leader[1]. They were better prospectors and fleet of foot when it came to moving on to more attractive sites. Artisan miners could still pop up overnight, abandoning fields and sometimes leaving workers unpaid.

Conditions for Cape workers were improving, but the upgrading was no doubt spurred on by Government Health and Safety Department reports slating Cape for the living conditions of workers, citing evidence of scurvy and malnutrition at the blue mines[2]. The asbestos mill at Prieska was the subject of particular focus. Being a railhead, it was also a shipping centre and Cape's mills still took in third party fibre from 'tributor' miners. In 1957 a third mill at Prieska, providing for greater dust control, was designed, and built by Atkinson and French together with extensive worker accommodation, which represented some progress. In the Transvaal, the market for brown asbestos was less competitive and Cape had the opportunity to develop greenfield sites in addition to the Penge mine. Penge produced a high output of superior quality fibre, but unlike other sites, involved a hefty royalty payment to the landowner, Transvaal Consolidated Land and Exploration. For Cape workers there was some security and Cape's subsidiary, Egnep, claimed to be the first company to provide housing, medical care, sanitation, and food for its entire workforce during the late fifties. Conditions for its workers here were claimed to be superior even to those in the gold mines.

Some of the technical improvements were initiated by secondees from Cape's minority shareholder, the Central Mining and Investment Corporation (CMIC). CMIC had been formed in 1905, to bring together several of Harry Oppenheimer's De Beers investments. It was a major player in gold mining and had access to mining techniques that were transferable. CMIC had assets of £25 million in 1952 and was the vehicle, alongside the British South Africa Company, for British mining investment in South Africa. In 1958 there were takeover talks linking it with Gold Fields of South Africa and alternatively SANLAM, the Afrikaner Nationalist investment vehicle[3]. These were seen off, and the outcome placed it firmly under the control of the Anglo American Corporation (Anglo), by then the predominant mining company in South Africa. Within twenty years Anglo was to secure minority holdings in all the major mining investment houses, including Gold Fields. This was significant for Cape, as Anglo was to play a role in its future as we will learn later. In the same year Cape gained further capacity through the acquisition of Consolidated Blue Asbestos Corporation, the prime purpose of which was to meet immediate fibre supply commitments in the USA.

The operational techniques in part dealt with the need at Egnep and Amosa to mine deeper in order to maintain the quality of ore, involving elaborate pumping and ventilation equipment. The 1956 Company Report comments 'During the next two years capital equipment at the mines will call for very substantial expenditures'. The 1957 Report refers to a vertical shaft being required at Penge. A further need was to meet the demand for higher quality grades of fibre, and this required improvements in the milling process. The hardness of brown asbestos meant that ductwork and milling equipment required constant repair and maintenance.

Cape's mines were in remote locations – its blue mines tucked away in the north of Cape Province and the amosite mines in the northern corner of the Transvaal. Rail and road access and power supply dictated the pace of expansion and the speed at which it could get the product to market. Asbestos mining suffered from a lack of investment relative to other mining interests. Cape could hardly raise the sort of capital being ploughed into gold and diamonds, but it could take advantage of consequential infrastructure improvements.

The fifties were to see a significant increase in the sale of bare fibre to the USA. Cape's sales to this destination exceeded US$6 million in 1956, largely channeled through its subsidiary North American Asbestos Corporation. The 1959 Company Report recorded that 'a very large contract was negotiated for blue and brown asbestos with the United States Government through the office of the Commodity Credit Corporation'. This was to top up strategic stocks of what was considered an essential commodity, particularly in Naval shipbuilding. Another developing export market, mainly for amosite, was Australia through the relationship with James Hardie. By now Hardie was producing Caposite under licence in Sydney.

1960 was a formative year in South Africa, with the Coalbrook mining disaster in which 435 coal miners died, Macmillan's 'Wind of Change' speech, the State of Emergency, Sharpeville Massacre, and the referendum for the establishment of a Republic. Apart from the Marikana massacre in the platinum mines at Rustenberg, the rioters did not seem to target the mines. Giles Newton commented in his 1959 report, published in 1960, that in the light of the rioting 'shareholders will be glad to learn that there was no anti-European incident of any sort at any of the company's mines. Conditions are of course totally different in the country areas from those in the industrial towns, and the general living conditions and amenities which we provide have earned for us an enviable reputation among the tribal Africans, who eagerly seek employment at our establishments.' This probably relied on reports from management in the field who would inevitably talk up conditions, but it perhaps points to the more paternalistic approach adopted by British companies, and the management ethos of Giles Newton and Lord Elton. The living conditions of workers did improve, so there was benevolence in their rule.

Products and Marketing

The 1950's was a period when there was major infrastructure, process plant and utility investment in the UK, all beneficial to Cape and its range of products. ICI developed its Wilton chemical complex, ICI Billingham its fertiliser and synthetic fibre ventures. Refineries were built by Shell at Teesport, Regent at Milford Haven and ICI at North Tees. In the South there was work on the BP Refinery on the Isle of Grain and Mobil at Coryton. The Central Electricity Generating Board (CEGB) was formed in 1958 to coordinate regional investments with central research facilities at Marchwood. Calder Hall, the first nuclear power plant, was commissioned in 1956 and Cape was to play an important part as a further nuclear fleet was rolled out. All these organisations were to become increasingly influential in the specification of the type of products Cape manufactured.

One of the most successful products of this period was Cape's Asbestolux. This product, which made effective use of the unique properties of amosite asbestos fibre, was a composite building panel produced in sheets. It had excellent fire-resistant properties providing for up to 4 hour fire resistance and its formulation had been devised by Cape at its Barking research facilities. It remains to this day in buildings, now subject to strict regulations as to protective maintenance. Asbestolux was a board in which amosite fibres, giving strength to the product, reinforced mixes of calcium silicate and diatomaceous earth. The asbestos fibre content was no more than 35% and helped to trap air such as to give it insulation properties as well as fire resistance. It was a fairly soft board (unlike asbestos cement) making it easy to cut. T&N in due course had a competing product – Turnabestos – but it was considered inferior; otherwise, there was no real competitor. By now it was in full production at the Uxbridge Flint Brick Company site, which could readily accommodate a continuous line incorporating Austrian Hatschek technology. This had been developed for asbestos cement board and key to the production of Asbestolux was Cape's adaptation of the equipment to accommodate the product's process technology. In 1959 a further £250,000 was being invested at Uxbridge in additional capacity and the original line at Barking re-commissioned. The product soon became a staple building board for a range of commercial and domestic applications -

mainly ceilings and partitions in sensitive fire areas - prompted by the insulation and fire preventative provisions of the emerging building regulations. It came in different thicknesses and densities depending on application. Its equivalent within the marine sector, Marinite was benefitting from the boom in shipbuilding. The QE2, in particular, had Marinite specified throughout, for bulkheads, partitions, and ceilings. These products represented a significant outlet for Cape's amosite fibres, reflected in the fact that in 1960 14% of UK imports of asbestos was amosite compared with only 3% in the USA[4]. Technology in the USA relied on chrysotile, with no comparative equivalents to Asbestolux in the board application.

The Company's Barking factory site (illustrated p.34), the largest in the Group, manufactured a number of legacy products, the main one being Caposite insulation, which came in pipe section and mattress form, and comprised up to 85% asbestos fibre coupled with magnesia or calcium silicate. The 1950's saw good demand for this product in power plants and refineries, being specified by major users. Whilst the material had temperature toleration advantages over glass and mineral wools it was by the end of the period beginning to lose out to these products. Cape's foresight in setting up its Sterling facility for the manufacture of Rocksil rock fibre insulation appeared to be paying off, and a third furnace was commissioned in 1959.

The Barking site dated back to 1913 and saw the development of many of the applications for asbestos fibre. In the fifties it had engineering and millwrights' workshops, research and development facilities in addition to administrative offices, canteens, and social/sports facilities. Extending to seven acres it housed the production of textiles (fireproof clothing), brake pads and produced the old Plutoboard in addition to Caposite. By the end of the 1950's many of these products were being superseded, produced at other plants, or discontinued and it supplemented Asbestolux production capacity. It was a jobbing facility at a time when volume demand required more sophisticated production techniques. In addition, Barking provided a base for an Outworks Department providing installation advice or service to important customers. Given the range of activities and type it is little wonder that Barking became identified with some of the worst aspects of the handling of asbestos and its link with disease.

Cape produced textiles, gaskets, ropes, a type of millboard and some Caposite at Acre Mill, Hebden Bridge, Yorkshire (illustrated p.34). Under pressure from the government, Cape had taken over the old mill in 1939 to meet the demand for filters for gas masks in the second world war. After the war demand fell and space became available to produce various textiles and, in due course, Caposite, which was in demand for the industrial complexes at Billingham and Wilton on the Northeast Coast. These textile products were becoming superceded and the 1959 company report notes that, although profitable, the Acre Mill contribution was modest. As in the case of Barking this was a site that would be linked with the worst health consequences of asbestos. A small but profitable business was located at Kentmere in the Lake District adjacent to deposits of diatomaceous earth. This is a sedimentary deposit that has a high silica content and has a wide range of industrial applications. In Cape's case it was used in the making of Asbestolux and plastic insulating compositions.

Cape had an historic link with the past in its plant in Italy[5]. Capamianto Spa in Turin could trace itself back to the early days of Cape when Italy was a pioneer in the development of asbestos. At the time of its inauguration Cape recognised that it needed to have knowledge of the applications for its fibre as well as outlets. To gain such expertise there was no better place than Italy, and the company acquired the established business of Messrs. Eltore Albasini near Turin. By now the subsidiary produced a similar range of products as Cape in the UK, and lead the market in Italy. Prior to and during the 1950's, the impression is given that the Italian management operated independently and had the better of Cape's management - the reports in the 1950's refer more to cultural difficulties than profits!

Another site was in South Africa at Benoni, near Johannesburg which produced some of the Cape products. Caposite (labelled Isolamianti) was also produced in France and in 1955 production of Caposite was initiated by Cape Asbestos (Canada) Ltd. on the USA border.

The one business that seemed to be out of kilter with the core business, was Weaver Manufacturing and Engineering at Bedford. This company was mainly involved with garage equipment. In 1956 it acquired the rights to the Kismet air pump and became Kismet Weaver. In 1960 Cape acquired William Turner (Kismet) Ltd which was known for its tyre pressure gauges and foot pumps. This was a period when car ownership was gathering pace, and the business clearly made a useful profit contribution. The management was afforded a great deal of autonomy, and as long as the business contributed, was left alone. At this time

Cape's range of brake and clutch linings was manufactured at Barking and sold as part of the general portfolio of asbestos based products alongside building and insulation products.

The thermal insulation contracting activities of the company centred around the Outworks Department at Barking. Cape had succumbed to the acquisition of marine contracting specialist Andersons Insulation of Liverpool in 1954. It raised issues of conflict of interest in competing with some of Cape's clients, but it ensured that Cape's products were firmly specified in the Barrow submarine facility and in the Clydeside shipyards, both of which were Anderson strongholds. Whether considered wise at the time, moving into contracting proved to be a diversification that ultimately enabled the company to survive, as we will see.

Hitherto, wherever possible, if installation services were required, the company sought to subcontract the site work to existing installation contractors[6]. One was William Kenyon with whom Cape was in joint venture in the Rocksil venture, and strong in power plant work in the Midlands. Others included McAndrew Wormold in the Northeast, Kitsons in Scotland, F Leroy in Manchester and Bernard Hastie in Cardiff. One of the earliest contracts in 1960 involved the building of the Texaco oil refinery in Pembrokeshire where Cape formed a consortium with Bernard Hastie Insulation. Cape supplied materials and Hastie the labour, given the client's requirement for an all-Welsh labour force. Such arrangements were not entirely successful, as the partner providing labour tended to give priority to his own contracts in allocating his best tradesmen, exposing Cape potentially to the charge of poor performance in the field. In Ireland the Company had to step in and purchase the business of M. A. Boylan Ltd. at the request of the constructors of the Whitegate Oil Refinery in Cork. This demonstrated the key role played by the insulation contractor in the final commissioning of these plants – a feature we will return to later. Overall Cape was still a reluctant installation contractor at this time.

During the decade steps were taken to set up local sales offices, sales hitherto having been largely directed from the London Office and through local agents. Glasgow Sales Office had been opened in 1948, by 1954 an office in Birmingham, and 1957 an office in Newcastle. These offices handled the whole sales portfolio which, whilst an improvement on what went before, was not ideal, as it was difficult to find salesmen able to master such a diverse range of products and services. Ken Bishop, Cape Insulation's Retail Sales Manager when he retired in 1984, recalled that, as a salesman in the fifties he had an old Jowett Javelin motor car and was expected to call upon anyone and everyone requiring anything from pipe insulation, to needles and twine and woven asbestos aprons and gauntlets. 'With this formidable list, together with a car-boot full of literature and samples, I visited lagging contractors, prisons, hospitals, railway carriage and engine builders, laundries and I don't know who else'[7].

 The old 'Spes Bona' logo appears to disappear from company literature and was replaced by the symbol displayed here. The three standing figures within the oval representation of fire were the figures Shadrach, Meshach and Abednego, who, the Prophet Daniel recounts, were thrown into a fiery furnace by Nebuchadnezzar but preserved from its affects. The untidy design was no doubt sourced in house and would have done little to enhance the brand!

So the period was one of buoyant market conditions, product development and expansion overseas.

Competition

Asbestos mining worldwide was expanding at a great rate and for many applications chrysotile was adequate. It could also be mixed with the more expensive blue and brown varieties. The main producers of chrysotile continued to be in Canada and Russia. Easier to mine, the lower pricing of the material limited the premium that the producers of blue and brown asbestos could charge.

In South Africa, Gefco had taken over as the market leader in blue asbestos, taking advantage of buoyant market conditions. Its UK business - Central Asbestos Company – was known in particular for its sprayed asbestos insulation under the Silbestos label. The Gefco annual report of 1957 showed a profit of £289,000 rising to £590,000 at the end of the decade[8]. It too invested in its mines during the period, having to follow Cape's lead in providing housing and facilities for workers.

Cape's main UK competitor, Turner and Newall (T&N) was largely complimentary, its mining activity directed towards chrysotile. There was a fair amount of intercompany trading, and Cape and T&N's hold on the industry was to draw the attention of the Mergers and Monopolies Commission (MMC)[9], of which more later. Criticism by Giles Newton of the Restrictive Trades Practices Act introduced in 1956, in the 1960 results announcement, almost invited MMC attention. Whilst T&N competed with Cape in many sectors, their particular strength was in asbestos cement ('TAC') and automotive products ('Ferodo'), both ranges utilising mainly chrysotile fibre. Cape had no presence in the asbestos cement sector and only a minor one in brake and clutch linings, the latter also featuring British Belting and Asbestos (BBA). Unlike Cape, who merely marketed fibre in the USA, T&N had acquired a stateside manufacturing presence, producing asbestos cement and brake linings.

Health and Safety

In 1953 asbestos appeared to be at the height of its powers in terms of its benefits and demand. In attention to health and safety, if anything Cape appeared to be ahead of public sentiment, and the health hazard was portrayed as being under control. Whilst its mines did not benefit from many of the precautions taken in Cape's UK factories, they did benefit from an effort to improve housing and welfare.

However, shortly after, the 1954 Annual Report of the UK's Chief Factory Inspector reported on deaths in which both asbestosis and lung cancer were present. The link was certainly not new as Dr. Merewether, by then Chief Inspector of Factories, had in 1947 reported a higher incidence of lung cancer in death cases associated with asbestos than silicosis. In 1955, the distinguished statistician and epidemiologist, Richard Doll, carried out a study at T&N's Rochdale plant that identified the notably 'higher risk' of lung cancer amongst asbestos workers. This suggested that men with lengthy exposure to asbestos had a tenfold risk of death by lung cancer. The industry liked to console itself with the argument that given the long latency period in the development of lung cancer, the effect of the dust controls under the 1931 Asbestos Regulations had brought the lung cancer problem under control. It was encouraged in this view by Doll himself who spoke of incidences becoming 'progressively less'[10]. The best that can be said is that the effect of the earlier dust control measures may have reduced the frequency of lung cancer. During this period, evidence was emerging of the link between smoking and lung cancer, and tuberculosis still lingered on, so it was not difficult to blur the causal link. Expert Witness Sir Alisdair Breckenridge in litigation[11] in which Cape was later involved, concluded

'It is probably reasonable to state that the view of the scientific community as of 1959 including leaders in the field of epidemiology such as Richard Doll, was that cases of asbestos related disease would be steadily declining with the passage of time following the decrease in exposure levels since the 1931 Asbestos Industry Regulations'. Author Jock McCulloch's perception[12] was more stark - 'by 1960 asbestos was used so widely and asbestos related disease such a huge problem that it was difficult to resolve'.

Whether Cape saw it as such a major problem at this stage is doubtful and the Directors would, I believe, have concurred with Sir Alisdair. However, Cape did continue to play an active role in dust control and, in 1957, alongside T&N and BBA, became a founding member in the Asbestosis Research Council (ARC). This was funded by the three companies and initially set up to coordinate work on dust sampling and monitoring. Academics from Reading University were joined in the Council by researchers from Cambridge. The first appointment of a Research Fellow at Cambridge was announced in 1961. In terms of disease, and as its title suggests, the focus of the Council, however, remained largely on asbestosis. In later years, the industry (also unions) was charged with a 'conspiracy of silence' over their awareness and disclosure of the risks attached to asbestos at this time. In the context of the UK and Cape this is possibly unfair as the evidence was not considered conclusive, and in carrying out the activities of the ARC they were not silent. But it could not be said that they approached the task with a great sense of urgency.

Meanwhile in South Africa, whilst mining continued apace, in 1953 a Committee on Silicosis and Pulmonary Disability was set up in the Department of Mines. Asbestos was a minor area of focus but under the Silicosis Act in 1954 asbestosis was included in the list of certifiable diseases. The Pneumoconiosis Act of 1956 formalised the status of asbestos mining as a controlled activity within the embrace of the Mining Inspectorate, and established the Pneumoconiosis Bureau. The existing provisions for compensation for asbestosis were rationalised and enforced. Cornish-Bowden, Cape's Managing Director was particularly upset by this, reportedly later having to pay out £60,000 in compensation for just one of the mines in a single year for 'old cases of asbestosis'[12]. This is a hefty sum and equivalent to over £1 million today. If indeed that was the amount, it would reflect a large number of cases, and no doubt directed principally, if not entirely, towards white workers. This alone would have contributed to a growing awareness within management of the incidence of asbestosis in the workforce.

The asbestos mining sector was small, remote, and left largely alone by the Inspectorate. Cape had a good relationship with the Department of Mines, so the interface took place more in Johannesburg than the field. The reality was that efforts to control dust and general working conditions in the asbestos mining sector were extremely poor. As we learnt in chapter 1, the use of women and juveniles to carry out the splitting of the ironstone from the fibre by hand and hammers, continued into the sixties, contrary to the provisions of the 1956 Mines Act. In a later TV documentary it was claimed that some 6% of a total 7,500 claimants from this period had commenced employment in the mines under the age of seven[13].

It is a little surprising that Cape then readily allowed members of the Inspectorate and the Pneumoconiosis Bureau access to its mines in conducting their own survey into the extent of asbestos related disease, now including cancer. The industry offered to fund the research being conducted to the tune of £25,000[12]. (The amount expended turned out to be less). It could be a reflection of Cape management's ignorance of went on in the mines. They certainly should have been aware that in the Northern Cape, disease was becoming an important political issue. In 1959 the results of the survey were reported at the Pneumoconiosis Conference held in Johannesburg, the consequences of which are recounted in the next chapter.

Management

Giles Newton directed the business for most of the decade but stepped up to Chairman in 1957. His choice for succession suggested the absence of an immediate candidate. He opted for Joint Managing Directors - R H Dent and T C Hale. Ronnie Dent, a qualified accountant, had joined the company as Company Secretary in 1946, and in 1953 he had been appointed to the Board as Director of Finance and Administration. Barely forty-four years of age, his appointment as a Managing Director was a bold move given the age profile of the senior management and their largely operational background. To balance the appointment the position was shared with Tom Hale, who was very much an operational man, and identified with the Barking site. Giles Newton clearly perceived Ronnie Dent as a man of promise, which he proved to be, as he went on to become Managing Director and Chairman in later years. To appoint Hale jointly was perhaps designed to assuage the concerns the rest of the senior management may have had over such a young man, and a Head Office accountant to boot! Dent soon made an impression and one of his first steps was to replace Claude Cornish-Bowden, Managing Director of the South African Mining entities, who ran the business very much as his own fiefdom. It was alleged by his successor that Cornish-Bowden had been negotiating with James Hardie of Australia the possible sale of Cape's mining interests, behind the Board's back.

Ronnie Dent must take some credit for the financial good health of the company as it came to the end of the decade, but the market had been buoyant, and it had been fairly easy to make good money. The Board's strategy revolved around asbestos and the mining mentality prevailed – justified in terms of the source of profit. It's shareholders and non-executive Directors were all of this background. But the added value business in terms of product range was ageing and over diversified. Some of its production facilities were falling behind in their ability to innovate, their standards and scale.

Between 1953 and 1960 Capital employed in the business increased from £8 million to £15 million. Trading Profit from £1 million to £1.8 million so it was a capital intensive business, but earnings represented a respectable 18% on capital employed. Profits however could be lumpy, particularly in the mining sector. But overall it had been a successful few years and shareholders were rewarded with rising dividends. For the other stakeholders – those who worked for Cape – the UK standard of living rose during the decade and there was considerable pride in working for the company.

Penge Mine, Eastern Transvaal. Housing and (below) Dust Collection units

Acre Mill, Hebden Bridge (*by kind permission Hebden Bridge Local History Society*)
Barking Site (*permission granted under license from Historic Environment Scotland*)

 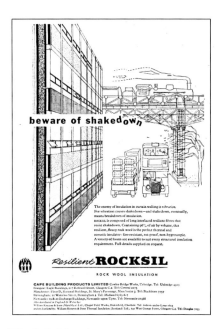

Noramite (Canada) and Rocksil Advertisements.

Don (Small & Parkes), and Trist
Draper Automotive Products

(Provided under License from Alamy)

Chapter 3

Peak Asbestos

'The blunder that cost thousands of lives and destroyed an industry was a management blunder, and the blunder was denial.'

Former Johns Manville Executive, Bill Sells. 'What asbestos taught me.'

The rejuvenation of the British economy after the war continued throughout the 1950's and 1960's and they were good years for those companies like Cape involved in infrastructure work. A similar picture prevailed in overseas markets. Cape's sales increased from £17.97 million to £45.97 million over the 1960-70 decade – a compound rate approaching 10% per annum at a time of moderate inflation. The mix changed, with mining declining as a proportion of sales but still providing over 30% of profits. The profit margin, which historically had held steady around the 10% level was reducing as the higher margin on asbestos fibre sales was diluted. But nevertheless Cape Asbestos was an attractive share to hold with the dividend rising from 5p in 1962 to 7p a share in 1970 and the price of the shares doubling over the decade.

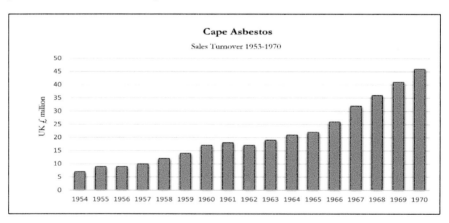

Cape Asbestos
Sales Turnover 1953-1970

Organisation and Management

Giles Newton, who had guided the Company over the past two decades had to retire as Chairman in 1961 as a result of ill health and Tom Hale, Joint Managing

Director, died. Tom was barely fifty-seven, and it was always believed that he was a victim of an asbestos related disease. Giles Newton was appointed to the honorary position of President. Ronnie Dent at the age of forty-nine became sole Managing Director and Deputy Chairman, and by 1963 Chairman and Managing Director. Stephen Pollen, Managing Director of CMIC and one of their two representatives on the Board, then became Deputy Chairman.

Giles Newton had served the company well. He had played an important part in widening the market for Cape's amphibole fibres, both supply and added value. Without him the company may have been just an inconsequential miner of a premium fibre with a limited market. He had a collegiate management style and in consequence a loyal team. He was particularly active in bringing the industry together to effect improvements in dust control, giving full backing to the Merewether Report and ensuing regulations. Unfortunately, his efforts were devoted to a cause which ultimately had an unhappy ending, but it would be unfair to charge him, or his team, with a level of concealment as to the health hazards associated with asbestos, it being at odds with the main body of evidence available to them at the time. There was no apparent distinction at that time between the relative hazards of Chrysotile and Amphibole fibres. But it would, though, have been difficult for them to throw off the ingrained notion that placed the unique fire protective qualities of asbestos on a pedestal.

Coming into the sixties. Giles Newton's board was something of a Gentleman's Club. Mining tended to attract either those looking for a bit of adventure in the field, or those engaged in mining finance in the City of London. Both came from the best private schools and were frequenters of the best London Clubs. Cape was no exception – on the Board there were old school chums Rupert St. George Riley[1] and George Courtauld[2]. They had played cricket together for their house at Malvern College. Both had distinguished war records in military intelligence with George being one of the original section heads in Section D, also in its successor, the Special Operations Executive (SOE). George had a liaison role with intelligence groups in France as did Rupert in Switzerland, using means of subterfuge to undermine the Nazi war effort. Mining Engineer Rupert had joined Cape in 1938 having spent time in the Canadian mining industry and after the war became Cape's Managing Director in South Africa. He drove competition Riley motor cars in the thirties and although he was believed to be a member of the Riley family, he was in fact a Cobbold, leading altogether an adventurous life. He was behind the car rallies organised by the Head Office '114 Park Street Social Club' that Giles Newton had initiated. George Courtauld was a member of the Courtauld family and a Director of Courtaulds Textiles. A decade or so earlier Giles Newton had introduced his son Michael to the organisation, and he was subsequently appointed to the Main Board. It is quite possible that Giles appointed Dent and Hale as stop gaps, pending a crowning of son Michael, but Ronnie Dent was gaining confidence in the role. By the end of the decade Rupert Riley and George Courtauld had gone, and we see a management structure firmly under Ronnie Dent's control, with a fair representation of Executive Directors. New recruits brought updated management techniques and expertise more appropriate to the changing nature of the business. Ronnie Dent was described as being a good delegator, allowing management freedom of action, analytical in approach with a preference to persuade rather than compel. By the end of the decade he was able to pass the Managing Director baton to Geoffrey Higham, who had joined the company in 1966 as Managing Director of the Building Products business, and by then a comparatively young forty-three. Such recruitment interviews generally took place over lunch at the 'Rag' – the Army and Navy Club, which had moved from St. James's Square to a new location off Pall Mall in 1962. Ronnie Dent and colleagues on the Board were to be seen there; Giles Newton might invite them to the Bath Club or George Courtauld to Whites. Reciprocal arrangements meant that they were also infrequent visitors to the Kimberley Club and in Johannesburg the Rand Club in South Africa[3]. Kimberley was the hub for the Northern Cape mining industry and the Rand for Transvaal mining interests.

Shareholders

The Central Mining and Investment Company (CMIC) held 16.9% of the shares in Cape prior to 1965. This hardly gave it control but it was widely understood that additional shares were owned by Anglo American Corporation (Anglo) associates in South Africa (including Transvaal Consolidated Land) which gave it more power over the company than CMIC's shareholding suggested. CMIC and Anglo had a further interest in Cape in that some of Cape's mining properties were leased, and associates of CMIC and Anglo received royalties in return for mineral rights. In 1965, Anglo merged the British South Africa Company, the Consolidated Mines Selection Company and CMIC, to form Charter Consolidated, registered in the UK. Charter was listed in London and comprised a jumble of Anglo investments which did not readily fit into its other principal areas of activity. One third of the new company's shares was owned by Anglo. By 1968 the Cape Asbestos Company Report is recording a substantial interest in its shares of 24% attributable to Charter Consolidated, and this subsequently rose to 25.3%. In 1969 Charter made an offer to Cape's shareholders to increase its holding. The proposed offer was worth £12.5 million for 50% of the balance of the shares it did not own (£2 per share). Shareholders were invited to tender up to 100% of their holdings subject to scaling back if the amount exceeded the 50%. This was accomplished with some ease given that there were still cross holdings within the Anglo Group, and the old James Hardie holding was available. So Charter achieved its objective of increasing its holding to 62.5%. The market was perplexed, but Charter explained the move as a means 'to provide a channel for the development of Charter's industrial interests and facilitate an expansion of activities in both groups'. Charter had UK activities in heaters and railtrack fastenings and their proposal seemed to imply synergy, but in truth there was little - then or subsequently. Presumably, by retaining the separate London listing for Cape, they felt they had a UK publicly listed vehicle in which to gather other industrial interests. This was not entirely credible as Cape was still perceived as a mining company, and one of a mineral which was becoming increasingly under scrutiny.

Ronnie Dent opposed the takeover, valuing the independence he enjoyed as head of a public company. But Charter moved in, with Sidney Spiro, Charter's Managing Director, becoming Cape's Deputy Chairman, with a further two representative directors from Charter – Lionel Stopford Sackville, P.C.D Burnell - and (later described as) 'urbane' Anthony Evelyn Hepper. A Royal Engineer, Tony had earlier worked at Courtaulds, and having caught the eye of George Courtauld, had being recruited as Cape's Manager at the Acre Mill, and subsequently Consulting Electrical and Mechanical Engineer at Cape's mines. In later years he was appointed Chairman of Upper Clyde Shipbuilders. This made for a swollen Board of thirteen including Executive Directors. Ronnie Dent's antipathy towards the takeover was not forgotten by Sidney Spiro.

As the decade evolved it becomes all the more inexplicable why Charter should seek to acquire a larger shareholding in Cape. It either meant they had an overriding and perhaps naïve belief in the future of asbestos, despite the revelations emerging from the Johannesburg Pneumoconiosis Conference in

1959, or that Anglo and the South African mining establishment wanted to gain better control of the asbestos disease narrative, given its potential consequences elsewhere in their portfolio of businesses. It may have been simply to spread its investments beyond South Africa, and utilise Cape's management in doing so.

Mining

The sixties was a period of substantial growth in the South African economy. Investment in the mining sector increased across the board. This, in part, reflected a movement of labour into a growing manufacturing sector, which affected wages in the mining industry. Anglo had become a dominant player in the economy which could only be to Cape's benefit[4]. However with the declaration of a Republic in 1961 power was moving away from the old mining houses and firmly into Nationalist hands.

The Cape Asbestos 1960 Company Report reminded readers that the export of crude fibre constituted the larger part of the Group's revenue, and in 1965 it recorded 10,000 employed in its mines. Reports during the 1960's describe a buoyant market with demand outstretching capacity. This was accompanied by

heavy capital expenditure. More than £2 million was invested in the amosite mines, mainly at Penge in the Transvaal, justified by the higher margins earned on amosite. A new dust collection unit was installed. The market continued to decline for the shorter blue fibre in favour of the longer amosite (brown), which was more suitable for the mix of market processes now prevailing. Importation of blue crocidolite asbestos into the UK ceased in 1970. By 1973 the UK Competition Commission was noting that 'Cape is the largest producer of amosite fibres and is responsible for 90% of total world production. About 30% of Cape's output comes to the United Kingdom, mainly for use in fire resistant insulation board[5]'. Some of these investments in the mines were problematic in operation and by the end of the decade there were indications that investment returns were not as anticipated. This may have reflected the fact that of the order of 40% of capital expenditure was now being directed towards dust control.

Managing the Mining Division from its London Office depended on having local trustworthy management in the field. The remote mines in the Northern Cape and Northeast Transvaal were located in the old Boer Republics, Afrikaners and their language tended to prevail. Tony Hepper recalled 'I had an office in Johannesburg and travelled to the mines in a small aircraft, or sometimes by car, but it took a long time. The mines were very isolated and operated in their own communities with their own power station, schools, and hospitals'[6]. Logistically there were obstacles to overcome and for capital projects it was necessary to place considerable trust in local managers and contractors. The Directors of the South African subsidiaries were the familiar UK faces who, although resident, were hardly hands on. Managing Director and Old Etonian Justin Mackeurtan, who had replaced Cornish-Bowden, was rarely seen at the workface, more commonly engaging with colleagues in the industry at the Rand or Country Club in Johannesburg. He claimed to know 'people in high places,' was comfortable in government circles, and soon learned to keep London at a distance. An Afrikaner and CMIC man, Louis Kuyper was the driving force in the field. If Giles Newton's team in 1953 was wary of the Nationalists and opposed to apartheid, by the sixties it would appear local management was more tolerant, if not aligned.

Ronnie Dent proudly reported he had made two visits one year to the South African business. Visits from senior management typically involved excursions to game reserves. It raises the question of not only how firm were the controls exercised by the company over these subsidiaries and mines, but also management's awareness of conditions. At the end of the previous decade, Cape's manager at its remote Pomfret mine, the eccentric Major Arthur Ackerman, was said to have ruled it 'as a private kingdom'[7] and insisted on being winched up from the mine with his dog in a cocopan (miners' trolley) rather than walk. Men's loyalty in the field tended to be to their colleagues and to the mining fraternity rather than the company that employed them.

But sales of the output grew with the opening of new international ventures in Mexico and Argentina (Bruno-Cape s.a.). Notable were sales in the USA where the Government made substantial purchases again in 1960 to support strategic stocks. However these subsequently began to tail off. Despite this, in 1968, the company was sufficiently confident to renew the royalty agreement on the land leased from Transvaal Consolidated Land (an Anglo affiliated company) for a further 25 years. But the decade as it turned out could be described as the heyday of asbestos mining as production was about to peak.

Products and Marketing

Ronnie Dent's decade at the helm featured a total commitment to asbestos, a scaling up of existing activities and a broadening of Cape's portfolio to include gaps in its added value product range. The extent to which this was the Board's intention at the beginning of the decade we will consider at the end of the chapter.

Engineering

The first step was the acquisition in 1960 of the Small & Parkes business in the brake lining sector. This involved the issue of 1,250,000 shares as consideration, valuing the business at just short of £1 million. Cape had ventured into this area of the market when it had acquired the Weaver Manufacturing and Engineering Company after the war. Cape Capasco heavy duty moulded brake liners and clutch friction facings were in great demand when steel allocation favoured the commercial vehicle market, but by the 1950's it was the domestic motor vehicle industry which was booming, and Cape did not have a competitive product; Small & Parkes did. Brake pads and clutch linings used chrysotile asbestos and in relatively modest quantities, so as an outlet for Cape's blue and brown asbestos it offered little in terms of fibre sales.

Small & Parkes had been founded in 1881 and produced an entire range of engine packings, belts, bearings and linings with a claimed 10% share of the world-wide market for friction products for the motor car industry, its main competitors being Ferodo (T&N) and Mintex (British Belting and Asbestos or BBA). Its technology was clearly ahead of Cape's in the woven type of brake lining, which was cheaper to produce, and more suited to domestic vehicles. It had a strong brand in 'Don.' A family business, although by then also a public company, it was headed by A. Herbert Parkes. As the senior family member he joined the Cape Board, shortly to be succeeded by his son Francis (Pat) Parkes as Managing Director. During the first two years the business, now forming, with Weaver, the Engineering Division of Cape under Divisional Managing Director Lionel Dawson, was a focus of investment at its Manchester factory and in expansion elsewhere. Towards the middle and end of the decade its contribution to profit was considered 'most satisfactory' and the business was growing internationally. Production of motor vehicles was expanding at a greater rate in Europe, notably Germany, and it tackled, a little belatedly, the European market through a joint venture with Johns Manville in Belgium – Don International s.a. In South Africa a subsidiary was set up – Tesco/Tecalmit (Pty.) Ltd. Don had outlets in India and New Zealand. A Joint Venture with Imperial-Eastman marketed hose couplings and fittings for hydraulic applications and Cape Marine Propulsion Ltd was set up to develop a new method of small boat power transmission. Not all of these appeared to be a great success, with the last two being liquidated by the end of the decade. The Kismet garage equipment business continued to perform well and in 1969 the Trist Draper Group of Companies in Bristol, which produced asbestos yarns for woven brake linings, was acquired, adding the brand name 'Top Dog'. Trist had a majority holding in the English Asbestos Company (Cape buying the remaining 25% from BBA) and a subsidiary named Transport Brakes Ltd., serving the railway industry. By the end of the decade the Engineering or Automotive Division, as it became known, comprised a third of Cape's overall sales turnover.

Building Products Sector

The second example of diversification lay in the boards and building products sector. At Uxbridge production continued of Asbestolux and flint bricks. Giles Newton commented in the 1960 annual statement that demand exceeded Cape's capacity to supply, production having been commenced again at Barking to supplement Uxbridge supply. Michael Newton was the Director responsible for the business but his strengths lay more in sales than production and he was replaced by recruit Geoffrey Higham who had a background in production engineering at Metal Box. The Uxbridge plant was upgraded and by 1967 output greatly increased. Michael subsequently headed up sales in the Insulation Division, a role in which he was very successful. The family connection enabled him to remain on the Main Board.

The sector in which Cape had no presence was asbestos cement sheeting and pipes which represented a substantial market for asbestos fibre (but mainly chrysotile). The opportunity arose in 1966 to acquire the Universal Asbestos Manufacturing Company Ltd (UAC). UAC had been set up by ex-employees of Bells United Asbestos when taken over by T&N in 1930. United Asbestos and Bells predated Cape and were pioneers in the mining and import of Canadian chrysotile fibre. UAC's Chairman, Stockbroker Frank Douglas and Financial Director, Richard Caine, were on a mission and through the Charter network persuaded Ronnie Dent to purchase the business, which was located at Watford and Bowburn, and produced a range of asbestos cement cladding, pipes and rainwater goods. For groundwater pipes the longer amosite asbestos fibres were required and UAC had a good working relationship with Cape as a supplier. Otherwise their asbestos needs were satisfied by chrysotile. The offer for UAC valued the company at £5.1 million based on an all share offer coupled with a sizable element of unsecured loan stock. Customers in the asbestos cement sector were used to having stock available on demand and producers struggled to match productive capacity with demand. This had been reflected in the profits of UAC, which having peaked at £574,000 in 1962, had dropped to £259,000 in 1966. Johns Manville Corporation had picked up an eighth of UAC's equity at an average of eighteen shillings a share against Cape's offer of fourteen shillings, so were expected to make a counter offer. Whether they now had doubts over the future of the business or whether it was because of troubles elsewhere (they were in court over asbestos cement price fixing issues with the US Government in the same year, part of which involved the import of foreign asbestos cement pipe), they accepted the offer. The price looked generous; but Cape shares were standing on a premium price to earnings ratio. UAC had just built a new factory on the site of the old Bowburn Colliery in County Durham increasing its capacity considerably. The business was not without problems, there being a need for investment at Watford, whilst Bowburn was failing to meet production expectations. Asbestos cement had by now become something of a commodity item with little differentiation amongst the major competitors, being T&N and Atlas (acquired by Eternit in 1975). UAC came with a business called Chancery Insulation - UAC had ventured into the field of structural fire protection alongside its cladding activities, forming this specialist subsidiary using spray techniques involving asbestos. This unit in due course became part of Cape's thermal insulation contracting business.

In 1960 Cape also acquired a plant at Queensferry, Deeside, which produced wood fibre insulation board, thus broadening the range of products offered to the building industry to include ceiling panels/tiles under the brand name 'negaflam'. Whilst not in the same league as Asbestolux for fire resistance, this was a much lighter product and suitable for suspended ceiling systems.

It was logical to bring together the newly acquired UAC business and the Boards unit in one Division and in 1969 Cape Universal Building Products was formed embracing all the companies. W R (Bill) Doughty was recruited by Geoffrey Higham (by then Managing Director of Cape) who had worked with him at Metal Box, to head up the combined business.

Adding asbestos cement products (as well as Don's brake linings) to Cape's portfolio meant that Cape's range of activities now largely mirrored T&N and between the two companies they dominated the market. It enabled Cape's sales turnover to double, although still modest at £35 million compared with T&N's £90 million. These acquisitions added fuel to the Mergers and Monopolies Commission Enquiry in 1968 into the sale of asbestos fibre and products in the UK. Whilst certain restrictions were placed on T&N, the eventual result in 1973 found that the operation of the market did not act against the public interest[8]. A main criticism related to mutual covenants and to restrictions placed on the seller under agreements for the transfer of businesses to T&N, one of which was Cape's textile interests from Acre Mill and Barking. A somewhat confusing entry in the 1972 Cape report by the Chairman read 'Since the end of the year the Monopolies Commission has reported and your company has received a clean bill, some references being, if only by inference, not wholly uncomplimentary'. Given that the two companies together with BBA were drawn together in defence of their health and safety record (see below) the possibility of some collusion in the marketplace is not beyond credulity. A focus of the MMC Enquiry was asbestos cement and here it appeared to conclude that the old SAIAC cartel had ceased to function after the war. Maybe UAC, which was not believed to be a member of the cartel, had played its part in its demise.

Insulation Division

For the Insulation Division the decade was a period of rationalisation with legacy products being phased out due to concerns amongst clients as to the safety issues surrounding asbestos. Towards the second half of the decade major end users became nervous of asbestos containing insulation materials. One after another they banned its use, ICI being the first followed by Shell, Esso, BP, CEGB, British Rail, The Ministry of Defence was slower to adopt the ban, particularly where using USA specifications (e.g. HMS Dreadnought and the first nuclear submarines). Major process plant contractors such as Foster Wheeler followed, excluding asbestos containing materials in their specifications. Caposite was losing ground to alternatives such as Cape's own Rocksil and to the calcium silicate pipe insulation manufactured by T&N's Washington Chemical Company and their 85% Magnesia based insulation. The latter was also manufactured by the Chemical & Insulating Co Ltd. which was a subsidiary of Darchem Ltd., a competitor in the insulation contracting sector. Cape began to catch up when it developed its own calcium silicate product – 'Caposil' - in 1967, but initially this still had a 25% asbestos content. Against this backcloth it became no longer sustainable or commercially viable to retain the facilities at Barking and Acre Mill. In 1966 a sale of the Barking site to the Local Authority was announced to facilitate a housing development, and the phasing out of Acre Mill commenced, to be completed by 1970 with demolition in 1976. Residual textile interests had been sold to T&N. By now it would have been clear to the Directors that these two factory sites concealed an appalling legacy of industrial disease. In addition, hindsight would levy the charge of a shameful record in not cleaning up the two sites, but the focus on the dangers of asbestos was still largely confined to its significance as an occupational hazard and little attention was given to environmental pollution at the time.

One bright spot was the further development of the Stirling facility producing Rocksil mineral wool insulation. Sales were at a record level in 1960. There were now four lines in operation and the product range was broadened. Other Companies had entered the market producing mainly glass fibre, the main one being Pilkingtons, so the market was becoming competitive with entrants having deep pockets for the capital investment involved.

The company's activities in thermal insulation contracting soldiered on, the acquisitions – Andersons and M A Boylan continued to perform - now supplemented by Chancery Insulation - but the Barking outworks activity was in a state of flux. Cape remained a reluctant contractor and it was an activity that was alien to the management culture, being mining and manufacturing driven. In his reference to contracting in the 1960 annual statement Giles Newton said, 'the competition for high temperature insulation contracts in both the nuclear and conventional power station fields continues to be so fierce that I am convinced the trade is in the absurd position of carrying out millions of pounds of business for a return which in many instances must be negligible'. The company sales force was attached to the regional offices and the personnel employed were more comfortable with counter sales rather than complex work requiring an added value labour input. The sales force was directed as far as possible to secure specifications and in this activity were particularly successful - some 20-30 years later the writer was still seeing international specifications referring to the brand names 'Caposite' and 'Rocksil'.

In Italy, Capamianto which historically had produced a very comprehensive range of asbestos products was proving a liability and the impression is given that Cape had lost control of the subsidiary. Reference to it becomes less as the decade progresses with a note in the 1968 accounts recording that it was being put into voluntary liquidation. It had been a great training school for the insulation industry in Italy, as several of its managers re-emerged in competing companies such as Riva & Mariani and Rossetti. Elsewhere, in South Africa, Cape Asbestos Insulations Pty and Caposite Applications Pty traded satisfactorily.

Overall the Insulation Division was a drain on profits during the decade and appeared to lack both leadership and direction.

Asbestos Legacy

By 1960 evidence was emerging of a further fatal disease associated with the handling of asbestos – mesothelioma. This became apparent at the Pneumoconiosis Conference in Johannesburg in 1959, the international conference arising from the Pneumoconiosis Bureau's investigation into the range of pulmonary diseases in the mining industry. Asbestos mining in fact constituted barely 5% of the value of South Africa's mining activities at this time, yet it became a focus of these conferences over the course of the decade. It has been suggested by some writers that asbestos mining was a stalking horse for mining activities such as gold which had for long been recognised as having serious silicosis and tuberculosis issues[9]. For powerful mining interests, if the pace of revelation of the ills of asbestos could be controlled this in turn would delay the exposure of similar issues elsewhere.

Mesothelioma is a cancer of the lining of the abdominal cavity or the membrane that surrounds the lungs and lines the inside of the chest cavity and is, with rare exceptions, incurable. Such tumours were uncommon and were to become particularly associated with asbestos. Dr J. C. (Chris) Wagner was born in South Africa and in consequence of his first-hand research in the field published a seminal paper in 1960 with fellow authors C. A. Sleggs and P. Marchand which became a well cited work in the history of industrial medicine[10]. This drew attention to the association between the development of mesothelioma and exposure to asbestos dust in people living in the Cape Province asbestos mining areas, and involving crocidolite. Wagner's research was a consequence of visits to Cape's Prieska mine where he had found faults in the recently built third mill and, more particularly in the crushing plant. Cape was to close the plant by the end of the decade. As noted in the last chapter the research was in part funded by Cape, Gefco and T&N who invited visits to their mines.

In the same year leading producers around the world including Cape came together to form the Asbestos Producers Advisory Group (APAG) to defend the industry. Apag's representative in South Africa, Fritz Baunach of Asbestco claimed that the mesothelioma scare was created by chrysotile producers trying to force South African fibre out of the market. Apag did much to curry Government support and proved a constant frustration to those engaged in further research in South Africa.

Cape's Managing Director in South Africa, Justin Mackuertan, knew Wagner and was privy to his findings. Dr. Walter Smither, Works Medical Officer at Barking was asked to make a visit to the mines in 1962. Smither was already aware of cases of mesothelioma arising in the Barking workforce, so the possibility of evidence in South Africa would not have been a surprise to him. Of his three weeks visit it appears that three days were spent at the mines (and the obligatory four days at the game reserves); his confidential report to the Board in London made it aware of the poor working conditions – 'At Prieska, the conditions around and about the mill are not good. The crusher is out of doors. Fibre comes in on the windward side of the mill and is crushed in the open. We saw this opening on several occasions and it was obvious that quite a cloud of dust was being produced and being blown away by a fairly strong wind towards the town - the mixer was raised from the floor of the general warehouse area and had a very dusty platform. Men were working below in a rain of dust'[11]. MacKuertan's response to critics in South Africa was that the Main Board Directors were aware of the problems and were dealing with them in a way such as 'to render further research unnecessary.' Despite Cape's previous cooperation in the research, MacKeurtan considered that no particular action was necessary; moreover he appeared to be supported by the mining establishment and inspectorate, so the response to these findings in South Africa was minimal. Mackeurtan apparently never accepted that asbestos exposure caused mesothelioma and subsequently played a significant role in suppressing the associated research. It has to be remembered that apartheid was now firmly entrenched, South Africa having declared itself a Republic in 1962, and the mining industry was underpinned by the weakest and most neglected in society. Given that Dr. Wagner now became focused on the UK, the attention given to research and regulation eased off in South Africa.

Wagner had caught the attention of John Gilson, Director of the Medical Research Council's Pneumoconiosis Research Unit (PRU) in South Wales and in 1962 Wagner joined Gilson's team, reflecting the fact that the UK was a more fertile ground for further research. He was pleased to do so - he considered that neither the mining industry nor the Government in South Africa were likely to show any great urgency in response to his findings. It was as if the whole issue was being 'offshored,' which no doubt would have suited the South African mining industry. This undoubtedly had the effect of extending the life of asbestos mining in South Africa and it was to be thirty years before the last of the mines in the Northen Cape were closed. The PRU collaboration spawned widespread further research publications, including from sources in the USA where Dr. Irving Selikoff's findings lead him to declare publicly that there is no 'safe level' of asbestos and that even one asbestos fibre could prove lethal.

Whilst there was not unanimity amongst researchers, there was sufficient concern and attention given to the issue that by the middle of the decade pressure arose to revise the UK 1931 regulations in the light of current evidence. As in the earlier period the industry was consulted with a view to seeking their cooperation in this process. Cape's involvement was largely through its founding membership, alongside T&N and BBA, of the Asbestosis Research Council. Walter Smither, on behalf of Cape was involved but it would appear that T&N

and BBA were more proactive in meeting the challenge represented by the research findings, Dr John Knox, T&N's Chief Medical Officer particularly so. By 1965 a great deal of progress had been made towards understanding the link between asbestos and mesothelioma, the causal link was becoming clear and Cape, in the 1965 Company Report, found it necessary to make a statement:

'There is one feature of our business which has received considerable publicity during the year, and this is the risk to health from exposure to asbestos dust. This risk is not new and has been the subject of Government regulations since 1931. Since then your company along with others in the industry, has taken great pains along with others in the industry, to introduce appliances and methods to control the emission of dust and to sponsor research into medical and other aspects of the problem. We are intensifying our efforts in this direction and shall continue to seek the best medical and scientific advice in order to protect our workers and to conform with the highest standards of safety and hygiene considered necessary in the handling of our products.'

There was widespread press attention to the issue, pressure at Government level and some through the Unions. The Directors must have been rattled at this stage, reflected in the rapid phasing out of Cape's worst legacy facilities at Barking and Acre Mill, but there would appear to be no further formal statement along these lines in Company Reports during the next few years. This was against the background of the review by the Ministry of Labour of the Asbestos Industry Regulations of 1931. An Advisory Panel was set up with an impressive list of members, for which T&N and Cape were invited to provide a representative. Cape's Medical Adviser, Walter Smither, was its initial appointee. He was becoming involved at a political level that was really beyond his comfort zone as Barking site's local GP and Works Doctor. By 1967 Cape recognised that a more senior executive should be involved and Dr. Richard Gaze, appointed to the Main Board in 1961, and its Chief Scientist, became Cape's Management member on the Asbestos Research Council (ARC). He then became actively engaged in the protracted discussions and consultation that took place culminating in the revised Asbestos Regulations in 1969[12]. Cape took a fairly hard line in defending its interests, perhaps more so than the ARC and T&N. In his submission on behalf of Cape, Gaze stated 'the present spate of publicity given to hazards associated with asbestos has a large emotional content, unfortunately kindled by a body of medical and quasi-medical opinion all too often taken as fully authoritative'[13], rejecting many of the initial proposals put forward by the Advisory Panel. In its final form, which Cape did accept, the Regulations in Technical Data Note Thirteen (TDN13) for the first time suggested a quantitative limit for asbestos dust from chrysotile and amosite at two fibres/millilitre (ml) of air over a four hour weighted exposure period, and tightened up on a range of ventilation procedures and associated protective equipment and clothing. The interpretation of this limit caused a great deal of controversy and only added to the number of potential victims of disease. The industry took it that working conditions were acceptable *up to* the two fibre limit whereas the regulation only advised that if working conditions were below the two fibre level the factory inspectorate would not seek to enforce the regulations (i.e. it did not mean that working conditions up to two fibres did not represent a danger to health). The industry had a year's grace to bring its processes to order. The limit for crocidolite (blue) was one tenth of that for chrysotile and amosite, which was virtually unachievable – a further reason for phasing it out.

The run up to the introduction of these regulations was the subject of a lot of focus in later litigation when the extent of mesothelioma sufferance became apparent. Evidence revealed at trial[14] showed the extent to which the ARC sought to prevaricate in order to protect the industry. Cape and others were shown to be evasive in some of their advice and publications, and constantly sought to water down the demands emerging during the regulatory drafting process. It showed that the ARC in an internal research document in 1969, had accepted the link between asbestos and mesothelioma and that 'elimination of the dust hazard is the only answer.' This could only suggest that the 1969 regulations represented merely the first step in achieving such a goal - later evidence suggested that 1 in 10 asbestos workers could contract an asbestos related disease at the two fibre/ml level. Whilst the most comprehensive review of the subject to date, the 1969 Regulations did not go far enough, lacked 'teeth' and were open to subjective interpretation.

The focus of the Advisory Panel and Regulations was on the occupational hazard of handling of asbestos in the factories. Environmental waste issues were not addressed and whilst regulation extended to 'works of engineering construction' its disciplines were only loosely monitored beyond the factories. A significant exposure to dust now was to be found on sites up and down the country. This was a period when high rise blocks of flats were being built, and considerations of fire in sharp focus. In Asbestolux and equivalent products, Architects had the answer to securing protection of the steelwork structures being utilised in their design. In addition Asbestolux would be specified for ceilings, ducts and partitions, all involving cutting the boards on site. During the period 1967-1973, 20% of the ceiling area of all new public buildings involved asbestos insulating board[15]. The site fabrication process gave rise to some of the most severe examples of dust ingestion. This was exemplified in Glasgow in 1967, when the Scottish Occupational Health Laboratory Service carried out a survey of the Red Road Building site, demonstrating the exposure to dust in the various activities[16]. It was the carpenters who faced the most risk and it was subsequently forecast that one in ten British carpenters born in the 1940's would die of cancer caused by asbestos[15]. Unfortunately more often or not the response was to add a supplementary rate per hour to wages rather than implement recommendations. The trade off here between providing highly effective fire protection as against worker health should have been avoided, and clearly Cape and others were negligent in not paying enough attention to instructions and disciplines attendant on the installation of their products. They were not alone in this, legally manufacturers were not required to draw attention to safety issues in the handling of their products through labelling, until the 1970's health and safety legislation.

It can be imagined that the Cape Board will have taken such a threat to its business very seriously. Its business was asbestos mining and processing, and its existence depended on it. It had taken steps to improve conditions in its factories. The industry argued that the benefits of asbestos outweighed its hazards. This was certainly an attitude adopted by many of Cape's Directors who had grown up with the concept of a 'magic mineral' protecting the world from the hazards of fire. Even the *Lancet*[17] in a June 1967 leader pointed out that any evaluation of the hazards of asbestos had to take into account its benefits in terms of safety from fire. Up until the late sixties Government and international performance standards in many instances could only be achieved with asbestos containing materials. Later in 1967 *The Times*[18] featured a supplement on asbestos which included a glowing report of a successful industry. This is believed to have arisen in part from the lobbying and involvement of the Asbestos Information Committee (AIC) which had been set up by T&N, Cape, BBA, and Central Asbestos to put the case for the industry. They hired top PR Consultants Hill and Knowlton who had cut their teeth on the tobacco industry.

The issue was one of particular medical complexity, and it was not difficult for a good PR practitioner to counter much of the evidence laid on the table. For the media it was not difficult to find a victim around whom a very sad tale could be told. The AIC efforts to discourage health warnings and labelling that warned of the dangers of asbestos reflected badly on Cape and the other companies, and can be seen as rearguard action of an industry in trouble.

For Cape there will have been some relief when the new regulations, came into being in 1969. Its struggle to meet them later came back to haunt it. The reality was however that mesothelioma sounded the death knell for asbestos as it was becoming apparent that merely trivial amounts of dust and from remote sources could be lethal. Regrettably imports of the material into the UK would linger on for some time, but Cape was now to be firmly on the defensive.

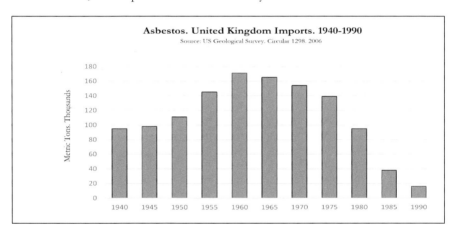

Asbestos. United Kingdom Imports. 1940-1990
Source: US Geological Survey. Circular 1298. 2006

Finances

Cape's defensiveness, to the extent of adopting the machiavellian antics of the AIC's PR Consultants, reflected its financial dependency on asbestos mining and obligation to shareholders. Profits from the sale of asbestos fibre were at record levels despite sales from this source representing a smaller proportion of the total. Profits were holding up nicely and had nearly doubled over the decade. The text of the 1970 Report declares that 'the successful mining of asbestos and export of fibre from South Africa is a major contributor to the results of the Group at this time'. It reads almost as a warning to those shareholders who might be questioning Cape's continuing role in the mining of asbestos. It would appear from the 1969 figures that mining earned profit margins in excess of 20%, the remainder of the business less than 10% so it was attractive, even if capital intensive. Asbestos was still embedded in the culture of the business, and had to be defended, at least in the short term.

Conclusion

Cape had made a deeper commitment to asbestos in a decade when all the warning signs were suggesting caution, if not diversification away from the fibre. Whether Ronnie Dent had such a strategic commitment in mind at the beginning of the decade is doubtful. The two acquisitions that deepened the commitment would appear to have been opportunistic. They turned out to be untimely and in the 'seemed a good idea at the time' category. The UAC acquisition, made at the same time as some of the most serious revelations of the harmful effects of asbestos, seems inexplicable, and evidence of the state of denial quoted beneath this chapter's heading above. Hindsight might suggest that in making significant investments in automotive and asbestos cement, Cape's product strategy was being directed towards the less harmful chrysotile applications for asbestos, but at that time it was not clear to the industry that such a differential between chrysotile and amosite was apparent. Dent was a numbers man, and it was on the numbers he was focused, particularly returns from the South African mines. Here he allowed the industry and Cape's management to cocoon its mining activity from the increasing duty of care pressures being applied elsewhere. Whether it was denial of the asbestos problem or a single minded focus on shareholder's returns (which were good), it was not an illustrious legacy to pass on to his successors. Whilst it would have taken a brave and far-seeing leader, this period was the one in which Cape could have taken action to avoid a lot of what was to come. Instead Cape had to man the barricades.

Chapter 4

The Journey Beyond Asbestos

The 1970's was a period in which the company withdrew from asbestos mining and emerged as a leading building and insulation products supplier and thermal insulation contractor. In 1970 the sale of asbestos fibre represented 56% of the trading profit of the company, a much higher percentage than in prior years, making up for a poor performance elsewhere. The Board must have wished the reverse were the case given the acquisitions in the previous decade. By the end of the seventies, though, the Mining Division had been sold and the Building and Insulation Division was the major earner, sales in the sector increasing by a factor of nearly ten. The laggard was automotive and engineering where sales and margins in real terms declined. Over the decade total sales increased from £45 million to £204 million in 1979 and trading profits from £3 million to £15 million; return on capital was now comfortably in double digits at 18%.

The main economic feature of the decade was the oil crisis in 1973 and the dramatic increase in the price of energy. This gave rise to a period of high inflation, the cost of living increasing by 190% over the decade. There was boom and bust, an IMF bail-out, a stock market crash (1972-74), strikes and the 'Winter of Discontent' in 1978/79. Similar pressures arose in South Africa, coupled with the death throes of apartheid. All of which represented a challenge for Cape's management. The rising cost of energy however was of benefit to Cape with its portfolio of energy saving products, added to which the infrastructure and building sector held up well.

Organisation and Management

Charter was now playing a more interventionist role in its majority controlled subsidiary. Ronnie Dent had opposed the takeover and South African Sidney Spiro, Charter's Managing Director, was looking to move him aside. They were seeking to combine the management of Cape with other industrial interests. Lionel Stopford Sackville, a scion of one of England's aristocratic families, was now Chairman of both Charter and Cape and recalled 'a luncheon attended by Charter's non-executive nominees to the Cape Board and the other non-Charter non-executives on Cape's Board, at which it was decided that Higham would replace Dent (as Managing Director) subject to Spiro 'canvassing' other executive directors, apart from Dent and Higham'[(1)]. Dent was at the meeting and agreed; Higham, he claimed, being his choice with Pat Parkes as Deputy. Ronnie Dent survived, as Chairman, whilst Sidney Spiro moved up as Charter's Chairman. Dent had by now become a Director of Charter and was asked to oversee two other Charter businesses.

So it was to be Managing Director Geoffrey Higham's decade, assuming the role on January 1st, 1971. He inherited a company heavily committed to asbestos but there had to be great doubts as to whether an asbestos based business could be sustained. He had a duty to shareholders and employees to build a future. Whether Ronnie Dent or Geoffrey Higham had a clear strategy to exit asbestos at the beginning of the decade is doubtful. They were not going to articulate such

a move whilst Cape retained the mining interests. The actual incidence of asbestos related disease was still low, given the latency delay, and evidence suggests they believed asbestos would have a continuing role and Cape could weather the storm. Midway through the decade however any defence of asbestos became rapidly untenable and as a result events took their course. When presented with means of disengagement the Directors did, to their credit, pursue them rigorously. For the manufacturing businesses, it was a decade offering considerable opportunity in existing markets, so there was no particular pressure to diversify. Ronnie Dent encouraged new business ventures put forward by his managers and took the view that if they had not succeeded in two years they could be terminated. There were however too many that had to be terminated, reflecting a lack of proper scrutiny at the proposal stage.

As a reflection of the lingering commitment to asbestos, it was not until 1974 that the corporate name was changed from Cape Asbestos to Cape Industries. This was claimed to be rather a reflection of the increasing role industrial processes played in the business than the fact that asbestos was getting a bad name, but the latter must have been the reason. By then, too, a new corporate logo had been introduced. It was similar to the previous 'biblical' symbol but without the three men and well overdue!

Mining

In 1977, world production of asbestos peaked at 4.8 million metric tons as did South African production at 380,000 metric tons, with Southern Africa being the third largest producer after Canada and Russia[2]. It was to be a decade characterised by increasing costs, albeit recovered in rising prices. In South Africa, black consciousness was reflected in strikes that affected the mining sector, and political unrest, culminating in the Soweto uprising in 1976. At the same time the mines became a drain on capital given demands elsewhere in the business. It was necessary to mine deeper to meet quality requirements. The quality of 'weathered' surface mined fibre no longer satisfied the demands of the building and insulation products sector. In 1974, £3.5 million was invested at Penge alone, deposits being mined at 1,296 ft. at the lowest level. All this affected profitability. The Charter 1975 Report recorded that Cape's African wages had increased by 90% in 1974, and were three times the rate applying in 1971 - against a backcloth of a shortage of labour. Demand remained strong enough to support higher prices, but there were beginning to be signs of a drop off in demand in the USA and the UK, reflecting safety issues. Some mines were becoming exhausted - the blue mine at Koegas, once the largest, closed in 1978.

Geoffrey Higham saw it as a priority to be more actively engaged in addressing issues in the Mining Division than his predecessor, and was unhappy with what he saw. By 1974 he had sidelined Justin Mackuertan and appointed Simon Doherty as Managing Director of Casap. Doherty had earlier been fed in as Mackeurtan's Personal Assistant, prior to his appointment having worked closely with Higham and Dr. Gaze at UK Head Office. Mackuertan could not be readily removed because of his connections, but the subsequent improvement in operational capability and profitability at the mines was very much down to Doherty, who also had a clear brief to report back to Gaze on progress made in dealing with dust control issues.

With demand dropping the writing was on the wall for asbestos mining; the Cape Board could see it and the political outlook in South Africa was looking precarious. South Africa was becoming isolated and for the chrysotile lobby it was easy to pillory amphibole asbestos and its main country of origin. A ban of blue and brown asbestos was threatened but South Africa found an unlikely ally in Russia, which needed crocidolite (blue) or amosite (brown) to mix with its own product. By the early seventies there were ominous signs of industrial disease claims (IDC) and litigation in the USA (see page 75) which could draw Cape in, so the search was on to seek a way out of asbestos mining. It was becoming less important in terms of Cape's own needs as it transitioned away from asbestos containing products, particularly those involving crocidolite and amosite. Consumption of amosite was at its greatest in the production of Asbestolux and Marinite, and as we will see these were replaced with asbestos free equivalents during the decade. Whereas, in 1969, 14% of the output of its mines was feedstock for product within the Group, by 1979 this had dropped to 1%. So while it is unlikely that it had been the Board's intention to dispose of the mines at the beginning of the decade, given the extent of the subsequent capital investment expended, by 1975 it was firmly in their mind, and for Charter there was a question of reputational damage by association.

Geoffrey Higham was tasked with finding a buyer and approached, amongst others, Asbestco of Switzerland who owned the KCB mines in South Africa. The reaction of Chairman Ernst Schmidheiny was dismissive, suggesting they too were looking to withdraw. (The last similar acquisition made by Ernst on behalf of Asbestco relied on a contract written on the back of a cigarette packet so any deal may well have not satisfied Cape's lawyers anyway!)[3]. A solution was engineered by Charter in the form of an acquisition by Transvaal Consolidated Land and Exploration Company (Transvaal), from whom Cape leased land and mineral rights. A slightly surprised Higham was able to finalise a deal to dispose of the business in 1979 for a net consideration of £15 million cash. Shareholders in Transvaal included Charter itself and Barlow Rand, the conglomerate, in which Anglo American also had a holding[4]. This strongly suggests that Anglo orchestrated the deal through Charter. It was in Anglo's commercial interest to limit scrutiny of asbestos mining to South Africa and maintain a degree of control over the industry. This was possible in that it now had stakes in all of the major mining investment houses.

Whilst the fact that the Mining Division had contributed £3.5 million of Cape's trading profit suggested a good deal for the buyer, in the circumstances and in hindsight it was a very timely deal for Cape. Cape did though have to provide a warranty of protection against industrial disease claims.

This then precipitated an avalanche of deals. This was as much a political move as it was a reflection of asbestos related health issues, or a pent up need for mine rationalisation. The Nationalists in South Africa had for long resented the power of Harry Oppenheimer's Anglo and encouraged Afrikaner business interests, one of which was Federal Mynbou (Fedmyn), a subsidiary of SANLAM and by now owner of General Mining or Gencor (in which Anglo also had a holding). Fedmyn already owned Cape's competitor Gefco and by 1981 controlled competitor Asbestco's KCB. Within two years of its purchase, Transvaal's parent Barlow Rand, sold the Cape business to Fedmyn. Fedmyn, through Gencor, now had a virtual monopoly. The industry was now firmly under the South African mining establishment's protective umbrella.

So ended Cape's involvement in the business activity for which it was originally formed. There were few tears shed as the company had moved on. Management now was far removed from the buccaneering band of mining engineers. Political and economic conditions were rapidly changing in South Africa and the country was beginning to catch up with the levels of awareness of asbestos related disease now apparent elsewhere. An epitaph written in the *Cape Review*[5] stated:

'Asbestos has played a fundamental role in the growth and development of Cape but also in the provision of products and materials which have been essential to the convenience and safety of everyday life. It is only through experience of asbestos that the science and technology of fire, heat and energy control has advanced and allowed, wherever practicable, the development of alternative materials to asbestos itself.'

This was an admission that all was over for the fibre, and at this point the only asbestos used in Cape's range of products was in asbestos cement cladding and automotive friction materials. It could now manage without blue and brown asbestos both of which were subject to a voluntary import ban in the UK.

Automotive & Engineering

The automotive and engineering activities of the company at the beginning of the decade comprised Small and Parkes, making Don and Capasco brake and clutch linings and disc pads, mainly as original equipment; the newly acquired Trist Draper, based in Bristol, serving the replacement market for automotive and rail, and Kismet, the successor of the old Weaver business, selling garage supplies. In Manchester Small & Parkes had its own R & D facilities, enhanced in 1971 by a test track.

Whereas in the 1960's UK car manufacturers dominated supply in the home market, by the end of the decade European manufacturers were gaining market share on quality and delivery grounds. UK motor car production peaked at 1.92 million vehicles in 1972. Whilst Small & Parkes had set up a subsidiary in Belgium – Don International s.a. - to service the European manufacturers, the business had its difficulties and never really gained a significant share of the original equipment market. Breaking the hold established suppliers had over customer accounts proved difficult. In 1973 it was reported 'the company's products are being manufactured under licence or by associates in an increasing number of countries which now include Belgium, Czechoslovakia, India, Jamaica, Japan, Malaysia, Kenya, New Zealand, South Africa and Spain'. The Belgian plant – Don International s.a - had subsidiary sales offices in Germany and France.

Given the growing after market for automotive parts and repairs, in 1972 the decision was taken to set up a chain of outlets for the distribution of specialist motor components, and Cape Distribution was formed, partly by acquiring existing businesses. By 1974 it had a national network of sixty-five outlets.

In 1975 the Small and Parkes name was dropped in favour of Don International to identify more readily with its major trademark. It is noteworthy that the name 'Cape' was very rarely referenced in its literature - a reflection of its independence. Success was being achieved in the mainland Europe market, but this was short lived, as the market suffered a downturn at the end of the end of the decade. Annual reports suggest a business that was over diversified, snatching at new opportunities without too much forethought. Any uplift in performance seemed to be subsequently matched by disappointment or downright failure. It was clearly a competitive and cyclical market tying up capital that could have been more productively employed elsewhere. BBA (British Belting and Asbestos) was a formidable competitor and by the 1980's claimed to be the world's largest supplier of brake pads to the automotive business. Cape Automotive's sales increased from £20 million to £57 million over the decade, but trading profit margins never exceeded 5%, ending up at 2.2% in 1979. It shared little in common with other Group businesses being more directly involved with consumer markets; the impression is given that the Small and Parkes executives were left to their own devices, whilst the main board's management's attention was focused elsewhere, and on businesses that they were more familiar with. Had it been a major outlet for Cape's mines there would have been hidden benefits, but its fibre needs were confined to chrysotile.

Building Products

By 1973 Cape had a remarkably diverse range of products for the building industry under the banner Cape Universal Building Products. It had the old Uxbridge flint brick business, a range of asbestos cement profile claddings for external use, pitch fibre pipes and rainwater goods (the old UAC business); Asbestolux board for partitions and ceilings, lay-in ceiling tiles of wood fibre and mineral wool, and high performance Marinite board at Germiston. In 1974 Cape acquired Johns Manville's 47% stake in the Marinite business. Cape claimed to be 'the world's leading producer of asbestos based non-combustible boards and panels providing vital fire protection in buildings and ships.'

A range of translucent sheets 'Unilux' had been added and in 1974 Cookson Sheet Metal Developments in Southampton was acquired and introduced profile sheet steel cladding. Cape's sales personnel could approach specifiers and contractors with a broad portfolio of products in a sector which at times was volatile but one which offered growth over the decade. By 1973 there was logic in splitting the business between Cape Universal Claddings catering for products for external applications (at Watford and Bowburn) and Cape Building Panels (at Uxbridge, Queensferry and Germiston) for products having internal applications including shipbuilding (Marinite), with particular emphasis on fire protection.

One of Cape's major markets was the farming sector where there a boom in the construction of concrete portal framed buildings clad with asbestos cement profile sheeting, the most common design provided by Atcost. Many of these buildings survive today without alteration, some now subject to redevelopment. For farm and industrial buildings Cape could provide drainage systems, rainwater goods and moulded fittings, cladding in asbestos cement, metal or unilux, internal partitioning, and ceilings – a one stop shop. As a result of heavy capital expenditure sales and profits rose rapidly in the second half of the decade, albeit boosted by inflation.

In 1972 the first of four patent applications made within the decade and covering asbestos-free building boards was filed by Vic Barrable, Cape Boards' Technical Director, the inventor being named as R.J. Zukowski, the Chief Technical Officer. These were to a broadly defined recipe incorporating 'selected fibres and fillers,' reinforcing the calcium silicate core. The difficulty was finding a fibre that would replicate the properties of asbestos. Several alternatives were researched and tested but the best of the bunch was found to be cellulose fibres and the chemically treated pulps as used in paper manufacture.

Having gone through the necessary testing procedures to meet the relevant standards, by the end of the decade Superlux as a replacement for Asbestolux, and Monolux for Marinite, were both being actively marketed, initially alongside the products they were replacing. The range was extended to include Masterboard and Vermiculux. Superlux met requirements where up to 4 hours fire resistance was required, Masterboard was a Class O building board for general building applications, Vermiculux satisfied a need for the fire protection of steel columns and beams (replacing the old asbestos based spray technique). Monolux could withstand temperatures up to 500 deg. C and was available as a board or cast into shapes The cost of Superlux and Masterboard was 15-18% more than Asbestolux and builders initially complained of greater fixing costs, so Asbestolux continued to be produced until the differential narrowed and market preference prevailed. The great advantage of these products was that they were moisture resistant compared with gypsum, the most used general building board. Cape could claim that they were the first company in the world to introduce an asbestos-free product that represented a direct replacement of asbestos based boards.

The innovative significance and quality of these asbestos free products was such that they are still produced today to broadly the same formula, format, and production technique. It is very much to the credit of the Barking and Uxbridge based R&D personnel that they emerged, and thus enabled Cape to abandon asbestos as fundamental to this side of its business. By the end of the decade there were marketing companies in France and Germany supporting sales. With the introduction of these asbestos-free replacements for Asbestolux, there was a further incentive to dispose of the mining business as nearly 85% of UK imports of Cape's amosite fibre in 1976 was directed towards the manufacture of fire resistant board[6]. Cape's other activities in asbestos cement and brake linings had only a very small requirement for amosite and could still procure the fibre from Cape's successor in South Africa.

The importance of the development of these products cannot be overestimated as it was now possible for specifiers to select asbestos-free alternatives. Hitherto under the International Convention for the Safety of Life at Sea, the only products capable of meeting its stringent fire tests were asbestos based [7]. It was not surprising then that the successful launch of this asbestos-free range of products was reflected in the receipt by Cape of the Queen's Award for Technical Achievement in 1980. Geoffrey Higham has stated that Cape was good at chemistry but poor at production; there was truth in this as market demand always tended to exceed the company's capacity to produce. But money was tight, and it was to his credit that he did make funds available to back these developments, at a time when Cape was beginning to struggle financially.

Insulation Products and Distribution

For Cape Insulation's Rocksil mineral fibre it was a decade when energy conservation became a major consideration on the back of oil price rises. Capacity at Stirling was again increased and the range of products expanded beyond the industrial sector into the commercial and home markets (e.g. 'Housewarm' loft insulation). Consumer goods such as electrical appliances opened further outlets for its products. The acoustic and fire protective features of the product made it a ready substitute for asbestos-based alternatives that were being phased out. Competition from glass fibre with deep pocketed producers such as Pilkington and Isover, was fierce. Whilst Rocksil rock fibre had an advantage in terms of fire resistance at elevated temperatures, this was only really of real benefit in the industrial sector. In the commercial sector (e.g. loft insulation) it could not pass on its higher production costs, so margins were slim. Given the heavy capital investment involved and time required to install a production line, it also proved difficult to achieve a fine balance between demand and capacity. Higham's comment on Cape's weakness at production applied here.

Cape continued to manufacture Caposil, the calcium silicate and asbestos fibre composite formed into pipe sections and slab that covered temperature ranges beyond the capability of Rocksil. By the end of the decade it was free of asbestos but as result, a rather crumbly product. This was complemented by the introduction of Capoflex, a non-asbestos ceramic fibre bought in from the Morgan Crucible Company.

The incentives initiated by the government covering the insulation of the housing stock encouraged Cape to take a stake in the booming sector covering home insulation, and in 1977 the business of Pattisons Insulation was acquired from its owner C.R. (Rod) Pattison. It was a useful outlet for Rocksil loft insulation. Pattisons ran a number of local depots and carried out installation work. The timing proved to be poor as a number of these government incentives were removed in 1980. Rod Pattison, remained the Managing Director of the business which was named Cape Insulation Services. A swashbuckling entrepreneur, he sat rather uncomfortably alongside the other sector managers. The local depots competed with distributors of Cape products such as Sheffield Insulation, which caused some resentment in the marketplace.

Insulation Contracting

In 1964 an Accountant by the name of John Farrell had been appointed at Head Office. His focus was very much on the rundown of the Barking site, and when the facility was closed the last of its activities standing was insulation contracting.. This business was concerned with industrial as opposed to commercial projects – e.g. oil refineries, power plants, shipbuilding, petrochemical, and other process industry applications. It was perceived as a risky, low margin activity at the rough end of the market and earlier dismissed by Giles Newton (see page 46). Farrell was sent to Barking to seek to get some control of this activity, and see whether it was a sustainable business. Whether his approach was overly zealous given the embedded culture at Cape's oldest site or not, he did not survive long and shortly left, only to be called back in 1968 to pick up the reins again. As related in the last chapter much of Cape's installation work had been sub-contracted, a major partner being Wm. Kenyon, based in Cheshire. Kenyon was a distributor of Cape products as well as an installer and enjoyed a close relationship with Cape, having been an original partner in the Rocksil mineral fibre project at Stirling. In 1971 Kenyon's took on a major contract at Burmah Oil's Ellesmere Port Refinery, through main contractor M.W. Kellogg, which proved beyond their capability and means. In return for accepting an assignment of the contract, Cape acquired the rest of their installation business, and shortly after merged it with the Andersons Insulation business to form Cape Contracts Ltd. This was a game changer as Kenyons had several key clients including ICI, Shell, BP and Courtaulds. In due course, Chancery Insulation, the old UAC subsidiary, was brought under the new umbrella. Farrell became the Managing Director. The business was headquartered at Cape's one remaining building at Barking – Cape Lodge - with depots now established in the key industrial areas. One feature of the market was to Cape's advantage. Projects were becoming much larger, and the smaller companies could neither finance the work nor afford to take on the risk. Cape, alongside Newalls Insulation and Darlington Insulation, were the main players at the top end of the market. Given the labour disputes that commonly affected the major sites, it was an unattractive business such that by 1975 T&N threw in the towel, and Cape was able to pick up its contracting business. This nearly doubled the size of Cape Contracts. Farrell had produced a formula on these deals with Kenyons and Newalls which ensured that any shortfall in the realisation of acquired work-in-progress was recoverable from the vendor. The consideration for the Newalls business did not exceed £750,000 and was satisfied by the issue of shares to Turner & Newall, with agreement by Charter Consolidated to purchase them for 40p each. This was at the nadir of the stock market and if T&N hung on to them they would have realised a sizable profit.

To understand how development of this business became so significant for Cape, it is necessary to look at how the market operated and its characteristics. The market mainly involved insulation for heat conservation which was a fairly simple process of applying a blanket or section of insulation to a pipe, dome, or flat surface. Some skill was then involved in the formation of a cementitious or metal finish. It was not highly skilled although the breed of men who formed the core of its labour were able to style themselves 'thermal insulation engineers' (TIE's), more commonly known as 'laggers' (those handling metal finishes – 'sheet metal workers'). They were heavily unionised under the GMWU, later GMB. It was a dirty and dusty activity involving poorly educated but proud men for whom it offered a reasonable wage[8]. Asbestos fibre came in through the London Docks and, given the market in the London area, many of the laggers came from the East End, particularly Barking and Dagenham where Cape's works was located. Glasgow, Newcastle and Liverpool were similar heartlands.

Lagging was one of the last activities in the building of a power plant, oil refinery or petrochemical plant – indeed any building involving insulation. This meant that the resourcing and planning of installation work could be a nightmare for the insulation contractor, as he was commonly subject to disruption and delays, involving sudden changes in manpower needs (exemplified in Kenyon's Burmah Oil contract). The power of the client or main contractor could be deployed to force the insulation contractor to work uneconomically, with consequent payment issues and delays. Partly in recognition of this, contractors got together in 1957 to form the Thermal Insulation Contractors Association (TICA) for the purpose of negotiating annual wage settlements with the Union and maintaining a closed shop to their advantage. The apprenticeship process was to involve four years training which restricted new entrants being rapidly inducted. Wage agreements were subsequently incorporated within the National Agreement 'Blue Book' covering the engineering construction industry. This at least gave each contractor parity in the wages they paid, a common charge per manhour, and thereby some power to resist wage demands when cornered during project execution.

John Farrell saw the other side of this contractual conundrum – insulation contractors had a countervailing power in being in a position to stand in the way of a client completing a project. TICA's relationship with the GMB ensured that work only went to time served laggers and their employers, so the insulation contractors controlled the labour pool. In this position Cape and others were able to demand proper compensation for their efforts in completing work that was subject to delay and disruption, where necessary holding the client to ransom by threatening his completion date.

A well publicised example was the CEGB's Isle of Grain Power Station under construction in 1976[9]. Designed to be the biggest oil fired power station in Europe, poor management of the project was matched only by the intransigence of organised labour. Laggers were at the forefront and the three insulation contractors on site were played one off against another. Farrell got agreement to the formation by the three contractors – Cape Contracts, Darlington Insulation and Newalls Insulation (by then acquired by Cape) of a consortium – CDN – to complete the work. At the time laggers at Grain were 90% less productive than men doing similar work elsewhere in the country and it is estimated that in 18 months on site CDN achieved the equivalent of only one month's production. Work stoppages arose over various issues including a scare that the glass fibre insulation being used was, as the successor to asbestos, dangerous to handle. It took nine years to complete the project with a massive overspend at taxpayer's expense. The tail wagged the dog and CDN were able to demand and get paid for the cost overruns attributable to the delays and circumstances that gave rise to the unproductive working. Despite this appalling example, however, projects did get finished, and when given a free run Cape could be relied upon to deliver up performance.

This commercial if not strong arm approach to project execution earnt Cape Contracts some attractive profits, and the Cape Board began to extol the virtues of an insulation contracting business. It had two negative effects, however. Firstly the Company earned a reputation for being commercially too aggressive. This was probably fair criticism, although previously it and others had been overly willing to roll over under client pressure. But it took another ten years or so to lose this reputation. Secondly it encouraged complacency and overly hasty diversification. Farrell had recruited some strong managers to run the UK industrial business, and encouraged by the Main Board he set his sights on creating further contracting businesses.

Towards the end of the decade a substantial opportunity rose for Cape in the burgeoning North Sea Oil and Gas sector. Cape Contracts seized the sales initiative engaging with both UK and US oil companies. A central sales force was established to approach both end users and contractors. This was a different world to working for the CEGB, ICI and land based Oil Refinery Companies. Engagement now was with worldly contractors such as Bechtel and Fluor and Operators such as Marathon and Occidental Oil. For a sales team hitherto based at Barking and more familiar with entertaining clients to an evening at the Catford 'dogs' followed by a drink at 'The Prospect of Whitby' at Wapping, it was now a London Office, the Club scene and a weekend grouse shooting!

The great benefit of its involvement in the offshore sector was the enlargement of its skills base. Natural gas related offshore installations and their onshore terminals required some specialised insulation techniques particularly in cold (cryogenic) insulation. They required an element of multi discipline activity (i.e. scaffolding might be included in the work scope, or a man may be required to perform more than one trade). They required high standards of safety. All these needs, and Cape's response in satisfying demand, formed the core and ethos of the business that was to evolve.

Work could be lumpy in the industrial sector and the business did carry out some work in the commercial field and this was enlarged on the acquisition of T&N's Newalls Insulation. Both Cape and Newalls undertook installation of some of their other manufactured products such as partitioning and suspended ceilings. Work was undertaken for mechanical contractors carrying out heating and ventilation work in buildings. There was also the old Chancery spray business operating in the fire protection sector. Encouraged no doubt by Ronnie Dent's two year trial philosophy, John Farrell set up a separate subsidiary – Cape Building Services Ltd – to give these businesses as Divisions an identity of their own. In addition the business of DHI Services, which supplied and installed insulated district heating mains, was acquired and placed within the new company.

The partitioning, suspended ceilings and spray fire protection business comprised the Structural Services Division. Partitioning and suspended ceilings was at the low end of the building trade – as was asbestos free 'Dry' fire protection involving boxing in columns and beams with Cape Vermiculux. However 'Wet' fire protection involving spray materials now free of asbestos and bought in materials such as 'Fendolite' or 'Mandolite.' This could be high risk work requiring technical expertise and carrying onerous warrantee provisions. The contracting side of Cape was short on the technical knowhow that existed at Uxbridge and the two businesses were arms-length profit centres. The Structural Services Division was persuaded by Architects Piano & Rogers to undertake the fire protection of the Centre Pompidou in Paris. This involved external steelwork, and it was Cape's task to fire protect by spray technique and cladding. It proved something of a disaster in achieving a watertight seal to the metal cladding, and a battle followed with the specifiers which ultimately went to arbitration. The business did not learn its lesson as to the folly in taking on prestige projects until it lost heavily on a further major contract - the partitioning at London Heathrow's Terminal 4; difficulties in sourcing labour and construction delays proved to be beyond the ability of management to control. By then Farrell pulled the plug having learnt some important lessons. Partitioning was for small local contractors and spray fire protection with no product of Cape's own and with its 10 year guarantees, too risky.

The heating and ventilating market was served by the Mechanical Services Division. Whilst this had the advantage of being serviced by Thermal Insulation

Engineers and sheet metal workers, their skills were slightly different than those in the industrial sector. The clientele were mechanical and electrical (M&E) contractors employed by the main building contractor. Contracts were generally small and involved a lot of congested and interrupted working, difficult clients and poor cashflow. M&E contractors were commercially hard nosed and they in turn were bullied by main contractors. The Division survived the decade largely as a result of securing all the work on the London Barbican Centre. The ultimate client was the 'Coal and Corn Committee' of the City of London and the project struggled with the extent and complexity of the M&E work, resulting in delays in completing the work. The complexity was such that 'as built' drawings bore very little resemblance to the design on which contracts were based. For those with an eye for a commercial opportunity, like Cape, there was money to be made. But once the project was finished it was clear that this was a one off and this too was a market for small local contractors.

In DHI Services its technique involved the injection of polyurethane insulation within a polypropylene sleeve, and its installation as a pre-insulated pipe in the field, the joints being injected with insulation foam on site. The initiative for this product arose from the creation of district heating schemes - a housing complex would be serviced by a central boiler circulating hot water underground to each unit - a popular concept with local authorities. The DHI pre-insulated piping system reduced the work on site. It was early days for the product, however, and there were some technical issues, but with the removal of government incentives the market began to dry up. Worst still were the 10 year guarantees inherent in the business which had to be honoured when the decision was taken to close the business and liquidate the company.

A further Newalls activity was the C.L. Whitaker Cold Store business in Grimsby. It survived as it had pioneered a process of injecting polyisocyanurate insulation between two metal skins providing for a pre-insulated wall or ceiling panel. This technique was deployed by Cape Building Products and its newly acquired subsidiary Cookson Sheet Metal Developments, in the production of pre-insulated profile sheet metal cladding. In consequence the business was transferred to Cape Building Products.

So Cape Building Services proved a failure, a lesson in misconceived strategy and its costs of closure for a year or so was hidden in the exceptional profits being made by Cape Contracts. One diversification towards the end of the decade that was a success however was scaffolding which will be dealt in future chapters.

A further new area of diversification established at this time within Cape Contracts was Cape Contracts International. Many of Cape's clients were undertaking projects overseas, and looked for support. This more often or not took the form of Cape being asked to design, specify and list all the insulation and cladding required for a project, supplying the material, an installation manual and provision of a number of supervisors to oversee local labour. This was particularly common in the power plant sector with Babcock and NEI building power plants overseas as far afield as Hong Kong, India, Iraq and Libya. The support of ECGD Government finance for many of these projects stipulated materials should be sourced in the UK which worked to the benefit of Cape's manufacturing businesses. In 1976 a contract was secured through Engineer Fluor for work at the Isfahan Oil Refinery in Iran on a turnkey supply and install basis thus involving a permanent establishment in Iran, utilising UK supervision and Iranian labour. By 1979 several projects had been undertaken in Iran, but with the Islamic Revolution Cape had to leave in a hurry. By this time a contract had been secured from Engineer Bechtel for low temperature insulation work at the gas gathering centres being constructed at remote sites Bu Hasa and Ruwais in Abu Dhabi, United Arab Emirates. This was all high risk work but proved the foundation of what was to become a worldwide project capability as we will see in later chapters.

At the same time John Farrell was dealing with a Dutch insulation contracting company -Verhoeff which had secured work on the Peterhead Power Station in Scotland. He secured Board approval to buy the company from the family owners. 'Jovial' Joop Heijnraets, Project Manager at Peterhead became the General Manager. Due diligence failed to recognize that the only real profit earner was a subsidiary in Curacao carrying out maintenance work for Royal Dutch Shell on the Netherlands Antilles Oil Refinery, and this business was not part of the deal. The company, operating out of Dordrecht, was a minor player in Holland with only one major client – Heineken. Its name was changed to Cape Contracts Nederlands BV.

Another diversification was asbestos removal. A consequence of the 1969 regulations was the pressure applied to Cape and others to remove asbestos containing insulation. This in itself offered market opportunity. Demand grew rapidly, and given the equipment needs to carry out the work, and perhaps a fear that by doing the work the company would build up further IDC problems for itself, the decision was taken to subcontract the work. This was not a success as the sub contractors performed poorly, both in terms of safe practice and their capacity to invest in good equipment. By 1976 Cape Environmental Services Ltd was formed as a separate entity. Cape subsequently played an active role in TICA's Asbestos Control and Abatement Division (ACAD).

Asbestos Legacy

Any feeling by the Cape Board that pressure might be off following the passing of the 1969 Asbestos Regulations, was soon struck a blow with the 1971 Granada TV's *World in Action* documentary devoted to Cape's Acre Mill which attacked the industry and the Factory Inspectorate. This was followed in 1975 by BBC's *'Killer Dust'*. Focus on Cape was somewhat diluted as a good part of the flack appeared to be taken by the Factory Inspectorate. The Inspectorate received an element of support from the medical profession, through the medium of the Lancet and the British Medical Journal, still citing some of the benefits derived from asbestos. This deflected critics from the industry which was clearly not meeting the two fibre per ml. dust limit imposed under the 1969 regulations (a failure evidenced in later litigation - see Chapter 12). Furthermore, under the 1974 Health and Safety at Work Act, an obligation was imposed on employers not only to maintain wide-ranging safe working conditions, but also provide environmental control of noxious substances. Renewed public focus on the dangers of asbestos resulted in the Government appointing Sir 'Bill' Simpson, Chairman of the Health and Safety Commission to head the Advisory Committee on Asbestos (ACA). The Committee took statements from a broad range of sources, including Cape and other manufacturers. The industry ramped up its PR in defence of the material. A report in two volumes[6] was issued in 1979 which made several recommendations. These amounted to a further disincentive to continue using asbestos and an encouragement to develop alternatives. In particular it proposed a ban on the import of blue asbestos and on the use of sprayed asbestos. It proposed a further reduction in the dust control limit to one fibre per ml (0.5 for amosite). The report was essentially a survey and the conclusions subject to enough caveats, giving the industry (and maybe the Government) further breathing space.

T&N by nature of its size and range of asbestos containing products had led the defence of the industry and had at an early stage engaged with the regulatory bodies. Cape too engaged but let T&N do much of the running, T&N having more at stake. Both companies had legacy sites that displayed the worst examples of negligence, but Cape played a low key game. It stuck to its argument that it had cooperated in the establishment and implementation of regulations, and had invested heavily in the necessary dust suppression equipment. It could now validly claim that it had been a pioneer in developing asbestos free products; in this it had an advantage over T&N which was a large, bureaucratic company, at times contemptuous, and slow to change.

In the 1974 Cape Company Report the Chairman is emphasising 'Asbestos and asbestos-based products make an essential contribution to society, through fire protection, energy conservation, safer transport and other fields', but by 1975 and prior to the formation of the Advisory Committee, we get a more placatory statement in response to some of the adverse press and TV commentary - 'I deeply regret that anyone may have suffered in any way as a result of working with this material. Your Company has always endeavoured to act responsibly in the matter, spending very large sums on the control of dust and taking a leading part in research into this problem. Advances in medical and scientific knowledge were taken into account in the drawing up of the new regulations which came into force in 1969 and these are fully enforced in our establishments. Nevertheless in view of the recent publicity, we welcome the proposed Government Inquiry.' The same report points to a record year in mining profits, providing again over 50% of the overall trading profits of the Company, so Cape was in no position to make any material change in its defensive narrative.

In the 1976 report further reference is made to the support given by Cape to the ACA. The 1979 Report refers to the ACA's findings but comments on the demanding dust emission standards and timescale for implementation. It could not resist the comment 'It appears to have done a great deal to rebut the ill-informed and strident criticism which has in recent years regrettably done so much to arouse public anxiety to an unjustified degree'.

Little is said of safety issues in South Africa, and it is clear that the focus of employee welfare and legacy industrial disease was now in the UK. In South Africa, compared with the UK, pressure from government and occupational safety bodies continued to be lax, until the unions showed some initiative on the demise of apartheid. Companies would claim that many of the workers at the mines were migrant workers, from beyond the borders of South Africa, so employee traceability was always an issue and records of later health issues non-existent. The record of Cape's management in South Africa was not good. The fact that they had initially engaged with the Pneumoconiosis Bureau's research only to dismiss its findings suggests they were far removed from the realities of the workface and more engaged in protecting the interests of the mining establishment. They behaved no differently from others in the industry and were symptomatic of a governing class underpinned by apartheid. Their actions probably allowed Cape to hang on for a few years and enable a successful sale of its mining assets, which was what, in effect, the shareholders were looking to them to do.

Industrial Disease Claims

The first personal injury claim related to negligence and asbestos in the UK was served in 1967 and involved seven workers employed by Gefco's UK subsidiary, Central Asbestos. Eventually subject to House of Lords Appeal, Central Asbestos was found to be in breach of the 1931 Regulations. The industry had been compensating victims quietly prior to that date, entitlement to compensation having been set out in the same Regulations. In the 1973 Cape Company Report we find the first references to the financial cost of dealing with industrial disease claims. The Report explains that hitherto the cost of compensation to victims had been paid out of working costs. The Chairman noted - 'Due principally to inflation and not, I am glad to say to any increase in numbers of people affected, these payments have risen to a very substantial figure'. In the notes to the accounts a provision of £3,500,000 was made 'which on present information should be sufficient to cover all future payments and against which all such payments will be charged'. The notes reveal that the actual cost incurred in the year 1973 was £600,000. A confusing statement in the 1975 accounts suggests that the provision is being eaten up rapidly and rather than increasing it, relies on the excuse that there are too many uncertainties in forecasting the likely liability. The Board was looking head on at an unquantifiable potential liability. At this time and in addition to asbestosis, lung cancer and mesothelioma, the presence of pleural plaque was considered a compensable condition[8]. Pleural plaques were small areas of thickened tissue in the lung lining or pleura. They were associated with asbestos working but were considered benign, although an indicator of possible more disabling disease. Pleural plaque was quite common amongst laggers in particular, and could involve a high volume of low value claims. Larger sums could be paid out if a claimant agreed a 'wrap-up' deal which embraced the risk of further disease manifesting itself. Pleural plaque was in due course to lose its status as a compensable condition.

It tends to be assumed that pressure to compensate victims was exclusively from external sources, but by this time the incidence of disease amongst retiree laggers that had worked for Cape was more than apparent to colleagues and management. When the Barking site was closed Cape retained a Victorian house – Cape Lodge – as the headquarters of Cape Contracts, John Farrell's base until the end of the decade. This was the home of the lagger fraternity that had been closely associated with the evolution of the asbestos industry in the UK. He would be regularly approached by employee representatives, doctors and local families and could thereby bring to the Cape Board a vivid account of the rising incident of disease and the demand for compensation, and possibly more so than the managers of the factories. Because of the dust control procedures applied, there were fewer cases amongst retiree factory employees, even though the factories were the source of the products laggers had to install in the field.

The 1973 Notes contain the first reference to litigation in the USA. 'The Company together with two of its subsidiaries has been named as a defendant in actions recently commenced in the USA which seek the recovery of very substantial damages. These actions are being strenuously contested. In the opinion of the Company's American legal advisors, the amounts claimed are highly speculative and conjectural and have no basis in law or in fact. The Directors are of the opinion that no material liability is likely to arise as a result of these actions and no provision has been made in the accounts in respect of any such liability.' This contingent liability wording was to remain a common statement in Cape's accounts for many years to come. Litigation in the USA had commenced with the success, after appeal, of asbestos worker Clarence Borel in an action against Fibreboard and other U.S. manufacturers in 1973, which coincided with the year that asbestos consumption in the USA peaked[2]. The U.S. industry was under increasing regulation after the Occupational Safety and Health Act had come into effect in 1970. By 1977 the momentum behind the drive for compensation in the U.S.A was gathering pace and further details were now revealed by Cape in relation to the litigation. It referred to a case in Texas[10]. The Tyler pipe insulation plant had produced pipe insulation utilising Cape's amosite fibre, mainly for nuclear submarines commissioned for the US Navy from 1954 to 1972 and was now the subject of claims for compensation on the part of workers exposed to disease. The Tyler employees, as factory workers, were not allowed by law to sue their employer, Pittsburg Plate Glass (PPG), but a means of getting round this was found by focusing on the chain of asbestos fibre supply. A number of companies involved in specification, supply and installation were cited including Cape's North American Asbestos Corporation (NAAC), Cape Industries itself and Egnep all of which were charged with supplying 'a defective product' - amosite fibre. (The US Government was also a defendant given its role in the use of asbestos in the shipyards). Cape was perceived as having deeper pockets than it actually had. It defended its corner and depositions by Chief Scientist Dr. Richard Gaze played a significant part in the outcome. (The plaintiff's American lawyer described Gaze as 'a tall, elegant and immaculately tailored man of fifty-seven who wore a Harris tweed suit and vest')[11]. His evidence helped to demonstrate that the factory operator (PPG) had been made aware of the dangers in the handling of asbestos. By submitting a defence, however, Cape had in effect allowed its corporate veil to be penetrated. Legal advice suggested the case against Cape had only a tenuous basis in law, but under threat of increasingly complexity and additional plaintiffs coming forward, Judge Steiger pressed defendants hard to make a deal. The outcome of this was that Cape Industries and its subsidiary agreed to be party to a settlement of which its share was US\$5.2 million (\$4.1 million of which was covered by insurance). This was a mistake as, although the parties made no admission of liability, it served as a precedent in terms of Cape appearing as a defendant in the USA. At Cape's November Board Meeting in 1977 it was minuted[12]: 'The Managing Director stated that, having regard to the legal opinion of Mr. J Fox-Andrews Q.C., it was proposed that in respect of any future United States claims not to contest the proceedings in American Courts and to accept the risk of a default judgement being given against the company, it being considered most unlikely that such a judgement would be enforced in an English Court'. It goes on to confirm the proposal to liquidate NAAC. The company had no alternative as Tyler 2 was shortly launched in the Texas Courts followed by the Hammond and Bloomington factory cases in 1982 – these involved punitive, in addition to compensatory damages, running into tens of millions of dollars. Had Cape been found liable the amounts involved would have destroyed the company. Henceforth Cape adopted the stance that NAAC no longer existed, Cape had no assets in the USA, and judgement was not enforceable on Cape in the UK. The Plaintiffs efforts to pursue Cape also in South Africa were somewhat thwarted by a South African law that prohibited disclosure of information about its strategically important industries. US litigation proved to be a running sore for a number of years as we will see. From then onwards the writer, alongside other Directors, was under instruction not to visit the USA on business for fear of being drawn into the litigation frenzy that followed.

In South Africa there had been some progress in formulating a basis of compensation for industrial disease. The Occupational Diseases in Mines and Works Act of 1973 replaced the 1962 Pneumoconiosis Act, tightening up the controls on safety in the workplace and establishing a compensation fund to which all controlled mines contributed. Whilst we learnt earlier that compensation had been available as far back as the 1911 South African Miners Phthysis Act, it was not until the 1956 Mines Act that asbestosis was formally recognised as a condition subject to compensation. The 1973 Act, being of the apartheid period makes particular distinction between the needs and entitlements of 'black', 'coloured' and 'white persons'. The requirements pertaining to black or coloured workers were vastly inferior to those applying to white miners. By the end of the decade compensation for an asbestos related condition varied between SR6,000 to SR30,000 (to a maximum SR70,000) depending on employment and racial status[13]. The amount of compensation subsequently paid was small given the fact that much of the workforce was migrant and not in a position to seek compensation from more than one employer. In 1979 when Cape's Prieska mine closed, the unemployed workers began to focus on its legacy and residents formed the Concerned People Against Asbestos (CPAA)[8] which began to look at the health and environmental issues surrounding the mining of the fibre.

In Summary

This had been a crucial decade for Cape. The asbestos bubble had burst and we can look back and take a view on the way management had handled it. The Board had obligations to all its stakeholders. It was clearly in the long term interest of shareholders to rid itself of the mines. Clearly it was also in their interest and the livelihood of employees to diversify away from asbestos based products and this it did, if slowly, but more rapidly than its competitors. Clearly it was in the interest of employees to engage in regulatory activity and implement safety measures, which it did even if confined largely to its own workforce and factories. But it was also in employees and shareholders interest to protect the business at hand and its conduct here opened it to the charge of resisting the transition away from asbestos, a view that was widespread in the public eye (the alleged 'ill-informed and strident criticism'). Later revelations (see Chapter 12) as to Cape's activities exceeding the TDN13 dust levels established in the 1969 Regulations suggest the criticism was well justified. Reading the written evidence submitted by Cape representatives to the Advisory Committee for Asbestos, they may well have been stretching the points of defence, been economical with the truth, or simply playing for time, but this was part of the process of managing the transition such as to ensure the survival of the Company and its people. Most significantly, the decade saw the increasing emergence of a further but significant stakeholder to be considered – the needs and demands of past employees as claimants.

This was Geoffrey Higham's decade and he deserves credit for removing the two most consequential legacy issues – mining and Asbestolux. Whether these figured as essential priorities in 1970 is doubtful, but when faced with the reality that the era of asbestos was over, action was taken. There was growth in the business and he saw the potential in insulation contracting. Shareholders had seen the share price more than double. But it was a period when he was increasingly absorbed with the fall out from the press disclosures and the mounting evidence of debilitating disease. He was now faced with the task of maintaining shareholder support whilst protecting employees and dealing with the needs of claimants at home and abroad. Despite the asbestos-related issues there is little evidence to suggest that this affected recruitment. Geoffrey Higham was an engaging personality, more so than his predecessor Ronnie Dent, and had the respect of those who worked for him. The Company had a good reputation as an employer with a low turnover of staff. He was careful to shield the operational units from the past, and if there was a necessity for evasive tactics in corporate dealings with the asbestos legacy, he never allowed it to infuse the culture of the ongoing business.

Chapter 5

A Decade of Reckoning

'What do I think about Cape? I hate 'em. I absolutely hate 'em. I don't know why I hate 'em because Cape is just a word'

Alice – A Fight for Life. ITV Yorkshire 1982

After the turbulent times in the previous decade the chickens come home to roost in the eighties. The recession in 1980/81 hit Cape hard. Cape's portfolio was vulnerable, particularly some of the diversifications and acquisitions of recent years. But nothing concentrated the mind of those directing the asbestos industry in the UK more than the ITV documentary 'Alice – A Fight for Life,' shown in 1982, which shaped events for many of those involved in asbestos. This had a profound affect on the industry, of which more later.

We left Cape in 1979 with a sales turnover of £204 million and a trading profit of £15 million. The performance of the company in the eighties mirrored the outcomes of the Thatcher Government years - wage control, pressures on productivity and the shedding of either twilight industries or those unable to compete. By the end of the new decade sales had reduced to £159 million and profits to £12.25 million. Capital employed reduced from £84.7million to £57.7 million. It was a decade in which the cards were reshuffled in the hope they came up trumps.

In 1979 Ronnie Dent had retired and Geoffrey Higham assumed the role of Chairman. His position as Managing Director was taken over by William 'Bill' Doughty. Bill Doughty had been recruited by Geoffrey Higham at the beginning of the decade and had been running Cape Building Products. Like Higham he was an ex-Metal Box man. As with Dent, Higham became a Director of Charter and assumed responsibility also for other Charter businesses which now involved several new investments, notably Shand and Anderson Strathclyde. The Charter Board continued to house a bevy of the great and the good in the Anglo empire, there being seventeen main board directors! Geoffrey Higham was recorded as stating[1]'I normally go to Cape on Monday and Tuesday and to Charter on Wednesday and Thursday and on Friday I do whatever is necessary.'

Insulation and the Acquisition of Newalls Insulation 1980.

In 1979 it was reported that sales had been booming for both Cape Insulation and Cape Insulation Services in the light of the cost of energy and government incentives. Decisions had been made to invest in expanding production. Cape's capital expenditure amounted to £14.9 Million in 1979, £13 million in 1980 and £14.4 million in 1981, a good level of which was devoted to the Insulation Division (Rocksil capacity was raised by 30% in 1979 with a further increase in 1980). Against this backcloth the opportunity arose in 1980 to buy what was left of the Turner and Newall insulation business – Newalls Insulation, which was the manufacturing entity. This comprised a facility at Washington, County Durham, manufacturing calcium silicate and glass fibre insulation, and one at Middlesbrough manufacturing glass fibre and slag wools. Since the proceeds of the sale of the asbestos mines (£15.5 million) had been more than swallowed up by capital expenditure it was necessary to go to the market with a rights issue of 1 to 4 shares at a price of 157p (the shares were traded at the time of the announcement at 190p). Charter Consolidated, who by now had 67.3% of the equity subscribed for and underwrote the issue.

The Newalls business had sales of £17 million and had made a loss of £100,000 in the previous year and was forecast to make a loss in the next year. The decision was made purely on the basis of the apparent market buoyancy in the late seventies. The products manufactured at Newall's Washington and Middlesbrough factories may have added to Cape's product range but were small scale. The Washington facility manufactured non-asbestos calcium silicate pipe sections and slabs. Branded 'Newtherm', this covered the top end of the temperature range. However, the market in Western Europe for calcium silicate insulation was small, as rock fibre (Cape's own Rocksil), had largely taken over. It remained popular in U.S. and Japanese specifications but being a fragile and bulky material, did not lend itself readily for export. At Washington there were two small scale glass fibre lines, but uncompetitive compared with the Pilkington plant and in the domestic sector competitors of Cape's Rocksil. The slag wool manufactured at Middlesbrough was in a narrow and dying market. However, acquiring Newalls gave Cape a 25% share of the overall insulation market with the other near 75% held by Pilkingtons. Others saw an opportunity in the UK market as BPB and Rockwool decided to enter the market at the same time, making for additional capacity .

This was against the backcloth of a new Conservative Government and clear signs of recession, exacerbated by the withdrawal of government energy conservation incentives. T&N's Chairman Stephen Gibbs expressed his concern at the outlook for the eighties in his statement in their 1979 Annual Report, just as discussions on the sale of Newalls to Cape was taking place. By 1982 he was reporting 'a terrible year for the Group' and T&N turned in a £19 million loss[2].

Culturally insulation was at the heart of Cape – Barking had been the centre of its universe and there remained a belief that this was a core activity. In the early days of Caposite, it needed the insulation business to promote and use its fibre. There had been a blind faith in the insulation market since the oil crisis in 1973 and the need for energy conservation. Sales bounded ahead, less so margins given that energy represented a sizable proportion of the production cost. There was justification in market confidence at the time, but it manifested itself in too broad a range of products across dissimilar markets and differing marketing arrangements. One example was the Cape Insulation Services domestic business involving loft and home insulation. It gave rise to conflict with Cape's distributors, it was 'low tech' and low margin and as soon as government incentives were removed, rapidly became a loss maker.

The loss of these incentives that had given such an impetus to the insulation of the UK's housing stock, in today's environment looks particularly shortsighted, with standards now far in excess of those prevailing then. Had the Government's initiatives at the time gone on and been expanded, Cape's insulation businesses may well have survived, if not flourished. In its press releases, Cape pointed to a fall in the market for its insulation products of 30% between 1979-1981, at a time when its own capacity to produce insulation material increased by over 40%! The business lost money in 1981 and barely covered its costs in 1982/83. By then Cape had bailed out of the Cape Insulation Services business. This venture into home insulation and local distribution had been misconceived from the beginning. Moreover, it was venturing into activities in which the Company did not have the necessary expertise, such as different forms of roof and cavity foam insulation. A somewhat cavalier management approach did not help, and after a number of depot closures and write-offs, the rump of the business was sold back to the management, from whom it had been acquired. A write-off of £1.35 million was noted in the 1983 accounts, arising from the withdrawal from cavity foam insulation alone, the technique not meeting the claims made in company literature.

As early as 1981, the Company was reporting a write-off of £4.5 million within the insulation division, and closures. The market appeared to improve a little in the next two years, but by 1985, shareholders were stunned by an announcement that parts of the insulation division would be closed down, with the main activity at Stirling, being sold to Pilkingtons for a consideration of £8 million. Out also went the Queensferry based wood fibre board activity. Exceptional costs amounting to £20.6 million were provided to cover the closure of the recently acquired Newalls Washington-based glass fibre facility and loss on the disposal of the Stirling and Queensferry-based businesses to Pilkingtons.

Based on what followed this may have been a reasonable deal for Cape as Pilkingtons within two years had closed the Stirling factory with the loss of three hundred jobs, whilst retaining the Queensferry site. Shortly afterwards Encon Insulation, a distributor of insulation products founded by two ex Cape employees, acquired the Stirling facility, ripped out the old Rocksil plant and installed glass fibre capacity under a £2 million investment. The number of employees at Stirling and Queensferry totalled 700 at peak; Superglass operated with seventy five. Encon's Superglass insulation proved a success and remains in production to this day. Knauf at Queensferry now produce mineral wool.

So ended a story that reflects poorly on the management of the business. In Rocksil rock fibre Cape had a superior product and it fitted well in the portfolio when Cape's market was largely confined to the industrial sector. For the general building sector and home insulation, its less expensive rival, glass fibre, was more than adequate. Cape had fallen for the incentives for investing at Stirling but for a bulky low weight product, transport costs were high compared with competitors located in the heart of England. Mineral fibre insulation whether rock or glass had become a commodity and Cape was just not equipped to fight it out with the likes of Pilkington, Rockwool, St. Gobain and Owens Corning. Production was hindered by too many different products, margins were always tight and marketing lacked focus - inflexibility and overmanning being the outcome. As the weakest producer at a time of a drastic reduction in demand it was the one to go. Insulation manufacture had remained at the core of Cape's business and its time, in fact, was up.

Automotive

Cape Automotive was already under pressure, displaying a drop in sales in 1980. A trading loss of £3.4 million was incurred and exceptional costs of £5.2 million recorded, half of which were redundancy payments. The business had a record of repetitive reorganisation and this time Don International and Trist Draper were brought together under the banner 'Cape Friction International Ltd.' Manufacturing was reduced to three locations – Manchester, Leeds and Bristol - and the three warehouses reduced to one central distribution centre in Warrington. Sweden was always the bright spot, but France and Germany were suffering also from a reduction in demand.

All this happened against a backcloth of the UK car industry moving from a position where, in 1968, 10% of the cars sold in the UK had been imports whereas, in 1980, it was 60%. Whilst Cape Automotive had recognised this in setting up outlets in Belgium, France and Germany there were established supply arrangements in place, difficult to break. Even when companies like Nissan set up in the UK in 1986 initial manufacture relied upon a significant element of imported parts. To make up for the loss of UK Original Equipment sales, the after-market became a dumping ground and very price competitive. Thus, we find ongoing losses in 1981 and 1982, with closures in Cape Distribution, reducing the number of branches from seventy two to twenty. Pat Parkes, as Managing Director, had been Higham's man and his Deputy (but never styled as such in company reports). Not so with Bill Doughty who considered he no longer had the answers and as a result Parkes resigned from the Board in 1981. A succession of managers then directed a process involving further corporate shuffling and closures.

In 1985 the Board responded to a proposal from competitor BBA to negotiate a way out of the business; it was sold for a consideration of £15.75 million, of which £3.5 million was due on completion, £7.0 million subject to post completion audit and £5.25 million after a five-year period. The book value of the assets sold was £20 million and the operating profit in the year 1984 £1.08 million. Cape had the benefit of the UK's net debtors but an immediate write down of £4 million was necessary. BBA must have viewed the purchase as justified on the grounds that it eliminated a competitor. It was a fairly courageous initiative in seeking to deal with the problem of overcapacity within the industry, but emboldened by the acquisition BBA went further and acquired Automotive Products in 1986.

Automotive had always been a bit of an odd ball in the Cape portfolio. There was certainly no cross fertilisation with other parts of the business and it had not been a significant purchaser of amosite fibre. Even when the UK car industry was at its height, the business was not making a satisfactory return. I doubt if Cape did a great deal for the business, and it certainly did not do much for Cape.

A Time of Reckoning

The shedding of the insulation manufacturing and automotive interests came at a cost. The financial fallout caused a delay in accounting to shareholders and a need to extend the year end from the previous 31st December 1984 to March 31st 1985, an extended *annus horribilis* for Geoffrey Higham and Bill Doughty. The interim statement issued therefore covered the 9 months period ending September 30th 1984. A loss of £33.3 million, made up of £6 million after tax trading losses and £27 million extraordinary costs, left shareholders in a state of shock. Worse was to come as the Automotive disposal did not arise until February 1985 and by this time Cape owed its bankers some £40 million. In March, the Company announced a capital reorganisation[(3)]. This took the form of a deeply discounted offer involving the issue of £10 million 8.4% interest convertible redeemable preference shares at par, based on one share for each 3 ordinary shares held. Conversion could take place as soon as 1986 based on 227 ordinary shares for every 100 of the preference shares, an effective conversion price of 44p. This was probably the best the company could do in the circumstances and still left it with a seriously depleted balance sheet. In the process it had to seek the permission of the Court for the cancellation of the share premium account and repay existing debenture stocks. The net effect, prior to the issue and Automotive disposal receipts, was that in the fifteen month period ending 31st March 1985, the net assets of the company declined from £60 million to £22 million, with £29 million of borrowings and finance leases falling due in one year. Cape was left with two divisions, Building Products and Insulation Contracting, and a consortium of bankers with a mortgage on the company.

Having Charter Consolidated to subscribe for their 67%, in effect underwrote the issue and gave bankers confidence, but it was to be touch and go for a year or more. For Charter it was a terrible year with not only Cape's woes but it had to accommodate a £50 million charge covering Johnson Matthey banking losses. It followed that in the same year Charter recruited J.W. (Jeffrey) Herbert to run their industrial interests, including Cape. Formerly a Director of Jaguar Rover Triumph, he joined from General Electric and became a non-executive Director of Cape. Charter's engagement with the business stepped up a gear with Herbert's arrival. Since there were now just the two businesses there was logic in not only selling the Head Office at Park Street but also reducing greatly the number of central staff. This included Geoffrey Higham as Chairman and Bill Doughty as Managing Director, who both resigned. Whilst to an extent authors of their own demise, they had faced a dramatic downturn in key markets in which the company operated, had maneuvered a way out and offloaded non-performing businesses, leaving a solid core for recovery. But they had not read the insulation and automotive markets well. Asbestos woes, of course, were a constant distraction. There had been too little due diligence on new proposals and ventures - this could possibly be attributed to Ronnie Dent's 'give them two years' trial and error approach. Jeffrey Herbert was the beneficiary in having a focused business left to him.

Both men were able to pursue successful careers after Cape, Geoffrey Higham as Chairman of The Rugby Group and a non-executive director of other companies, whilst Bill Doughty received a knighthood as Sir William in chairing the Northwest Thames Regional Health Authority. So ended a style of management which still had traces of the patrician days of the Mining Houses. The uniformed doorman at Park Street, the bone china tea service, the luncheon forum, and staff carefully vetted by the ex Naval Commander Personnel Manager. An Executive that was satisfied by bonus free salaries - modest by today's standards - the most notable perk being a chauffeur who, in more than one case, had better gardening than driving credentials!

Against this backcloth the Building Products business was performing well, particularly the Uxbridge based business in asbestos free boards now that production of Asbestolux had ceased. In 1981 the experienced Tom McKain, who had been with the Company for 10 years, was running both the exterior claddings and interior fire protection board businesses and was appointed to the Main Board. A great horse racing man, Windsor evening races were a popular forum for entertaining and corporate gatherings.

External Building Products

In 1980 the business of Stenni (UK) at Blackburn was acquired adding a range of coloured building façade panels to the portfolio. The product was of reinforced glass fibre stone composite composition and covered the top end of the façade market. The business appeared to prosper during the decade and by 1990 had a factory at Longwy, on the Franco-German border.

At Cooksons Sheet Metal Developments, the company was pioneering the development of pre-insulated metal profile claddings, and sales of Unishield metal cladding increased by 30% in 1983 from a low base. This business operated from a jobbing shop in Bishops Waltham and involved the continuous rolling of interlocking metal profiles. The founding managers of the business were good inventive technicians but needed Cape to fund and direct its future development. But Cape mistakenly allowed them to continue to run the business, and the outcome was constant retooling to deliver an ever-expanding range of metal profiles. At the same time, the process of applying polyisocyanurate foam insulation between two sheets was problematic and prone to cavity formation or delamination. The effectiveness of pre-insulated cladding relied very much on the method of jointing and overlapping adjacent sheets, and this was subject to many changes in design. As a result, it took some time to produce a stable product line, but once it was considered this had been achieved, volume production was set up at UAC's Tolpits Lane, Watford, factory. Even then it proved problematic, and others were entering the market with access to cheaper feedstock. It would have taken a rather more significant investment to become a major player, and Cape had other priorities. The Tolpits Lane line was closed down in 1985 culminating in write offs in the business amounting to £4.9 million in 1985. However, production continued at Bishops Waltham and under the name Cape Metal Products returned to its jobbing roots producing specialised profiles and stampings. The business was declared non-strategic in 1990 and sold for £5.77 million, giving rise to a surplus on disposal, partly aided by the potential development of the site. At the time of acquiring this business the concept was right as the product in time displaced asbestos/fibre cement sheeting, but it was a capital-intensive volume game and Cape did not have the wherewithal.

The collapse in the market experienced in the Insulation Division also affected the Cape Universal Claddings asbestos cement cladding and pitch fibre pipe business. Overcapacity and price levels forced the closure of the pitch fibre pipe part of the Bowburn, Co. Durham plant in 1983. By then the market for corrugated asbestos cement cladding was at a level equivalent to 50% of 1979 volumes. Demand reduction meant that it was no longer viable to maintain both production lines - at Bowburn, and Tolpits Lane Watford - and the latter was the one to go. So corrugated asbestos cement manufacture ceased at Watford in 1984, the cost of which were accounted for in the £3.3 million of extraordinary costs incurred by the company in 1984.

An added consideration was now the resistance to any cladding product containing asbestos. Efforts had been directed for some time towards finding an alternative to asbestos fibre in asbestos cement sheeting. This was not easy as apart from the strength and durability of asbestos, its content provided for the formation of a 'filter mat' in the manufacturing process and good dispersion in the slurry mix. None of the tested substitute fibres could match these qualities, and the non-asbestos replacement products experienced teething problems involving cracking and delamination. National Gypsum's US patent of 1982 referred to eleven possible fibre substitutes including cotton, polypropylene and glass. Cape eventually teamed up with James Hardie of Australia, historically an important outlet for Cape's asbestos fibre. An asbestos free corrugated product was jointly developed incorporating cellulose fibres, and which carried the brand name 'Unicem'. This was by no means unique and competitors such as TAC and Atlas (now Eternit) produced virtually the same product. Manufacture at Bowburn took place alongside the old asbestos line while it was being launched and market acceptance tested. Manufacture continued to the end of the decade but in a market characterised by over-capacity, the business failed to achieve an acceptable level of profitability and was quietly phased out, with some fairly modest closure costs in 1990/1. T&N's subsidiary TAC was of course pleased to see a competitor off and were described as 'helpful' in the process.

As long as the company retained the historic UAC site at Bowburn it was associated with asbestos, so it was keen to rid itself of the factory property. Cape could now at last say that it no longer manufactured asbestos containing products. Unfortunately, asbestos cement was grouped in the public mind – and still is - with the insulation and fire protection products incorporating high concentrations of blue and brown asbestos. But with asbestos cement the asbestos content in the portland cement slurry was 10 to 1, it was largely chrysotile and fibres were firmly encapsulated within the cement. Thus, the widespread existence of many of those buildings clad with asbestos cement today. As a capital-intensive activity, it had never served Cape well, either as an outlet for asbestos fibre or as a business with any unique selling features. In due course Belgium based Eternit acquired both Atlas and TAC (Turner & Newalls) in the UK, and dominated the market.

One legacy from the old UAC business – Cape had acquired with the business a long lease on a modern office building in the centre of Watford. The lease extended to the year 2000. It was a logical location for Cape's Head Office and a base for Divisional heads. It remained as 'Cape House' for the rest of the period of the lease.

In 1987 Cape acquired T.S.C Vitratech at Corby for an initial consideration of £500,000, a manufacturer of vitreous enamel cladding panels, an upmarket façade product produced in a variety of colours. Cape's extended marketing reach enabled it in 1988 to a secure a major contract for the Route 5 tunnel contract in Hong Kong.

So, by the end of the decade Cape's offering in external building products was reduced to high end façade products of vitreous enamel, GRP and metal.

Internal & Structural Products

In contrast the Cape Boards companies thrived. The decade was heralded by the acquisition of a small private company in Wellingborough, Northants – Durasteel Ltd. Cape Durasteel, as it became, had developed a rigid board providing up to 4 hours fire resistance. A core of asbestos-free fibre reinforced cement was enclosed within perforated steel sheets on both sides. It was the ideal product for blast proof enclosures on- and offshore. Its performance could only be matched by much thicker heavyweight structures, so it was effective where space was at a premium. It was an ideal complement to the existing Cape range of Superlux and Monolux board.

Margins were generous and sales of the product grew at a rate of 20% per annum over the decade, it having become established in the specifications of the CEGB and major oil companies. At a time when cities were competing for the highest skyscraper, it was commonly specified as a means of enclosing the fire sensitive services core, and lifts. In the second half of the decade a range of fire doors was introduced. Exports thrived, an example being the Petronas Twin Towers in Kuala Lumpur, Malaysia, then the tallest building in the world, where Cape also carried out installation. Spearheaded by a charismatic salesman and Managing Director, Tony Ashcroft, the business was a notable success for Cape at a time when there were more product failures than successes. Ashcroft ("I bleed Durasteel!") is recalled for his sales video which commenced with a showing of a test demonstrating the product's blast proof qualities, the resounding sound of which was sufficient to draw the attention of the most disinterested viewer. Durasteel is still widely specified and used today.

We left the previous decade with Cape having successfully launched the new asbestos-free board products – Supalux, Masterboard and Monolux. Greeted enthusiastically by specifiers in the UK and overseas, in consequence Cape Boards Deutschland, Cape Boards France and Cape Boards Nederlands were set up and staffed by nationals, and an international sales force assembled to take advantage of opportunities beyond Europe. The decade commenced with the announcement of Cape Boards largest order for Supalux and Vermiculux at the innovative Dinorwig hydro power station for £227,000. Exports were soon rising at a rate of fifty per cent per annum and despite the UK recession, home sales maintained. The growth of the business was supported by sustained investment at the Uxbridge facility. At the end of the decade Tom McKain was smart enough to drive through an £8 million capex proposal covering two new Hatschek production lines, which were to come on stream in the next decade - just in time to avoid a squeeze on investment as the parent company entered another tight financial phase. The Main Board were also smart enough to recognise they had a winner in the Uxbridge product line.

By 1988 the company had set up its own marketing outlet in Hong Kong – CBPI (Far East) and was securing orders against mainly Japanese competition, given its technological lead in asbestos-free products. The rigidity and the moisture proof properties of the range of boards made it ideal for high humidity environments. Shipping also to Singapore, Masterboard and Supalux were to be found on the Mass Transit System, Raffles City, social housing, and in schools. Shipping of such bulky materials became viable as container shipping took hold, there being ample capacity for Europe to Far East return trade at competitive prices. At one stage the price for a return 40 ft. container to Singapore dropped to just over US$100.

It was also a period of growth for the Monulux products produced at Germiston, now under the corporate identity Cape Industrial Products - volatility in shipbuilding being made up by strong sales in the aluminium and metals sector. Also within the Industrial Products Group was the old calcium silicate insulation slab and pipe section manufacturing unit at Washington. Despite Cape being the only supplier left in Europe the market was fairly narrow and declining.

By 1989 these combined manufacturing activities were generating sales of £81 million and operating profits of £11.8 million, having achieved double digit growth in sales and profit over the decade. A new house style was needed and introduced initially at Cape Boards - a bold 'Cape' in red underlined by a strip on to which the activity or company name could be inserted.

Industrial Services UK

Cape Contracts, the established UK Insulation Contracting Company had now grown to embrace several activities in the area of industrial services both in the UK and overseas. It had a decade of ups and downs with few activities operating at a stable level of profitability at one time. By the end of the decade and with annual sales of £78.9 million and profits of £3.1 million it was the poor relation given the excellent performance put in by Building Products. Managing Director, John Farrell, as an accountant, ran a tight ship financially and it was generally possible to run a work-in-progress credit such that the business could be cash positive. It made limited demands on Group funding at a time when cash was tight. By the end of the decade a new Company was formed – Cape Industrial Services (CIS) to embrace the contracting activities.

In the last chapter the company's entry into the scaffolding business was noted and by 1980 this was well established. This arose as a natural adjunct to insulation contracting, as clearly a complimentary trade was the provision of access for the process of painting and insulating pipes and vessels. Scaffolding for industrial applications (i.e. oil and gas, petrochemical and power generation) involved complex configurations as opposed to 'Town' or commercial work (e.g. office buildings) and therefore greater skill. It involved clients who were particularly concerned with safety and would look for evidence that scaffolding had been designed in accordance with applicable standards. Cape's entrance into the market was encouraged by its involvement with the North Sea construction sector, where there was a multi-disciplinary need as well as a demand for exacting standards of safety. A specialised scaffold design team provided clients with the necessary load and wind load data to demonstrate conformity to British Standards, which were considered among the best in the world, if not the best. The margins to be obtained from scaffolding were higher than insulation but it was of course more capital intensive, and its growth required substantial ongoing investment at a time when the company's finances were being stretched. Lower risk returns were to be obtained through scaffold and associated plant hire, and the business commenced setting up hire depots throughout the country. A series of regional acquisitions were made including Kennedys, Altitude Scaffolding and Western Scaffolding. The scaffold hire depots however required a level of investment that was not necessarily available at the time, and a different type of management.

In terms of equipment, the market in which the company operated required tailor-made scaffold structures involving scaffold tube and fittings. The alternative – 'system' scaffold was suitable for commercial work, being less labour intensive to erect. It however required investment in many special pieces. For Cape's tube and fittings, there was a substantial historic stock available; the capex involved was less than with the system type of scaffold being acquired by competitors, such as SGB, serving a broader market. In due course Cape had its own drop forged fittings made to British Standards by forgemasters Burtons (see illustration, page 107).

Tom Austin, and subsequently Mike Needham as Managing Directors of Cape Scaffolding, were both Accountants by training and thus well equipped to deal with the balance sheet idiosyncrasies of a scaffolding business and the need for care in the security of its assets. So, despite funding constraints Cape Scaffolding powered ahead during the decade becoming an independent scaffolding company, engaged directly with its own customers as well as sites on which Cape Contracts was engaged. It did give Cape a particular edge over competitors in offering a dual discipline package. Cape had found a top end niche which raised it above the traditional perceptions of scaffolding and scaffolders – this was a smartly uniformed workforce, disciplined in wearing the correct safety apparel and committed to good practice.

In 1983 a further discipline was added – Industrial Painting – when a 51% holding was acquired in Hunting Painting Contractors, the balance of the shares being acquired later. This business had been operating within the family owned Hunting Group for over 50 years and had useful approvals within the Defence and Oil sectors. It was overdiversified, working in a number of sectors (it had a speciality in electricity pylons) with little discrimination as to risk and profitability. This appeared a natural addition to Cape's multi-discipline stable as clearly painting immediately preceded insulation and might utilise the same scaffolding. In 1989 a further acquisition – Ardon Painting - was added.

The business retained the Hunting name in view of its reputation and became HPC Coatings Ltd. with its own depots. It involved equipment and technologies new to Cape, and did not quite meet expectations as a complimentary business. The reason for this probably arises from the fact that the main driver behind industrial painting was always the manufacturers – e.g. Hempel, International Paints, Jotun etc. – and their paints were already named in Oil and Petrochemical Company specifications. This meant that contractors had little leverage in material choice or pricing and the only means of effecting savings was through coverage in application, which, if liberties were taken, would be revealed under rigorous independent inspection. The material cost is high relative to labour, and this restricts the added value available. The equipment required – compressors and spray equipment – could be hired by smaller competitors so overall Cape had little economic moat as a contractor. In addition, there could be remedial work under guarantee, the responsibility of which was always disputed. Altogether the business disappointed and HPC gradually got merged into the rest of Cape Contracts activities, the discipline being called upon where Cape secured a multi discipline contract (usually maintenance) involving painting. It had been an inexpensive acquisition, but a good learning experience and painting remained in the portfolio.

This was a decade when Cape took full advantage of the opportunities in the Scottish offshore industry and the fabrication yards in the Northeast of England. An opportunist sales force combined with strong operational back up jumped in where others feared to tread. Clients wanted a multi-discipline capability and this was amply demonstrated in Cape securing orders for the fitting out of accommodation modules. Given the high standard of fire protection and insulation required, the need for access scaffolding and corrosion protection, Cape was well positioned to meet a demand for a 'turnkey' service which even extended to internals such as beds and curtains. The rush to get rigs completed set tight deadlines which Cape was able to meet. On the rigs clients looked to hire men who could handle a number of disciplines – insulation, scaffolding, painting, security, safety, catering. At its Aberdeen base Cape set up a training school and established itself as first choice contractor for ongoing maintenance with industry leaders such as Shell and BP. Labour adapted and demarcation barriers broke down. This was a business with barriers to entry and competition limited – the other major competitor – Rigblast – tending to focus on corrosion protection. The success of the operation was very much to the credit of the Director in charge – John Welsh – fearless in tackling any challenge. Welsh boasted a capability extending to over twenty different trades.

Standards had to be high in the offshore industry, so Aberdeen was an early practitioner and qualifier in the implementation of British Standard 5750, Quality Systems which had been introduced in 1979 (later becoming the international standard ISO 9001). This then set a standard that was to become established within the whole of Cape's industrial services business, and BS 5750 Accreditation became mandatory for each unit, including overseas. By 1988 existing safety procedures were greatly tightened up offshore as a result of the Piper Alpha disaster. Cape again pioneered the adoption of the standards being developed by the British Standards Institute, culminating in the eventual international standard OHSA 18001. Cape in Aberdeen was the role model and set standards which were to serve the Company well in succeeding years.

Cape Contracts was clear market leader in industrial insulation contracting in 1980, but the absorption of Newalls had encouraged other entrants. Cape had shown the way to managing risk and secured better project financing terms such that the barriers to entry were reduced. Cape had taught the industry how to run a business in this sector on minimal working capital. A young entrepreneur Bob Woods had set up Norbury Insulation in the early seventies and undermining prices and standards, taken market share. The business developed rapidly with some imaginative accounting to a point where it was to be floated on the London Stock Exchange. To give it credibility Bob Woods came across Irish Peer, the 6th Earl of Norbury. Lord Norbury, who appeared to have limited experience in such a capacity, was down to be Chairman. Switching his interest to racehorses, Bob finally presided over the company's liquidation in 1987. Deborah Services was established in 1979 and in 1985 Chieftain Insulation established on Tyneside by Peter Wardle, a former Managing Director of Cape Contracts. To an extent the market welcomed these companies as Cape's reputation had suffered due to an overly commercial attitude in project execution. But, as a result, margins were undermined, and some loss of market share was experienced. This affected the results of the business in the middle of the decade when Cape was struggling to survive.

The market however was changing to Cape's benefit. Firstly, many of the plants constructed in the fifties and sixties were now requiring an elevated level of maintenance. Clients were experimenting with various forms of maintenance contract. Whilst each site had a base load of planned maintenance, the precise scope of work to be undertaken at a point in time might be unclear, and emergencies could easily arise. This gave rise to term contracts generally of three or five year duration which required the contractor to maintain a presence on site at all times, ready to carry out work against a schedule of agreed rates – a formula that allowed the contractor to recover all his costs at a profit, assuming his contractual rates proved adequate. This was relatively risk-free work and provided a base load of activity for the contractor. Because of the commitment of resources required it also raised barriers of entry. Cape began to focus on this type of work for which it was well suited, particularly as it could now offer a multi-discipline capability. It meant that it could be more selective in undertaking high risk project work. There were though risks in maintenance contracts - the contract in theory had a 'nil' value, meaning that the client only called on services when needed, and in times when budgets were tight the level of activity could be cut back considerably.

The second reason the market was changing was the uplifting of standards generally, and here again with its offshore experience, Cape was well placed.

Industrial Services. South Africa

Cape retained a few businesses in South Africa after it had disposed of its mining activities, one of which was an insulation contracting business – Cape Contracts Pty. Ltd. based at Benoni. The business grew on the back of the rapid expansion of power generation monopoly Eskom during the seventies and eighties, much of it involving Babcock Power Ltd of the UK with whom Cape had a strong relationship. In 1983 (at the same time as HPC was acquired in the UK) the company acquired the business of Industrial Painters (Secunda) Pty., trading as Reef Industrial Painters, for a consideration of £734,000. Among its assets was a private aircraft which suggested there was room to increase margins! It can only be assumed that John Farrell had put a very convincing case to the Board for this diversification. If the acquisition had been presented for approval a year later, it is unlikely the Board would have been prepared to entertain investment in South Africa. Cape Contracts Pty. did prosper, only to be cut short by Cape's decision to abandon South Africa in common with other UK companies. The imposition of international sanctions against the apartheid policies of the Nationalist Government post 1984 coupled with asbestos related issues resulted in Cape disposing of its interest in Cape Contracts and Reef to its managers, at a price that suggested desperation. Not surprisingly this proved to be a good deal for management, as the business of Cape Contracts Pty. survives today, claiming to be the market leaders. However, had Cape hung on, the business would probably have been exposed to later litigation. This also affected Cape's other remaining business in South Africa – Capil Products (Pty) Ltd -which was disposed of for a cash consideration of £776,000. Capil had been quietly trading very profitably and its product range included an excellent domestic heater (see illustration page 106). The name 'Capil' was identified with the heater in the way the name 'Hoover' was attached to the vacuum cleaner. These heaters incorporated a heating element protected by asbestos board and were to be found in most dwellings including those in townships. It was not that efficient as a heater but was indestructible, fireproof and good for drying clothes! The product continued to use asbestos board and many survive today.

With this departure Cape sought to distance itself from a country that had been its spiritual home, leaving a legacy of which few would be proud.

Industrial Services. Europe

In the last decade we noted the foray into the Netherlands in the form of Cape Contracts Nederlands B.V. The company's presence had been boosted by the acquisition of the assets of Bestobell-Todd B.V., but disaster hit the business in 1983 – it had taken over as a resident contractor in the Rijn-Schelde-Verolme shipyard at Rozenburg Island, Rotterdam. The shipyard had been losing substantial sums of money for several years, constantly bailed out by the Government. The plug was pulled in 1983 and Cape had to write off £1.7 million debt and work in progress. The business had not been going that well and in its anxiety to fill the order book, management had ignored some of the risks.

Competitors claimed they had led Cape into the trap. The business continued to struggle through the remainder of the decade, with frequent management changes. A further move into mainland Europe took place in 1980 when Cape formed Société Cape Contracts S.A. in St Quentin, in France. This business took in the assets of a local company that had acted as a sub-contractor to Cape on the Centre Pompidou fire protection contract. Cape's Project Manager Pat O'Kane became the first General Manager of Socap. It was a small operation in a marketplace dominated by Wanner Isofi. It operated in the Northwest of France as a minor regional player.

For many years Cape had had a presence in Dublin, Eire – an operation that acted in effect as an agent for all the Cape companies. This meant that it tended to be accountable to none and run its own affairs, without contributing much in terms of profit. Its Managing Director, Terry Hayden however was a man of great charm and enthusiasm so a trip to Dublin was always a pleasure, but rather ran the business as his own fiefdom. On any major insulation contracting projects it needed the assistance of the UK or international business and by this time most of the major power plant and oil refinery installations had been completed. Terry Hayden acquired the business in a management buyout in 1986. The business spanned both Eire and the North of Ireland; the latter retained a depot for Cape Contracts.

Industrial Services. International

This was the decade in which the international footprint of Cape's industrial services capability was established. They were pioneering days – almost as if the spirit of venturing forth that characterised Cape's early mining days still lingered in the DNA of the business. In 1980 it had a branch office in Abu Dhabi looking after the work being carried out on Gasco's Gas Gathering projects at Ruwais and Bu Hasa. These contracts placed a responsibility on Cape to provide all materials, labour and a number of support services, frequently including the provision of labour accommodation camps, given the isolation of sites. Initially Cape brought in UK labour to carry out the insulation work which, being at low temperatures, required particular skill in installation. It was soon apparent that for availability and cost reasons it was necessary to resource the business with third country nationals, initially Indians. Projects involved tremendous challenges and the company was on a short learning curve. The writer recalls being called to a site meeting in the desert remoteness of Bu Hasa, on Boxing Day in 1981, at the request of Gasco Project Director Bouchami, due to Cape's faltering contract performance. Christmas Day evening had been spent imprisoned in the site security office, the company having failed to secure gate passes for third country workers smuggled on site to supplement a recalcitrant UK expatriate workforce. A call from Cape's Branch Office Sponsor, H.E. Khalfan Khamis Al Amemi, retired Head of Police, resolved the matter!

Throughout the Gulf, Foreign and National Oil Companies were beginning to invest in their oil refineries as demand for diesel grew, in upstream petrochemicals and in natural gas, on and offshore. A project in Abu Dhabi in which Cape got involved in the early 1980's apart from Gasco's gas gathering installations was the LNG (Liquid Natural Gas) Plant on Das Island, part owned by BP. This involved a process of refrigerating natural gas to a temperature of minus 180 deg.C. in order to liquefy it. In this state it became economical to transport the product by tanker. This involved complex cryogenic insulation systems which Cape had the technical skills to handle. This pioneering work proved very important in the Gulf and Far East as we will see later.

Within the decade businesses were set up in Qatar, Kuwait and Saudi Arabia, no longer as branch offices but by locally registered companies. To qualify for the award of contracts, handle government affairs more effectively and assume tax efficient status, each business would take the form of 51% or more local ownership. A local partner would be sought, and, alongside the Articles and Memorandum, a side agreement would be negotiated whereby a sponsorship fee (usually a percentage of sales) was paid to the partner in lieu of his profit (or loss!) share. Financing would be the responsibility of the foreign partner. The legality of some of these agreements were not entirely secure but with the right partner a productive and secure relationship could be established. Auditors always reminded Cape's corporate management that in law only 49% of the assets and the profit were due to Cape but generally accepted the consolidation of 100% of profit, if not assets. In the early days, the power and influence of the partner was important as work could often be secured through their relationships and influence over buying decisions. But the more powerful the partner, the higher the sponsorship fee. A key demand on the partner would be access to government departments particularly when seeking work visas for migrant workers, vehicle licences and powers of attorney.

In these early days it was not unusual to be approached for commissions and in some cases, they had to be paid, the difficulty always being to make sure that there was value for money to be derived. Cape, as a public company tended to be at a disadvantage here in that its international competitors were mainly private companies, and some were overtly open in their willingness to pay bribes. Where this was necessary Cape stuck to the rule - no cash payments, only against invoice from a registered intermediary. There had to be an exception to this in local government affairs where it was necessary to effect cash payments at government offices to secure visas, driving licences etc. A National would be employed in the capacity of Public Relations Officer (PRO) to deal with this. Fortunately, over time the payment of commissions died out, as client organisations became more professional.

As a UK company Cape did benefit from the historical presence of Britain in the Gulf, a language that was widely understood and the fact that some of the local oil companies had strong British ties. British technical standards prevailed, and the reputation of British companies was generally good. Whilst this acted in Cape's favour, its role was frequently as a second-tier contractor working for a main contractor. Here contractors from USA, Japan, Italy, Germany and France tended to hold sway and would favour their own national companies as their sub-contractors. As a result, Cape's main competitors were from these countries. However, they would tend to operate under the umbrella of the main contractor and leave on project completion. Cape took a deliberate decision to establish independent 'roots' in each of the Gulf States – making for a permanent establishment of management and labour. With the oil price crash in 1986 this looked to be a foolhardy strategy but by hanging on throughout the downturn, Cape stole a march on its competitors, as it meant that when the market picked up, Cape was there and up and running. The market did pick up at the end of the decade as we will see in the next chapter.

In 1988 Cape Contracts Overseas (CCOL) which looked after the Gulf and continued to conduct a supply and supervision business from its Watford base received Cape's second Queens Award, this time for Export. One of its contracts involved providing materials and supervision for the insulation of cryogenic tanks in Argentina for Gas del Estado in which British Gas held an equity share. The work was finished but not paid for when the Falklands War broke out. The writer was one of the first to get a visa after the end of the war to secure the debt. Cape later established a joint venture business in Argentina but found it could add little to the market, there being local contractors better able to deal with the commercial issues (mainly currency!) that constantly arose.

Industrial Services. Australia

In 1986, CCOL management noted a particular opportunity for its expertise in cryogenic (sub-zero) insulation systems when it sought prequalification for work on a major Liquid Natural Gas (LNG) Export terminal to be constructed on the North West Shelf at Karratha, Western Australia, for Woodside Energy, the shareholders of which included Shell and Japanese trading houses. Japan was a pioneer in liquid gas production and transport and represented the main market for LNG at the time. The Main Contractor consortium for the project included M.W. Kellogg of the USA, JGC of Japan and Clough Engineering of Perth. From a situation where the insulation works were considered a 'shoe-in' for Nichias, a Japanese contractor, Cape was able to win what in those days was a significant contract valued at £23 million. Key to its success was offering to set up a factory at Geraldton W.A. to manufacture the polyisocyanurate insulation required for the sub-zero plant and pre-insulate pipe spools (see illustration page 108). This helped to meet the requirement for Australian content, as did the formation of a 50/50% Joint Venture with Clough Engineering to carry out the work. Given labour relations in Australia, construction project contracts were let on a basis whereby costs were reimbursable subject to penalties/bonuses earnt against target budgets. This project proved to be very profitable and provided a learning experience in the technology that laid a further foundation for success beyond the decade. For those who initially pursued the order flying economy via Bombay to Perth by Air India, the prospect of a return flight business class by British Airways beckoned!

Asbestos Legacy

For those fortunate enough to be directing the Building Products and Industrial Services businesses it was a decade in which they were given their head, and subject to good stock/work-in-progress control and cash management, their funding requirements were largely met. But for the Chairman, Chief Executive and Main Board the legacy issues surrounding asbestos and the demands of the other two stakeholders – shareholders and claimants – were becoming all consuming.

We left Cape absorbing the conclusions of the Simpson Committee in 1979, having disposed of its asbestos mining interests. The last paragraph in the 1980 Cape Review article entitled 'Whence asbestos?' states 'Looking into the 1980's therefore Cape is set to make an ever increasing contribution to energy conservation, the protection of life and property against fire and, through the continued and essential use of asbestos, the provision of safety critical automotive components for world markets'[(4)]. This is a somewhat surprising comment as by then the Directors must have held the view that asbestos was not essential to its future and it would have set its course on the eradication of the fibre from all its products. It was perhaps seeking to justify why at that time it still retained chrysotile asbestos fibre in its building and automotive products. In the use of chrysotile, the Simpson Committee concluded that subject to the prescribed control measures being followed, there was no greater risk to employees than in other comparative industries. However, this was being questioned by 1982 and a further enquiry set up. Arguments continued on the subject of a new limit of one fibre per ml. of air for chrysotile and 0.5 for amosite.

At the same time Yorkshire TV screened *'Alice – A Fight for Life'* a devastating exposure of the last months of Alice Jefferson, a 47 year-old mother of two, who died in 1982 from Mesothelioma[(5)]. One of the most consequential features of the programme was the revelation that Alice had worked at Cape's Acre Mill at the age of seventeen for barely three months, thereby demonstrating how such limited exposure could still give rise to fatal disease manifesting itself some 30 years later. It presented Cape in a very bad light in the way its lawyers were allowed to fight the claim for compensation. Overnight £60 million was wiped off the share values of UK asbestos companies. Whilst the documentary focused public attention on Cape, the programme makers made it into an industry exposé, accusing T&N of concealing risks at its Rochdale factory. Cyril Smith, the larger than life but discredited Rochdale MP came to T&N's defence and in the process somewhat diverted attention from Cape. T&N were still actively promoting asbestos in their products, believing prior to the televising of the programme that they had largely seen off the health scare.

If Cape's Directors, after the Alice documentary, had any doubts as to the need to eradicate asbestos from the business, these would now have been abandoned. They could at least tell a slightly better tale. They could point to a record of disengagement from asbestos. Unlike T&N, it no longer mined or supplied fibre and after the sale of the Automotive Division, had a range of asbestos free products (apart from asbestos cement). It was able, smugly, to comment in its 1986 report 'A more positive approach by Governments in banning the use of asbestos based building products where suitable alternatives are available would have considerable benefit'. This was somewhat hypocritical, the main beneficiary being Cape which was in the unique position of providing asbestos-free alternatives.

The Asbestos (Licensing) Regulations 1983 required those continuing to use asbestos containing materials to obtain a licence from the Health & Safety Executive, and employees to undergo statutory medical examination. The Asbestos (Prohibitions) Regulations in 1985 formally banned the import of amosite and crocidolite, reinforced by the Asbestos Product Safety Regulations of 1985 and 1987. Further legislation followed with the Control of Asbestos at Work Regulations in 1987 subsequently amended in 1992, 2002 and 2006 gradually reduced the acceptable level of amosite fibre down to a single control limit of 0.1 fibres per ml. measured over four hours, and applying to all types of asbestos. These hardly affected Cape other than in its removal business, by which time it could be said the horse had bolted. The number of claimants now emerging only drew attention to the inaction over the years, in which the industry was complicit.

In the USA, the focus on the asbestos legacy was encapsulated in New Yorker Reporter Paul Brodeur's 1985 publication *'Outrageous Misconduct, the Asbestos Industry on Trial'*[6]. A charge against the industry 'of corporate malfeasance and inhumanity to man that is unparalleled in the annals of the private-enterprise system' smacked somewhat of hyperbole and only hardened attitudes in its defence. (For a defensive view of asbestos, readers are directed towards Rachel Maines' *'Asbestos and Fire, Technological Trade-offs and the Body at Risk'*[7])

In South Africa it was as if the industry had closed its eyes to the outside world. Doug Todd, Cape's former mine manager and a leading light in the asbestos mining fraternity, when interviewed in 1980 stated:

'Here in South Africa, health officials and the asbestos industry worked hard to counter risks in our mills and our mines. We developed new milling machines that reduced dust to a minimum and packed fibre in specially secured bales that would not be opened until they reached their destination. Down in the mines the asbestos was kept wet and ventilation was much improved. As a result of this asbestosis is becoming rare, and the asbestos industry is well on its way to redeeming itself".[8] Such a vignette can only evoke the comment 'out of sight out of mind' given the industry's dependence on migrant labour.

The revelations surrounding asbestos focused attention also on competing products such as mineral wool (Cape 'Rocksil'), glass and ceramic fibres. The potential health hazards associated with working with these materials was the subject of research by the International Agency for Research on Cancer (IRAC). For a number of years the asbestos lobby could raise doubts in users minds. It was however some time before it was generally concluded that, whilst very much in the nuisance dust category, it was not considered that mineral or glass fibre constituted a carcinogenic risk[9].

Industrial Disease Claims

In the USA, following the Tyler 1 Texas Court ruling in 1978 covered in the previous chapter, a further 206 plaintiffs instituted actions against the same defendants, including again Cape Asbestos and Capasco (known as 'Tyler 2'). In line with corporate policy, neither company took part in the proceedings, claiming that the court lacked jurisdiction. They were prepared to allow default judgements to be entered and defend their corner in a UK court, should action be brought. Prior to the institution of these actions, Cape's sales outlet - North American Asbestos Corporation (NAAC) was placed into liquidation. It was replaced by CPC, an Illinois Corporation, the shares of which were held by the former Chief Executive of NAAC and AMC, a Lichtenstein registered corporation, and then in trust for Cape subsidiary, Cape International Overseas Ltd. These selling arrangements continued until Cape sold its asbestos mines in 1979. Whilst such corporate gerrymandering would appear somewhat blatant in its intent, it seemed to provide for trading continuity without seriously undermining Cape's defence.

As in the case of Tyler 1, Judge Steiger took an active role in pushing for a settlement and supported the Plaintiffs in seeking to include the United States Government as a Defendant, given their role as prominent specifiers and purchasers of fibre. In 1983 the parties then engineered a default judgement against Cape, for an amount in excess of which the parties had previously agreed to settle, leaving the US Government to bear the cost of pursuing the Cape entities in the UK and/or South Africa. The default judgement amounted to $15.5 million. '*Now its US Govt v Cape*' ran the *Observer* headline[10] as the Plaintiffs, of whom the first named was Adams, sought recovery in the UK High Court. This was not going to be easy, there being no treaty or comity between the U.S and England concerning reciprocal enforcement of judgements. The writ '*Adams and Others v Cape Industries*' was served in 1984[11]. There then commenced a period of great uncertainty for Cape for by the time judgement was entered in 1988 a total of $63 million of default judgements had been served on Cape in the USA, including the first instance of punitive damages. After a long High Court hearing, Justice Scott found that the method adopted by the Texas court in assessing the quantum of the default judgement was, in the context of English Law, contrary to natural justice. More importantly he concluded that the default judgement was not a judgement enforceable in the UK courts. The Times Law Report put it[12]:

'An English court had no jurisdiction to enforce a default judgement obtained against an English Company where that company was neither resident in nor had submitted to the jurisdiction of the foreign court, nor where the enforcement of the judgement would offend against natural justice.'

Whilst on the face of it this was a major relief from Cape's point of view, Justice Scott was highly critical of the process under which the default judgement had been derived, and it left a lingering doubt as to whether, had the process been legally more robust, the result may have been different. In 1989, the plaintiffs appealed and, fortunately for Cape, this too failed. This was not considered an end to potential litigation from US sources and the threat was still a matter for consideration a decade or more later. The outcome of the case, however, was significant as it dealt with an issue – the penetrability of the corporate veil – that had ramifications for other multi-national companies, so there was relief in the outcome. It has been relied upon in many similar instances, although questioned in certain cases on the grounds of morality. It could well be argued that Cape did play a part in the provision of a material that caused injury and death, and it sought to evade liability through corporate and legal juggling. But the alternative was corporate suicide in what was a legal maze in State and Federal Courts.

Now that the precedent for the award of punitive damages had been set, awards in the USA were now at a level which threatened the financial viability of all the companies involved, and their insurers. The main player, the Manville Corporation (Cape's former partner Johns Manville) filed for Chapter 11 of the Federal Bankruptcy Code in 1982, and a long-drawn-out process commenced seeking to bring order into the handling of claims. This drew in the US Government given its role in specifying asbestos. Manville's 'high projection' of potential liabilities implied 120,000 suits and $5 billion of damages – five times the company's net worth[13]. The UK's T&N soon too was in the thick of it. Unlike Cape the company could not hide behind the corporate veil, having substantial assets in the USA as both a manufacturer and fibre supplier. Action against T&N gathered momentum, and at the end of the decade it was facing claims of £160 million compensatory and £200 million punitive damages on just two prominent New York buildings for Prudential and Chase Manhattan.

It was not surprising that asbestos-related litigants in America should seek to engage Cape's parent Charter as a Defendant in actions given its substantial presence in the USA. In the first case brought against Charter in a Pennsylvania Court the decision went against it, but was reversed on appeal. A further case in New Jersey concluded there was insufficient grounds for penetrating the corporate veil. The case against Charter fell down on the issue of the extent of control over Cape exercised by the Directors of Charter, and this was seen to be limited to major decisions and appointments. The shear size of the Charter Board helped to dilute the control factor, given its one Cape Executive representative! Charter continued to be named in other cases but appeared to be able to rely on these precedents.[14]. The impact of the litigation will no doubt have leant urgency to the deliberations within the Board at Charter as to a means of disentangling itself from Cape.

In the UK, claims for compensation continued apace but had yet not achieved a peak. The latency period of up to 40 years from an individual's first exposure, would suggest that given the peak period of employees exposed to asbestos being between 1955 and 1975, there would be a gradual increase in claims from 1990 onwards, which is what in fact happened. Cape's recourse to insurance to cover the cost of claims was limited. Employers' Liability insurance only became compulsory after the 1969 Employers' Liability (Compulsory Insurance) Act. Both Cape and T&N had at times taken a somewhat arrogant approach to insurance, believing they could control the level of compensation better and minimise publicity if they self-insured. T&N actually got insurers to administer their compensation scheme with the negotiation as to the amount being undertaken by the Company. By 1990 there was a desperate search for old insurance policies within Cape which achieved some success, one being the policies of the Iron Trades Insurance Company, which eventually was forced into liquidation under the weight of claims. The Policyholder Protection Act in 1975 had established a Board which ensured that a fund was set up, supported by a levy which protected policyholders against a collapse of an insurance company; however pre-1972 exposure was precluded.

Cape continued to meet UK claims and top up its IDC provision annually. Compensation was paid according to a scale based on the period of exposure and type of disease, ranging from pleural plaque, asbestosis, lung cancer to mesothelioma. Whilst it might be expected that many of the claims emanated from the manufacturing business and those who had worked in Cape's factories, this was not the case given the attention paid to dust control in the production areas. The bulk of claims was coming from those who had worked on sites for Cape Contracts – laggers – where little protection had been afforded.

Corporate

Earlier we noted that Jeffrey Herbert from Cape's major shareholder, Charter, had assumed the role of Chairman of Cape with the Joint Managing Directors, Tom McKain for Building Products and John Farrell for contracting, reporting to him. Charter's chairman at this time was Merchant Banker Jocelyn Hambro and Chief Executive John Clarke, a mining man. They had adopted a policy of disposing of mining interests and acquiring a portfolio of mainly UK based industrial interests. They had bid successfully for Andersons Strathclyde and increased their stake in Johnson Matthey. In Herbert, Clarke had the good sense to bring in an experienced operator outside the mining fraternity, to look after the industrial interests, including Cape, Shand, Pandrol and MKR Holdings. The Anglo connection was still strong, evidenced by the fact that Gavin Relly, Chairman of Anglo and two Oppenheimer family members were on the Board so there was clearly heavyweight support to develop Anglo's interests outside South Africa. However, men who had grown up in the quasi monopolies that Anglo presided over, were not exactly familiar with the cut and thrust of the industries they were now becoming involved in. Their record was not good, but Jeffrey Herbert certainly got to grips with Cape, rebuilding the balance sheet and restoring the dividend. Charter converted its Cape preference shares and its shareholding rose briefly to 74%. Being from the Arnold Weinstock GEC stable, Herbert was focused on financial performance, and the writer recalls budget meetings the first of which was announced with three key action points – 'cash, cash and cash' - which was understandable in the context of what had happened within Cape.

The turnaround in the company's finances was remarkable and this was due mainly to the outstanding performance of the Building Products business. The dividend had been restored and the balance sheet improved with the aid of a revaluation of Group properties. Substantial growth in export and international sales were offsetting static markets at home. Whilst sales turnover was split 50/50 between the two divisions, 75% of the operating profit of £12.25 million came from Building Products. Jeffrey Herbert could perhaps feel that his initial task was complete, and he recruited a Chief Executive, Michael Farebrother, to run the business. Mike joined from the Chloride Group where he had been Managing Director of the Industrial Operations Division and had also worked at Jaguar Rover Triumph with Jeffrey Herbert.

The 1980's represented a watershed in the transition away from an asbestos mindset. Hitherto there were senior executives remaining who knew what asbestos was. Had seen, if not felt the silken fibres; had interfaced with wheezing sufferers; had attended colleague's funerals; and had had to tackle the difficult ethical decisions involved. There were increasing numbers of sufferers amongst Cape's time-served laggers and the death of former executives Richard Gaze and Vic Barrable in 1982 and 1985, both of mesothelioma and comparatively young men, certainly concentrated minds. It was not only Union Officials who had black ties in their office drawers.

For the new managers of the business it was now all about industrial disease compensation; the fellowship of victims had given way to the fellowship of actuaries, lawyers and accountants.

**Bowburn Asbestos
Cement Factory
(demolished in 1992)**

*(Illustrations by kind permission of
the Bowburn Local History Society)*

Capil Heater (below)

Koegas Mine on closure (right)

Cape Scaffolding involved installations of great complexity. Drop forged scaffold couplers used worldwide were made to strict British Standard specification.

Woodside's Northwest Shelf LNG Export facility involved Cape setting up a factory at Geraldton, Western Australia, for the manufacture of polyisocyanate insulation and pre-insulation of pipe spools. 1988.

(Courtesy Woodside Energy Ltd)

Chapter 6

Lull before the Storm

The company entered the 1990's in a stronger financial position, with contented shareholders and a new corporate identity – simply 'Cape' rather than 'Cape Industries'. Earnings and dividends had risen rapidly in the last half of the previous decade and in 1990 Jeffrey Herbert could announce earnings of 27.7p per share and a 25% hike in the dividend. A new Chief Executive, Michael Farebrother, articulated a strategy built around building products and industrial services. At the turn of the decade, and despite losing their appeal in the High Court, the U.S litigants had one last go by referring their appeal to the House of Lords, but were refused[15]. So, the Board may well have felt the company was no longer vulnerable to existential claims for compensation. Whilst the senior executives could claim no responsibility for the actions of their predecessors, they would soon find that the corporate body could not. Whilst sales did increase over the decade from £159 million in 1989 to £233 million in 1999, operating profit reduced to £9 million from £12.25 million hiding some hefty provisions. Shareholders funds were static over the decade.

Organisation

In 1990 Jeffrey Herbert moved up to the position of Chief Executive of Charter PLC – no doubt a reward for the success of the industrial businesses under his control. He had recognised he needed to recruit a Chief Executive for Cape, thus the appointment of Michael Farebrother. Cape's two Managing Directors – John Farrell looking after Industrial Services and Tom McKain, Building Products - were nearing retirement age and probably too specialist in each of their fields to be considered for the Chief Executive role. Farebrother clearly had a brief to develop the business and considered this best done by bringing in new blood and widening his span of control. Tom McKain retired, and John Farrell was sidelined to the role of Business Development Director, only subsequently to retire in 1991. The structure set up introduced, alongside Building Products and Industrial Services, a new Division – Cape Architectural Products - which was to benefit from an early acquisition.

Mike Farebrother had an attractive leadership style, was a good delegator and had a clear strategy for the Group involving international expansion. He was not a great detail man, and his intuition could fail him. The Industrial Services business was split into three units – Cape Contracts Europe, Cape Scaffolding Europe and Cape East, the later covering the international business. Cape East was to be located in S E Asia; Singapore being seen as the place to be. Cape Building Products continued to run the Uxbridge and Germiston based boards business alongside the new Architectural Products Division. Farebrother's brief included acquisition and managing directors were encouraged to seek out suitable candidates. His Finance Director – F.K.J. (Keith) Jackson – would appear to have been somewhat thrust upon him by Charter. An economist rather than accountant, Jackson was an Anglo man with experience in a financial capacity in Malaysia and the Far East, largely in the mining sector. With limited hands-on experience in Cape's field of activity, Keith Jackson would have benefited from Accountant John Farrell's counsel when evaluating some of the acquisitions and diversifications that followed.

Cape Architectural Products

In 1990 Mike Farebrother brought in an old colleague, Tim Bowdler, who had worked for him at Chloride Motive Power to run the new Division – Cape Architectural Products. Bowdler had great energy and flair and had the right attributes to build a business by growth and acquisition. Their first action together was to acquire Thermo Acoustic Products (TAP) of Stafford, whose main product line was ceiling tiles. TAP was owned by Trafalgar House, Nigel Broakes' conglomerate, whose activities ranged from construction and property to shipping and engineering. By 1990 borrowings were catching up, and it was looking for buyers of peripheral businesses such as TAP. Together with TAP came the Echostop Systems business based at Frome. The combined cost was £8.1 million.

The Architectural Division took in the existing businesses - Stenni, now named Cape Façade, it having to drop the Stenni brand having no longer any link with the products originator, Steni A/S of Norway. Its resin bonded façade panels were now produced in Stafford and in Longwy, France. It took in Cape Vitratech and Cape Insulation Products, the calcium silicate insulation manufacturing unit

- hardly an architectural product. It was however developing new products including phenolic foam insulation which helped to utilise space at the old Washington factory. It was also developing the 'modlag' variant of the old range of calcium silicate insulation for the nuclear submarines under construction at Barrow, giving the product a new lease of life. Cape Industrial Services was the resident installation contractor in the yard.

The timing was not good as by 1991 the UK economy was in recession followed by 'Black Wednesday' in 1992 when speculators 'broke' the pound. This was almost a repeat of the start of the previous decade when Cape invested in growth in advance of a recession. Cape TAP Ceilings, as it became known, faced an immediate downturn in its market. By 1995 its product range was reduced when it took advantage of the opportunity to sell its successful metal ceiling business, which was becoming something of a commodity line, to Armstrong Metal Ceilings for a consideration of £3.7 million plus stock.

Cape Building Products

For Cape Building Products an acquisition was made 'to strengthen Cape's strategic position in Germany.' The business was 'Siborit Gesellschaft fur Calciumsilikate GmbH' to be integrated with Cape's existing sales company in Germany. The business manufactured high density calcium silicate board and moulded fittings for the aluminium and metal industries. The range complemented, and to an extent duplicated, the output (Monolux) of Cape Industrial Products at Germiston. This solved a management problem in Cape Boards Germany, the Managing Director, Klaus Koch of Siborit taking both roles. The cost of the acquisition was £2.26 million. C A (Sandy) Hutchinson who was now Managing Director of Cape Boards saw the acquisition as a means of penetrating the German market and taking advantage of the perceived technical strengths of Siborit. In view of the downturn in the UK, which had affected Cape at Germiston, the decision was taken to switch some production capacity to Cape Siborit. This proved a mistake as we hear of technical problems arising at Siborit in 1992. Cape Boards at Uxbridge also faced a downturn in the UK market with sales dropping 18% in 1992 but offset by exports which accounted for 41% of sales. In 1994 the business of Pyrok was acquired from the receiver for a cash consideration of £3.2 million. Pyrok manufactured cement bonded particle boards at its factory in South Wales which had fire resistance and acoustic properties, and which complemented the Masterboard and Supalux product lines. Meanwhile Cape Durasteel went from strength to strength.

In France, the Netherlands and Germany the sales companies were achieving good market penetration, Cape's competitors in the field still had not caught up. A new office in Cologne was established. Further sales companies were being established and the market in the USA was thought to have great potential. Advice however received from lawyers in New York soon put paid to the notion.

By 1993, Tim Bowdler had taken over responsibility for both Building Products and Architectural Products and the Divisions combined, but within a year he was away – assuming the position of Managing Director of Johnson Press. This was quite a step up for him and a little surprising as he had little or no experience in the newspaper industry. It was a measure however of his abilities that after changing jobs frequently in his career to date he settled into a role which clearly suited him. He spent over a decade in the thankless task of seeking to consolidate the regional newspaper industry.

Industrial Services UK

As outlined in the last chapter the company's activities offshore had force fed a culture of quality and safety that was rolled out elsewhere within the business. International Oil and Petrochemical Companies demanded these ambitious standards, so by setting itself the target of being best in class, Cape would be able to differentiate itself and offer a service that could potentially carry a premium. It had been the first Company in its field in the UK to secure the latest accreditations in quality and safety. This gave it a competitive edge with major international clients. Just as importantly it helped to raise the status of its trade. Laggers and scaffolders hitherto had been next to labourers in the hierarchy on a site. Often perceived as troublesome and scruffy in appearance, they were now seen in neat overalls, with the latest safety protection equipment and their work subject to disciplined and strict quality inspection. This helped to attract new recruits and a further feeling of pride in their work. This, together with Cape's ability to put together a multi-discipline capability, proved to be a critical factor in it becoming over the next twenty years the leader in its field. Cape was beginning to build barriers to entry in what had historically been a very competitive low technology market.

The UK insulation contracting business was rebranded Cape Contracts Europe and scaffolding - Cape Scaffolding Europe. Before John Farrell retired he had initiated the pursuit and subsequent acquisition of one of its major competitors – Darlington Insulation (by then Darchem Contracting) - in 1992, from the William Baird Group for a consideration of £8.25 million. This figure was adjustable as work-in-progress was realised, and the recoveries exceeded £2 million. It was a well-conceived purchase and increased Cape's regional coverage in the North of England and its overall UK work volume of activity by fifty per cent. It attempted to maintain the old Darlington Insulation name for the business and operate it alongside Cape, but the market was not to be fooled and whilst the acquisition was highly successful, there was inevitably some loss of market share. The only caveat was a cap of the purchase price agreed on Baird's liability for asbestos related claims; this ultimately proved inadequate. Reflecting the growing move away from projects to maintenance, the business of Maintenance Insulation, based at Oldham was also acquired from its owners for a consideration of £825,000. A further acquisition of the assets of Joseph Nadin Contracting took Cape's market share to just over 40%.

Following on from the Darchem purchase, Darchem had another business – R B Hilton, a refractory company based at Greenwich in London. Colonel Hilton had built this business up after the war and it had a particularly good reputation in this specialist area. Refractory work involves the supply and installation of very high temperature internal linings for furnaces, boilers and pressure vessels. The work is critical in terms of timing, quality and performance, and involves expensive materials and critical levels of inspection. The Greenwich plant was disposed of, and an office set up in Dunstable to house staff but in the process key members of staff were lost. It did however introduce a new activity in the form of heat tracing, trading under the name of Electroheat. The refractory side however was somewhat out on a limb and the expertise not familiar to Cape personnel. The later acquired Middle East R B Hilton business (see page 122) proved more rewarding. A far-seeing management might have recognised value in a further Darchem insulation business in the nuclear field - Darchem Engineering - but this business was sold to the Weir Group.

The margins in insulation contracting were not constant and Cape had its fair share of loss-making projects, as indeed had Darchem. Cape was still recovering from the reputational effects of its heavy-handed commercial approach in the previous decade, and many clients now had their defences in place. The Managing Director, Accountant Mike Needham, structured the business to provide for two Regional Directors covering the country enabling him to pursue opportunities in Europe.

Cape Scaffolding was still of a lesser scale and had a minimal presence in the South of England. In 1991 Kennedys Scaffolding was acquired from Travis Perkins for £1.2 million which filled this gap. By this time Cape Offshore Services had been formed to cover the offshore services business based in Aberdeen and it was decided, given the emphasis on safety, to place it under the control of Cape Scaffolding Europe. The old Hunting painting business morphed into Cape Specialist Coatings Ltd, and the distinctiveness of the hire and sale business was recognised in segregating this activity as Cape Hire Ltd.

Despite the name 'Cape Scaffolding Europe' no attempts were made to develop a European scaffolding business. There was logic in this as scaffolding equipment and technique differed on the continent; the UK still relied largely on 'tube and fittings' – tailor made scaffolding – whereas on the continent 'system' type scaffold was generally used. It was later found that in the Netherlands scaffold dimensional standards were different since they catered for the fact that statistically the Dutch were taller! As an offshoot of Cape's North Shields Office, a business was set up in Norway – Cape A/S. There was over-optimism that Cape's standards and expertise in the sector would be welcomed, and the first contract secured was for insulation services to Norske Skög at its pulp and paper plants. There were problems in manning the contract and local management failed to deliver on their promises.

Industrial Services, Netherlands

The difficulties managing the Cape Contracts Nederlands insulation contracting business on Holland continued. A cartel existed which made it difficult to compete with the larger companies. Through its international contacts in Kuwait Oil Company (KOC) Cape was able to break into the oil refining maintenance sector at KOC's Europort Refinery, but taking on the cartel meant that a low price was obtained. Based on, 'if you can't beat them join them', the solution opted for was to take advantage of an offer for sale of Cleton Insulation B.V. based in Vlaadingen, near Rotterdam, with branches in the North of Holland, Belgium and Germany. Cleton was number two in the market behind Hertel B.V. and had originally been a family company. It had been the subject of a takeover by Norbury Insulation of the UK, only to end up under their liquidation, but subsequently bought by the conglomerate NBM. Cape paid £4.36 million for the Cleton business which had a solid asset base and had earned a prior year profit of £541,000. Cleton brought in good maintenance contracts including two of the largest with Shell and Gasunie. The business was combined with Cape Contracts Nederlands (CCN) and the Managing Director of CCN was given the task of integrating the two businesses.

The management of Cleton was extremely wary of shareholders, particularly foreign shareholders, after their experience with Norbury. Attempts to improve work in progress controls and methods of accounting and operational management faced resistance. Some reflected a belief on Cape's part that the methods and controls appropriate to the UK business were appropriate in Holland. It would have been better getting to grips with the detail of the systems already in place, some of which were perfectly adequate. Whilst these changes were taking place it was found that for many years prior to Cape's ownership, members of Cleton Management were shareholders and had control of a labour sub - contractor providing services to Cleton. This, it was claimed, had been established by them as a 'bolt hole' under the threat of liquidation under Norbury. After a court action an agreement was reached with the personnel concerned, involving compensation for Cape. The management team remained in place - probably a mistake as it had the effect of making UK and local management wary of each other. However, the Cleton acquisition at last brought Cape scale in Holland, although in Belgium and Germany Cleton was a minor player.

Whilst at times some collusion had existed in the UK within the insulation contracting sector it was insignificant compared with the Continent. In some cases, clients condoned the practice. On a major site, ongoing maintenance required close cooperation and trust between contractor and client personnel.

Most contracts involved a five-year term and over the period relationships were formed. When it came to renewal of the contract competitors might 'protect' the price of the incumbent contractor in exchange for similar protection elsewhere. It was not unknown for a client to turn a blind eye to this or manipulate tender evaluation to make sure the incumbent contractor retained the contract, and thus avoid the alternative of disruption of personnel and new relationships. This meant that prices were inflated but not significantly so as the client's personnel were under some considerable budgetary pressure. It meant that Cleton and its competitors were cushioned from some of the comparative competitive cost pressures that applied within the UK.

Industrial Services, Germany & France

Earlier we learnt of Cape's developing capability in asbestos removal as Cape Environmental. The enterprising Director of Cape Contract's Southern Region had established a track record of high level asbestos removal projects in the South of England including hospitals and at Ford, Dagenham. Cape had invested in equipment and laboratory testing, and this helped to distinguish it from some of the small operators. In Europe asbestos removal was only beginning and Cape was well ahead of local practitioners. Through Dagenham contacts, Cape became aware of an asbestos removal requirement at Opel AG's Russellheim's site in Germany. It successfully secured the contract which involved stripping 40,000 square metres of asbestos-containing fire protection board in the paint shops. At that time local companies were short of expertise and manpower. UK labour was relatively cheap and easy to bring in on a temporary work basis. Opel was impressed with Cape's well organised site management, and the total lack of disruption to production schedules, allowing the line to continue whilst Cape operatives worked two metres above the production area 24 hours a day. It was highly successful, and the company received one of GM's 'Supplier of the Year' awards. A subsidiary, Cape Entsorgungstechnik GmbH, was formed, the word meaning 'disposal technology.' The business secured further work but projects let in the public sector were being let on a schedule of rates basis, unlike the GM work which was cost reimbursable. A major contract on the public hospital at Aachen proved the undoing of the business. The client's engineers resented the award of the contract to Cape against the higher priced contractor favoured by line management, and work was constantly interrupted given the day to day needs of a working hospital. Cape was seen by competitors as too much of a disruptor and they had the influence to help it suffer a significant loss. The experience was sufficient for Cape to call time on the business.

In acquiring Cleton Insulation a foothold had been secured in Germany but only just across the border at Meppen in the Northeast of Holland, hardly in the heartland of the Ruhr. Cape Entsorgungstechnik had been set up and this had brought the company into contact with the Ucke family, local owners of Hessisches Isolierwerk Gebr. Ucke GmbH based in Borken, further south but still not at the heart of industrial Germany. This was a small business, 75% of which initially was acquired in 1992 for a consideration of £571,000 and the remaining 25% two years later. Although perceived as a starter operation for Cape to enter the general insulation contracting market, the motives for buying were more to do with creating a base for the Entsorgungstechnik activity. It was hurriedly conceived, and its attractions were partly based on its lucrative maintenance contract with the local power station. Within two years the power station was closed down, the likelihood of which the previous owners were probably aware. Like many of the acquisitions at this time it said little for Cape's due diligence. When Cape Entsogungstechnik ended so did Hessisches.

Whilst it would appear logical to bring together the Cleton presence in Germany with the Hessisches operations under common management, Cleton management made it quite clear that they did not want to step on the toes of their German competitors for fear of retaliation in Holland. Such were the loyalties of the cartel! In consequence the Hessisches business was managed from the UK. The activities of industrial services and the manufacturing companies were so different in Europe that there was no sense in seeking to combine the German businesses of each Division under common management.

In France, the Socap business was making modest progress under Francophile, Pat O'Kane. In 1991, the business of Capel was acquired for £252,000 giving the company a base in Normandy and a further business was acquired in Marseilles. It brought prequalification for work on the nuclear power stations for EDF, the major purchaser of insulation and related services in France. It also brought problematic labour relations. Socap claimed that, with this acquisition, it became number two in France. If it did it was way behind the market leader Wanner Isofi. The performance of the unit was erratic.

Industrial Services, International
Southeast Asia and Australia

Mike Farebrother gathered together the international industrial services activities under the name of Cape East, the word 'East' signifying, in common with the perception of the time, that Asia in particular represented the future. The business certainly could not go west in view of the USA litigation, apart from which its competitors there were largely State-based, and the market would have been difficult to penetrate. The restraint on visits to the USA for Company personnel was awkward as the company worked for principal U.S contractors such as Bechtel, M W Kellogg and Foster Wheeler. At times it was necessary for the writer to visit their offices in Houston and San Francisco, and this was carried out a little clandestinely, literally on a day return basis.

In line with this strategy an office was set up at the new Gateway building in Singapore and the Managing Director of the business, Pat O'Donnell, was to be housed there. In addition to expanding the industrial services business the office was to take over the marketing of Cape Building Products boards range. For board products, a company was set up in Malaysia alongside agents in Thailand, Hong Kong and Taiwan. As a centre for housing expatriate staff Singapore was expensive, but this encouraged the development of local staff.

For industrial services, a local Cape company had been set up in Thailand and work obtained on the Esso Sriracha Oil Refinery through Engineers Foster Wheeler. This was an introduction through Esso, at their Fawley UK refinery, which provided management services to the Thai Refinery. This contract involved both scaffolding and insulation. Scaffolding was a new discipline for Cape personnel in the Far East, and their caution was reflected in some generous pricing for the work. Execution of the contract proved lucrative, and a means of developing a Thai labour force under UK personnel supervision. Given the location, it was not difficult to attract UK supervisors to Thailand and the business proved highly successful as the Maptaput industrial zone expanded over the next decade. Cape became market leader, and the business remains to this day. A similar introduction through Shell and Caltex at their Batangas Refineries in the Philippines provided an opportunity for Cape to set up a business providing insulation, painting and scaffolding services on a maintenance basis.

A business was set up in Hong Kong as a Joint Venture with Hong Kong United Dockyards. Historically Cape had supplied insulation materials and supervision through Babcock Power for the various phases of the Castle Peak Power plant expansion. It was encouraged to establish a presence to undertake the installation of these materials. Work was secured from China Light & Power and Esso on Tsing Yi Island. Had the company done its due diligence properly it would have established that the labour pool for this type of work was monopolised by two labour sub-contractor organisations, with dubious connections, who had a cast iron hold on labour supply and Cape was forced to hire through them at uncompetitive rates. In addition, despite its attempts, the use of bamboo scaffolding could not be ousted in favour of Cape's own equipment. There was very little wrong with bamboo scaffolding in terms of strength and assembly, only the way in which personnel scrambled over it!

In Western Australia Cape had successfully completed the insulation and scaffolding work on Trains 1 and 2 of Woodside's N.W. Shelf LNG plant built at Karratha. From an organisation employing over five hundred men the question arose as to what next to do in the market which was far too small to justify a permanent presence. The solution was to form a joint venture with a local company Modern Matthews which was strong in the heating, ventilating and air conditioning sector. Cape Modern as it became, was hardly a money maker, but it enabled Cape to have a local presence to undertake maintenance and be in place for further expansionary phases in the LNG sector.

The development of LNG provided Cape with an important strategic avenue that would underpin the development of its industrial services business internationally. The LNG process, and its temperatures down to -180 deg. celsius, required high performance insulation, more often or not provided by polyisocyanurate insulation formed into pipe shells and slabs. The insulation could alternatively be sprayed on the pipe in layers. The outer covering or vapour seal would involve various finishes of metal or glass reinforced plastics, and was crucial to the integrity of the system. Compared with the 'hot' insulation of boilers and high temperature apparatus it is a highly skilled activity and critical in performance. In developing expertise in this area in the UK, Abu Dhabi and Australia, Cape was able to take advantage of the expansion of both Export and Import LNG terminals. High barriers of entry ensured that business in this sector gained rapid momentum. The market for the Company's services in LNG was not an easy one to tackle as much of the initial investment was directed towards serving the demand in Japan for imported LNG. Japanese trading houses and engineering companies played a key role and as a result much of the subcontract work was awarded to Japanese contractors – competitors of Cape. Two Japanese main contractors dominated the field – Japanese Gas Corporation and Chiyoda Corporation. As early as 1987 Cape was making regular visits to Japan, its first salesman to visit being an old Cape Insulation sales director by the name of Ernest Broad, who had worked for Michael Newton. Immaculately turned out, with fine manners, he was well received as the epitome of an English gentleman. It then took five to ten years to establish an effective working relationship and gain the confidence of Japanese Trading Houses and contractors.

The Cape East initiative in Singapore gave further impetus to the sale of Cape Boards products with annual shipments of over one thousand 40ft containers of Masterboard and Superlux. An all-Singaporean sales team were highly effective. Penetration of the local market for industrial services was less successful. As early as 1975 Cape Contracts at its Barking Office had had the opportunity of teaming up with a local Singapore Company to develop an insulation contracting business. Personnel were brought over to the UK from Singapore and trained. They promptly returned and set up their own businesses! One - EK Chung - subsequently joined Cape in a Joint Venture – Cape Sing-Lung Construction - and from this small operation Cape was able to learn about the market and the hold that local Chinese companies had over the sector. Labour was always an issue given the need to secure work visas for migrant labour from Thailand or India. Very regrettably, momentum was interrupted by the early death of Pat O'Donnell, the Managing Director from cancer.

Middle East - The Gulf States

Meanwhile the Company's business in the Middle East was going from strength to strength. The fact that Cape had stayed on throughout the market downturn and established roots meant that it had the capacity available on the ground, whereas its competitors had to start afresh. This was not easy for them as it involved setting up a permanent trading entity, obtaining work visas and importing equipment. Cape also had the labour. From the early days it had learnt that, given the Gulf States' dependence on migrant labour, to undertake work it had to have its own Third Country National (TCN) permanent labour force, and not be dependent on labour brokers or sub contractors. The establishment of its own labour force, trained on a multi-discipline basis, was to prove the key to its success. This was no easy task as it was first necessary to get a block of work visas, and for this the company would be greatly dependent on the strength of the local partner. Cape opted initially for Indian workers who had proved productive and willing to be trained. To recruit Indian workers, Indian law required recruitment to be carried out through registered Indian labour brokers. Brokers were generally corrupt, frequently taking money off the men (in many cases their first year's wages). Cape learnt to establish its own trade testing centres and narrow down recruitment through one or two reliable agents. Local laws in the Gulf States laid down that foreign contractors such as Cape were totally responsible for their recruits, from airflights to accommodation and food, medical and repatriation. The law provided for a maximum sixty hour working week, prescribed the hours of paid overtime, entitlement to leave and end of service gratuity. For accommodation Cape had established a capability of building complete accommodation camps, including all medical, recreational, laundry and catering facilities.

The treatment of migrant labour in the Gulf has become the source of a certain amount of criticism in recent years. However, the rules for a foreign company were stringent, and the labour laws afforded a great deal of protection to migrant workers, who could resort to the local law in cases of breach. Unfortunately locally owned companies were not always required to show the same respect for the regulations. Migrant workers were certainly more open to exploitation by their own labour brokers than by foreign company employers in the host country. As we see later the opportunities for its TCN labour to develop skills and earn promotion was a further key element of Cape's success.

In Kuwait the company had in the late eighties undertaken a major contract as part of Kuwait Oil Company's Al Ahmadi refinery modernisation. It had secured the scaffolding contract which grew in scale substantially. At that time, it was possible to secure rates of reimbursement that covered the total cost of new or secondhand scaffolding. The stock of scaffolding provided a base load of equipment that was to serve the company well for many years. The contract was complete when Iraq invaded the country in 1990 and the only work being handled by the business was in fact in Iraq, where Cape had undertaken a lot of work over the years. Cape's Manager – Milivoj Vujic, a Yugoslav - managed to get out via Baghdad bringing Cape's Indian workers. Vujic moved to Abu Dhabi to promote the company to Hydromontaza - a prominent Yugoslav contractor. This was not a success as Hydromontaza was Croatian and Milivoj was a Serb! He was able to migrate to Australia with Cape's support.

A contract had also been undertaken in Jordan at Aqaba on the Red Sea involving a fertiliser plant and for a French Contractor – Spie Batignolles. The contract was in delay and the client particularly difficult. A dispute arose which eventually went to arbitration in Geneva. This was under Arabic law and whilst Spie relied on onerous contractual clauses, which Cape had accepted at the time of signing the contract, Cape found that Arabic Law dwelt less on the written word and more on what was 'in the minds of the parties' prior to signing the contract. In consequence Cape won its case, but given the management time and expense involved never repeated the arbitration process!

In Bahrain as a consequence of the Darchem Contracting acquisition, but separately, the business of R.B Hilton Middle East was acquired, essentially a refractories business. It was loss-making and its only meaningful asset was a branch office in Bahrain where it had secured the term maintenance on the Bahrain Petroleum Company (Bapco) Oil Refinery. This was the oldest oil refinery in the Gulf dating back to 1936 and required a lot of ongoing maintenance and asbestos removal. R B Hilton was under threat of contract termination and Cape management had to step in quickly. The existing management were found to be seriously wanting - not uncommon in the Gulf when not closely monitored. Under new management the presence at Bapco formed the basis of a highly successful business over the following years. R B Hilton still carry out maintenance on the site (2022). It presented particular challenges as Bahrain was not, despite the refinery, a substantial oil producer and its people needed work and a source of income. It gave Cape the opportunity of developing an indigenous labour force, mostly Shia as against the Sunni ruling class. Above all R B Hilton introduced refractories expertise to Cape's business portfolio in the Gulf and strengthened its multi-discipline offering.

R B Hilton Middle East had established a business in Saudi Arabia. This was only active to the extent that the Bahrain business was called upon to undertake refractory shutdown work on major Saudi sites on a short-term visit basis. Whilst in Bahrain it was possible to operate as a Branch Office of a UK company and repatriate profits free of tax, in Saudi Arabia as in other Gulf States the only commercially effective way of operating was as a Local Company, 51% owned by a Saudi National. R B Hilton had such a company which proved a more effective vehicle than Cape Contracts Arabia Ltd, previously set up in Dhahran. The latter company had struggled because of the oil crisis and been forced to take on activities beyond its core capability. The specialist refractory activity was a far more attractive sector of the market and Cape Contracts Arabia was phased out in favour of the R B Hilton business. The R B Hilton name was a highly reputable brand name in the critical area of refractories, and despite pressure to rebrand it, the business, as market leader in its field, continues to operate under this name. This, however, is also due to the fact that to change the name of an existing business in the Gulf States can be a bureaucratic minefield! R B Hilton Middle East was loss making and acquired for £400,000. By refocusing the Bahrain business and making effective use of the R B Hilton Saudi established unit, a payback of two years was achieved.

The centre of the company's business in the Gulf remained in Abu Dhabi, where its reputation had been established on the back of the Abu Dhabi Gas Industries (Adgas) and Abu Dhabi National Oil Company (Adnoc) developments at Das Island, Ruwais and Bu Hasa. The company had established a solid base, to the extent of importing the polyisocyanurate insulation manufacturing equipment utilised on the N.W. Shelf LNG project in Australia. A factory and yard were established in the new Mussafah Trading estate. The management under Welshman John Hockin - a veteran of Cape in Iran - had set out a full multi-disciplinary stall, including, insulation, painting, scaffolding and refractories. Some of the earlier oil and gas installations were now requiring maintenance and Cape was there to provide a full capability. Its competitors had failed to set themselves up on a permanent basis, with a stable workforce, and were initially no match for Cape.

Steps had been taken in 1988 to enter the market in neighbouring Qatar. Qatar had oil and gas assets- unlike Bahrain - but at this time the Qatar Petroleum

Company's oil refinery at Umm Said was the extent of industry activity, and Doha itself was a sleepy town with few attractions to appeal to either visitors or business. Cape first foray was a shutdown on the QGPC refinery in 1990 which proved a disaster as it was unable to provide adequate manpower given Gulf War mobility restrictions. The big opportunity for Cape arose in 1992 when the first three LNG trains for Qatargas were under construction at Ras Laffan. Cape's client here was Main Contractor Chiyoda Corporation of Japan, and its sales effort in Japan was rewarded with a contract for a substantial portion of the insulation and scaffolding works, valued at over £20 million. As insurance Chiyoda awarded the remaining work to its favoured Japanese contractor and competitor of Cape – a company called Meisei. The contract required quality standards to BS5750 and Meisei was unable to cope with this and as a result could not get approval to start on site. The problem was solved by paying Cape to handle their quality manual and provide various in-country services. Such was Cape's local strength that Meisei then subcontracted further work to Cape and in consequence played no further part in these projects for Chiyoda in the Gulf.

As in the case of many large projects the work was subject to delays. This can cause profound consequences for finishing trades such as insulation. Inevitably there are commercial disputes as the insulation contractor will be required to accelerate work, and provide additional manpower to achieve a revised congested programme. On the project manpower peaked at over one thousand, creating the need to ship in four Birmingham City Corporation Busses to transport workers from the camp to jobsite! (see illustration page 154). Chiyoda were not used to the commercial pressure it was necessary for Cape to apply to recover the extra cost of delayed and disrupted working; (the alternative being a sizeable loss on the project). Despite the fraught dialogue that took place, Cape completed the work on time, earnt a bonus, and learnt a great deal from working with Japanese clients. It found that their prime focus was on performance and if that was delivered, they were good payers and sympathetic to claims for valid additional compensation. Not sophisticated in their project systems they were good at invoking a positive on-site culture focused on delivery. Cape's sales in the Gulf and the reputation earned on this project, made it now the clear market leader. As in the case of Abu Dhabi, to carry out the work a local company had been formed in which Cape's shareholding was 49% - Cape East W.L.L. – the partner being a member of the ruling Al-Thani family.

By this time Cape's permanent TCN's workforce in the Gulf exceeded one thousand men, mainly of Indian but also of Pakistani, Nepalese and Indonesian nationality. By the end of the decade the progress of Indians in assuming managerial roles was reflected in the appointment of Hemachandran as Operations Manager in Abu Dhabi and Samir Chopra in the same role in Qatar, later to become Cape's local Directors. Some UK Expatriates were employed in Project Manager roles, but superintendents were all TCN's.

Corporate

In 1994 the year end changed from 31st March to 31st December. This was explained as bringing Cape in line with shareholder Charter. The results for 1995 were solid with sales of £244 million, Trading Profit of £12.4 million and a significantly increased dividend of 11p. The Convertible preference shares issued in 1986 had been converted into ordinary shares providing a generous return to shareholders over and above their 8.4% yield. The balance sheet was sound, management had been incentivised with share options, and shareholders were tempted by a carrot being dangled in the form of the potential development of a motorway service station on surplus land, adjacent to the M25 at the Uxbridge site. (Planning permission was never granted and there remain no motorway service areas on the M25). The 1995 annual report made no new references to any asbestos related issues and great optimism was expressed as to the international prospects for the business. Over in Charter Consolidated, 65% shareholder, however, changes were afoot as we shall see in the next chapter.

Safer buildings and boats thanks to Cape

FOR 40 of Cape's 100 years it has supplied thousands of ships around the world with fire protection panels, ensuring safer journeys for crew and passengers.

The Germinston Works at Cape Industrial Products Limited in Glasgow has built marine boards for walls and ceilings since 1952. Marine manager George Potter, said: "The boom time was in the 1950s and Sixties after the Second World War when all the Western countries were re-building their merchant fleet."

It was during this time, in the late 1960s, Cape won the prestigious contract to provide fire boards for the QE2 and some years later for the other high-profile vessel, Canberra.

Cape Durasteel Limited was also involved in the marine business, selling fire protection walls for the off shore business, which doubled in the early Seventies. Doug Eldrige, who worked as administration manager at the time, said: "We sold considerable quantities for the installation of oil rigs and did work for companies such as Shell and Phillips Petroleum."

Today, Cape Industrial focuses mainly on the industrial market with about 40 per cent of its business linked to the marine sector. Nearly all marine work is for export, reflecting the decline in Britain's shipbuilding industry.

Meanwhile, the construction market has been served for nearly 50 years by Cape Boards Limited in Uxbridge. It launched a fire resistant board, Asbestolux, to this market in 1951. In 1970 the company embarked on a major research and development programme to develop an asbestos free board. The first, Supalux, was launched in 1976.

In the late Seventies the Cape Boards established companies in France, Germany and Netherlands. Another milestone came in 1980 when Cape Boards won The Queen's Award for Technological Achievement for the development of asbestos free products.

A £2.2 million high tech production line was opened in 1983 and two years later a second line was added, replacing the existing

HISTORIC... an artist's impression of The Minories in 1893; the location of Cape's first office

five production lines.

These days more than half of the company's business comes from overseas. It has worked on many international airports, including Frankfurt and Munich, and other large buildings such as the National Museum in Singapore, the Hilton Hotel in Jakarta, Raffles Hotel and the large commercial centre Suntec City in Singapore.

On the Centenary of the Company, Cape was emphasising its role in protecting ships and buildings from fire.

(Illustrations courtesy of publishers Key Communications)

126

CAPE NEWS

The newspaper for employees of Cape PLC   July 1993

Chief Executive's Review: Michael Farebrother on Cape's performance over the past year

TURN TO CENTRE PAGES

Cape improves its performance

Jeffrey Herbert

IT has been the worst building recession since the war – but Cape's resilience has won through, says Chairman Jeffrey Herbert.

In his statement in the company's 1993 Group Annual Report, he said: "Cape has had a satisfactory year with an increase of 21% in sales and an increase of 5% in profit before interest and tax."

Cape's expansion into overseas markets, the acquisition of new companies

AT A GLANCE

Cape's results, in brief
Turnover: UP 21% to £245m
Overseas sales: UP 34% to £107m
Profit before interest and tax: UP 5% to £11.9m
Final dividend: UP 3% to 7.75p

and the organic growth of companies offering industrial services has resulted in increased turnover.

"Overseas sales are up by 34% and

now account for 44% of turnover compared with 39% last year," he said.

Profits generated by all Cape companies – with the exception of Cape Ceiling and Cape Boards Siborit – were an improvement on last year. But the losses generated by these two operations, combined with restructuring costs, restricted the overall increase in operating profits to £527,000.

Cape has had to face significant demands on cash resources this year.

"The growth in the industrial services operations has placed an additional

Below: **John Farrell**
Cape Contracts Pioneer

Complex project right on target

THE biggest construction project in the UK is on schedule with Cape Scaffolding providing a complex design structure for the Drax Power Station Site near Selby in Yorkshire

Cape Scaffolding has supplied 150 miles of tube, 62,000 boards and 200,000 fittings for the £770 million Flue Gas Desulphurisation Plant. The Babcock contract includes the provision of scaffold structures for four of the six absorber towers and associated structures.

Operations Director Julian Gammage, who is responsible for the contract, said: "It's a very big job and we are employing about 70 scaffolders to work on the site until late 1996."

Challenges

One of the greatest challenges this project presented was the sheer logistics of it. "The absorber towers are very big structures and we had to design and build full internal and external scaffolds to facilitate all operations including the rubber linings inside the tower." The absorber towers, which are 155 feet high, are part of the process plant which is designed to remove 90% of the sulphur dioxide in the flue gases. The plant will be fully operational in 1996 when it will have the capacity to reduce 280,000 tonnes of sulphur dioxide a year when using coal with a sulphur content of 2.8%.

The scaffolding structure erected at Drax Power Station in Yorkshire

Visits paid off: £8m contract secured

The Abu Dhabi team with Regional Director John Hockin

CAPE East Abu Dhabi have been awarded an £8 million contract by Chiyoda Corporation of Japan, for the supply and installation of thermal insulation on the new LNG Plant to be built in Qatar. Qatar is one of the small-

Chapter 7

The Storm

The 85th anniversary of the Company was celebrated in great style in 1978 at the Dorchester Hotel, and attended by the great and the good amongst clients and the industry. No such extravagance accompanied the celebration of the Centenary in 1993, it being on the eve of a period that would involve traumatic events for the company. It began with changes at Charter Consolidated, Cape's major shareholder. It will be recalled that Charter was a spinout from the Anglo American Corporation of South Africa. Anglo continued to hold shares in Charter, the majority of which were held by its subsidiary Minorco, whose direct holding was 35%. In 1993 Charter had a 38.5% interest in Johnson Matthey which it sold, yielding £330 million and an exceptional profit of £218 million. This enabled it to buy out the Minorco shareholding by means of a loan note subsequently redeemed for £235 million and then purchase the whole of the share capital in Esab AB, a leading manufacturer of welding equipment and consumables, for £445 million. Under a Scheme of Arrangement it formed a new holding company with the name Charter PLC.

It was hardly a coincidence that this took place at the time of the accession of the African National Congress to power in South Africa (RSA). Anglo feared that their business activities could be the subject of nationalisation, and took steps to ensure that should this happen it would not embrace subsidiary companies. Whilst Charter had been set up to bring together Anglo's interests in Europe, Australia and Africa outside the RSA, it was to Minorco that it had looked to house its assets, largely in the USA. Whereas Charter had hardly been a notable success, Minorco had prospered and now became Anglo's prime vehicle for gathering up their assets in the RSA and elsewhere, being quoted on the Luxembourg stock exchange. By the end of the decade Minorco, combined with what remained within Anglo to form the Anglo American Corporation we know today, whereas Charter was later swallowed up by a U.S conglomerate - Colfax Corporation – which had been attracted by the Esab business, but which ultimately spun off all the businesses including Esab.

Quite early on in his involvement with Cape, Jeffrey Herbert would have been aware that Charter's investment in Cape was potentially toxic. Since 1984, Charter themselves, perceived as Cape's parent, had been warding off a series of asbestos related claims in the USA. They would have been contemplating a means of shedding this troublesome investment holding. Cape's situation and performance since had been such that it was not particularly attractive to a potential investor. In 1996 a way was found. The reasons Charter gave in the proposal document covering the sale were rather feeble and almost the opposite of the reasons given in 1969 for the initial enlargement of its holding – (1) the need to focus on its (Charter's) manufacturing interests (but Cape had a profitable manufacturing business) and (2) to concentrate on businesses which were wholly owned (in which case why not buy out the remaining equity in Cape?). The real reason, of course, lay in its nervousness about the asbestos legacy. This was referred to in the proposal document's small print and its reference to 'a background of litigation.' In the context of the litigation, the timing was good, as by this time the perception was that the US litigation had come to an end, which, given the passage of time, in fact proved to be true. That this coincided with Charter's disengagement with Anglo is pertinent. Anglo may well have wished to distance itself from Cape for fear that the legacy of its asbestos mining activity would catch up with it in the new South Africa. This would not be lost on Charter which could take a similar view. Both will have been aware of the possibility of further impending litigation having followed recent cases in the London Courts relating to South Africa (see page 133).

Charter had a choice of seeking to sell the holding to another investor or dispose of the shares by open offer. The UK stock market was at a low in 1995, but rising, which might suggest the latter, but time was not on their side; a quicker more certain route was to find an investor. Lazard and Kleinwort Benson were entrusted with the task. The only serious bite seemed to come from a boutique private equity house – Rutland Trust PLC - but even then not to the extent of Charter's total shareholding. The deal on offer was that Rutland would acquire 25% of the equity of Cape (in effect 30% of Charter's stake) for 130p per share (a consideration of £17.66 million). This could rise to 30% given that Rutland were underwriters for a further 5%. The balance of the Charter shares were to be placed by Kleinwort's with institutional shareholders, at a price of 130p, underwritten by them. Rutland were to provide management services comprising a Chairman, Chief Executive and Finance Director for a fee of £650,000 per annum.

This placed a value on Cape of £71 million, a business having net assets of £62.5 million, sales of £244 million and trading profits of £12 million and an exit p/e of under ten. The apparent low valuation suggests desperation on the part of Charter, but for them it was a quick and neat solution. The fact that Rutland, who were gaining a reputation in private equity, had taken this stake, and would assume the role of managers, was clearly an attraction in the disposal of the rest of the shares to institutions, which was successfully achieved. Schroder and M&G (already with a 10% holding in Charter) ended up with 11% each and Framlington with 9%, attracted by what looked to be a solid yield.

So what attracted Rutland to the deal? They obviously considered Cape had two profitable businesses with good market traction. Any private equity house will have the seeds of an exit strategy in mind in acquiring a business, and subsequent events suggested Rutland envisaged either selling or floating the individual businesses at a premium. This was no doubt outlined in their pitch to potential shareholders at the time of the placing. But they must have been conscious of the asbestos link if only because of the small print in respect of the US litigation. But also the annual charge of industrial disease compensation. This was rising but had averaged £1.5 million p.a. over the previous five years so at that level was probably considered manageable. But thorough due diligence would have shown up substantial risks of further litigation and demand for compensation. Actuaries would have told them of the likelihood of rising claims in the development of asbestos related disease, given the latency factor. Looking across at competitor T&N, the Board here had decided to make an 'unexpected and exceptionally high' charge for industrial disease compensation amounting to £140 million in their 1994 accounts, albeit mainly in respect of the USA.

In terms of due diligence. Rutland relied on what was provided to them by Charter. Given that Rutland were to provide management, the incumbent Chief Executive Michael Farebrother and Finance Director Keith Jackson were to leave and therefore played no part in the sale process as representatives of Cape. Cape was represented in the negotiations by two Non-Executive Directors – Michael Millward, a former Director of John Laing PLC and Sir Michael Grylls, a Member of Parliament since 1970, and Michael Pitt-Payne, Company Secretary, known as the 'Three Michaels'.

Farebrother and Jackson were to receive payments for loss of office - Farebrother receiving £703,645 and Jackson £378,551. Of these amounts over 50%, the Cape Annual Report stated, was received 'from third parties'. Not surprisingly this was Charter. Despite this incentivisation arrangement on behalf of Charter, Jeffrey Herbert took great pains to emphasise in the press release that neither he nor Jackson had taken any part in the decision making as to the action of Charter in disposing of their holding. Rutland must have been aware of these arrangements as the deal negotiated replaced the existing management with it's own under the service agreement.

Rutland formally took over the business in July 1996. The Rutland secondees comprised Michael Langdon, founder of Rutland as Chairman, Christopher Dowling as Chief Executive and Paul Cartwright as Finance Director. The press release issued at the time gave advanced notice of their intention to focus on Cape's core markets and dispose of peripheral businesses, and forewarned of an exceptional write down of £15 million. Dividend policy was to be brought 'in line with the building industry.' Independent Directors Sir Michael Grylls MP and Michael Millwood were retained from the old Board, the other Charter nominees resigning.

Rutland's strategy was soon revealed as lawyers were instructed to look at demerger opportunities. The advice of US lawyers was sought on the prospect of either Division, if demerged and incorporated as a separate entity, being able to trade in the USA without fear of litigation. This was mainly directed towards an intended demerger of the Industrial Services Division. (A better understanding of the market would have suggested that the opportunities for Cape Industrial Services' style of operation was probably limited in the USA). The advice would appear to have been negative, other than the prospect of sales of Board Products through an arms length Distributor. At the same time advice was sought from London lawyers as to the risks attached to segregating and of disposing of the Industrial Services business – i.e. the risk of asbestos litigation flowing through to any newco formed for the purposes of demerger. Rutland then looked at two options. The first involved a separate Industrial Services

Division holding company being created and comprising companies which did not have historic asbestos liabilities. The holding company would then be demerged by trade sale or share offer. The retained group, comprising the Building Products business and other Group companies having the asbestos liabilities, would continue and meet ongoing claims. Option two involved the same procedure in relation to the Industrial Services Division but the segregation of the companies with asbestos liabilities (the 'tainted' companies) from the Building Products Division, setting aside a fund to satisfy the actuarial liabilities of the relevant companies; alternatively not setting up such a fund. Rutland opted for (1) and Charterhouse Securities and Kleinwort Benson were invited to commence the process of demerging the Industrial Services business with a view to flotation on the London Stock Exchange. This proceeded at pace and it was later reported that a total £1.2 million was expended by Head Office on fees relating to the process.

In the meantime Rutland had set about simplifying the management structure following the departure of Michael Farebrother. The Building Products Division now incorporating Architectural, was headed up by recruit Peter Morton joining from BPB Industries in 1997. The Industrial Services was headed up by Managing Directors Paul Ainley (UK) and Peter Gartside (International). For the purposes of the potential flotation Paul Ainley was to assume the role of Chief Executive of the business and steps were taken to prepare a Long Form report under instructions given to Cooper & Lybrand.

On taking over, Rutland set about implementing the restructuring that had been predicated in their press release and presentations to investors. In the annual report for 1996 the two divisional activities were presented as clear profit centres. Manufacturing reported an operating profit of £6 million on £71 million of sales with capital employed of £34 million, Industrial Services with comparative figures of £8 million, £152 million and £30 million. But exceptional costs covering wholesale restructuring came in at £17.2 million. Of this, £2.5 million represented prior year under accrual of compensation for industrial disease. The rest covered several items involving the write down of assets and losses on disposal of businesses. Out went what remained of the Ceilings business, acquired by a management buyout. This disposal was not a total disaster, given the previous sale of the metals range, as the proceeds did not fall too short of the initial consideration. In Industrial Services the businesses of Hessisches in Germany and Socap in France went. Cape A/S in Norway was closed. They were small unprofitable players. By then the European businesses had been transferred across to the management of the international side of the business. The previous approach had been too much based on the successful UK model; attempts to force it on these European companies had failed to consider some of the cultural nuances, and their acquisitions had been questionable.

In such a way, it took private equity, in the form of Rutland, to see the business with fresh eyes and no more so than in its declared acceptance of the company's liability for industrial disease compensation in the UK. Whilst Cape had been paying compensation for many years it was historically hidden as a 'working cost' and the Directors tended to shy away from describing it as an enduring liability. Rutland, in its dealings with shareholders and employees made it quite clear that it was a liability that had to be recognised, and as a result paved the way for the setting up of a fund to deal with it. It could be said that a line was firmly drawn under the denial that had featured under Charter in the past. For Cape's management, the motivational energy and ambition characteristic of private equity introduced by Rutland had an immediate effect. The year 1997 produced improved results, with the Industrial Services Division increasing profits by 20%, providing for an attractive trend in presenting the case for flotation. Earnings per share at 15.7p represented a good earnings yield on Rutland's 130p entry price. But the year also brought news of yet another threat related to its past which had the potential to prove terminal.

In March 1997 notice of court proceedings was served against Cape in the UK, by five South African residents, supported by UK legal aid, who claimed they had suffered injury because of Cape's asbestos mining activities in South Africa. Amongst the five claimants, Matlaweng Mohlala had been a child worker in the mines and Rachel Lubbe was the wife of Shalk Lubbe, Company Secretary at Cape's Penge mine. She had died of lung cancer and the action, in her name, was being conducted by her husband[1]. London lawyers Leigh Day brought the case. Set up by Martyn Day and Sarah Leigh in 1987, this legal practice had earned a reputation for pursuing human rights cases. They were described in the Observer as being 'a thorn in the side of the multinationals'[2]. Richard Meeran, a partner in the practice headed up the South African litigation. It was prefaced by the attention brought about by Earthlife Africa, an environmentalist group formed in 1988 focusing on the activities of a British Company, Thor Chemicals, which had set up a mercury recycling plant at Cato-Ridge near Durban in 1988. Thor had closed its plant at Margate in the UK in 1987 under threat of prosecution from the HSE, given the exposure of workers to excessive levels of mercury. It had then been relocated at Cato-Ridge in South Africa using the same processes. Following the poisoning and death of two victims at the Cato-Ridge plant the company was fined the equivalent of £3,000 in South Africa, for breaches of health and safety regulations. In 1994, compensation claims on the part of twenty workers were lodged in the UK High Court against the Chairman and Parent Company in the UK and Leigh Day represented the plaintiffs[3]. In the meantime President Mandela had initiated a Commission of Inquiry into Thor Chemicals. In 1997 an out of court settlement was reached involving compensation totalling £1.3 million with further claims and an appeal to follow.

The outward effect of this was to encourage further action to be taken against other UK parent companies, where negligence in relation to their workers in South Africa could be identified. Thor was a small prize financially but it received a great deal of publicity, which may well have encouraged those involved to pick up further briefs. There were potentially much bigger targets – those companies responsible for the prevalence of silicosis related disease in the wider mining sector. Within a year a further case in 1995[4] took on one of the major UK based mining houses – Rio Tinto Zinc (RTZ) – and involved a single claimant suffering from cancer who had worked at RTZ's uranium mine in Namibia. The case twice went to appeal and in 1996 the House of Lords found that the case could be heard in a Court in England. In the background was the South African Commission of Enquiry into Safety and Health in the Mining Industry, which had commenced in 1993 and which was to result in the Mine and Safety Act of 1996. This was very critical of practices particularly in the gold and coal industry.

In the case of asbestos, the return of anti-apartheid activist Dr Ahmed Renderee from research work in Canada, brought him to the attention of the then Director General of Health in the Northern Cape Province[5]. He was asked to make the first large scale assessment of asbestos workers in Prieska, Cape's notorious mine location. It was no coincidence that this coincided with the issue of the court proceedings in London against Cape PLC involving the five South African residents, two from Prieska site and three from Penge[6]. This initiative had the support of the CPAA (Concerned People Against Asbestos) which had been active since the closure of the Prieska mine in 1979. The asbestos workers claimed they had been exposed to levels of asbestos dust thirty times in excess of UK legal limits without protective gear, and suffered injury as a result. Leigh Day had secured UK legal aid for the claimants, there being no forum available in South Africa to pursue their claims, or legal aid available. The South African Government had a backlog of issues in the post-apartheid period and even if the misdemeanors of the mining industry were on the list, asbestos mining at its peak in 1977 had only represented some 3% of overall minerals production, so it was not at the forefront of their attention. In January 1998, the UK High Court granted Cape's application to have the proceedings stayed, enabling the claims to be heard in South Africa. This decision however was reversed by the Court of Appeal in July 1998, which was upheld by the House of Lords in December 1998.

On top of this in October 1997 a writ was served in the UK High Court by Vincenzina Girondo and three other former workers who had been employed at Cape's former subsidiary Capamiento at its Turin factory in Italy. Capamiento had been liquidated in 1977. Article 2 of the Brussels Convention provided that such a case could be heard in the English Courts. At the same time manslaughter proceedings had been instituted in Milan against the Italian Managing Director. The proceedings had been suspended as the Managing Director had been diagnosed with alzheimer's disease. The plaintiffs won their case in the UK and a settlement was reached. In due course a process of establishing compensation funded by the taxpayer and by means of a pension multiplier and workers compensation was established in Italy and further claims against Cape did not materialise. The facility to sue management for negligence or 'intentional homicide' however remained, as Executives and Directors of the Italian Eternit business learnt, being awarded prison sentences over the period of 2005-2012.

The South African cases received a great deal of attention and publicity. There was consternation in many quarters that foreign workers could secure UK legal aid. UK Parent Companies, particularly the mining houses, feared that the corporate veil could be pierced and they could be exposed to enormous damages for the activities of overseas subsidiaries. For Cape it was potentially existential as it was clearly a test case that would, if successful, produce an avalanche of potential claimants, which is what occurred. Between 1997 and 1999 a further eleven writs were served involving 3000 workers. Cape put the best legal brains to work on its defence and in 1998 accrued £3.3 million towards the legal costs.

Rutland's management were stunned – they appeared to have no inkling of this in evaluating the case for investing in Cape, nor is it likely to have arisen from their due diligence. If Charter had remained on board they would have had the Anglo connection to draw on at such a time. But Rutland should have been aware of the implications for Cape of the Thor and RTZ London hearings. To their investors it reflected badly on Rutland's judgement so it did harm their reputation. Moreover in preparing Cape's defence it caused detailed analysis of the corporate structure and the 'corporate veil' and this further demonstrated what they were already becoming increasingly aware of – that it was going to become extremely difficult to demerge Cape Industrial Services such that it would be beyond the reach of potential claimants. The intended demerger was already in danger of being dropped as it looked as though the business would be placed in the construction sector, and valuation expectations were not looking attractive. Despite attempts to have the business categorised in the support services sector, expected to offer a higher valuation, the appetite for public offers in 1997 was beginning to fall off. So the demerger plan was put aside and Rutland saw their essential task was to see the South African broadside off. They had no real alternative, and as a private equity house with a good ethical record to maintain they approached the challenge mindfully, backed by the best legal advice. Lawyers eagerly sought the brief as there was an expectation of further claims in this practice area.

To the management of the industrial services business the abandonment of the demerger option was not a great disappointment. Given the type of business it was they were hands-on operational people rather than corporatists. Had the demerger gone ahead it would have no doubt involved new 'city wise' management with possible unintended consequences. As it was, and given Rutland's style, the industrial services management was allowed considerable freedom to run and develop the business, which they did. For many years the whole IDC issue in fact afforded them protection against diversions and pressures from without or within. For the Manufacturing Division the position was similar but, unlike industrial services, the business was capital intensive and the implications would be more significant.

Rutland could see that none of their immediate plans could be realised and that they were going to be in for a rather longer haul. To tie down two of their key Executives at Cape was a sub optimal use of resources. A Chief Executive – Ian Maclellan - was recruited and an internal candidate – Ian Widdowson - promoted to Finance Director. Maclellan, a chartered accountant, joined in July 1997. His most recent role had been as Chief Executive of Ibstock PLC.

Manufacturing

In taking over Rutland must have thought they had, in the manufacturing business, a steady earner with potential to expand; good margins had been earned in the manufacture of some first class products – Superlux, Masterboard, Vermiculux, Durasteel, Monolux, the Siborit products and now Pyrok. Operating profit margins consistently hit the 10% mark and sales moved ahead in 1996. It turned out that Michael Farebrother had left something of a management vacuum and loss of momentum. After the loss of Tim Bowdler, Rutland found in Peter Morton, ex BPB Industries (British Plasterboard), someone knowledgeable in the industry to take the helm and at the end of 1997 the manufacturing businesses were brought together under a single entity – Cape Calsil Group Ltd. - of which he was Managing Director. However one by one the range of products seemed to take a knock. Reference to the strength of the £Sterling in the years to follow was too readily given as the reason for the decline of what was an export dependent business.

Cape Boards

For Superlux and Masterboard there were some product improvements in 1995 and 1996, but by now competitors such as Promat and BPB were beginning to catch up. Promat was producing similar boards, BPB offered a moisture resistant plasterboard and Knauf has a board based on perlite. These were companies with deep pockets. At Cape, product innovation and R&D had fallen behind and a renewed focus probably came too late. At Uxbridge, with volumes falling off there was a need for changes in work practices to get costs down, the workforce having got used to some hefty overtime payments. The newly acquired business of Pyrok however benefitted from being exposed to Cape's sales network.

Export levels to the Far East held up initially despite shipping costs beginning to creep up and the strength of the £Sterling. This was due to success in tackling further markets in SE Asia – Taiwan, Thailand and Malaysia. In 1997 sales to the Taiwan market exceeded one million square metres[7] and the attractions of the market prompted Cape to put together a joint venture, with Agent Goldsun Construction and Development Co. Ltd. Ian Maclellan in the 1998 Annual report hailed this as the answer to falling volumes in the Far East, stating that a joint factory was being set up, with Cape engineers directing its design and

 refurbishment. This was a 50/50 joint venture, incorporated in Taiwan, and from the PLC accounts the investment could not have amounted to much. Cape provided the technology and Goldsun the factory. The initial focus was be on Masterboard. The rationale for doing this was sound – to ship bulky relatively low value building products halfway around

the world could not last. Taiwan was seen to be the gateway to China as well as a good production location for Southeast Asia. The timing was too late. Cape's sales success had been very much down to it's pioneering development of asbestos free calcium silicate boards in the seventies. In the Far East in 1995 it was still competing against asbestos containing board sourced from Japan. Japan was behind in asbestos replacement, but strong in calcium silicate technology. It was not until 1995 that amosite asbestos was banned in Japan, so there was an incentive to develop substitutes. By the time the Goldsun JV was incorporated similar asbestos-free products were available, a plant having been set up in Taiwan with Japanese technology by Taisyou International Business Co., which rapidly became the market leader. Cape's input to Goldsun would have been the slurry recipe and mix and means of running the machines to achieve the correct quality. Having done this, Cape appeared to lose control of the operation, whether through weaknesses in the deal that was struck or the disengagement of Cape's Singapore based regional management. The latter saw the establishment of the JV as an Uxbridge initiative and continued to market UK produced board against the Goldsun product. The end result was that it was a double failure with

Goldsun and others taking the market and Cape failing to gain from the JV. An impairment was noted in the 2001 accounts amounting to £2.5 million which looks to have related to the Joint Venture and subsequently it was noted in 2002 that Cape's 50% share had been sold for a consideration of £500,000. Cape Goldsun calcium silicate boards are still marketed by Goldsun associate. Wellpool Co., who, interestingly, have a subsidiary called Cape Co. Ltd. in Taiwan. Its present website claims 'Wellpool's calcium silicate board technology is licensed from the century old 100 year old English building materials maker Cape Asbestos'. It boasts an output of 3.4 million boards per annum. Whilst the seeds of this venture had been sown before Maclellan and Morton's arrival, they appeared not to have had time to control the modus operandi of the venture such that it delivered on its promise. It certainly did not.

Durasteel

The Architect of Durasteel's success, Tony Ashcroft, had clashed with Michael Farebrother who was looking to get behind the management moat he had erected around the business. Ashcroft wanted to run it as a lower volume high margin business whereas Farebrother thought it could be taken a lot further. When Peter Morton took over he saw the opportunity of rationalising his production units and bringing Durasteel into Uxbridge from Wellingborough, since Uxbridge had spare capacity and labour. The assumption was that the product could be produced on the Hatschek machine, representing a major step up from the old batch production. This however proved a problem given the high portland cement content which clogged machines. Another disaster.

Of greater significance was the decision by Durasteel management to take on a £14 million contract for tunnel and ventilation ductwork fire protection for the Jubilee Extension Underground Line in London. The Client had pushed Durasteel management into accepting a supply and installation contract. The company had no experience of undertaking a major installation contract, and still maintained Ashcroft's supreme confidence in its capabilities. They could have wisely consulted commercial people in the Industrial Services Division, or sought to employ them as sub-contractors, but they blithely went ahead. As we learnt in earlier chapters a poorly managed subcontract role on major projects can lead to commercial suicide. Like many such projects the construction of the

Jubilee Line was subject to delays and changes which neither the contract Durasteel had entered into, nor the commercial acumen of the project management, allowed it to earn a fair return for its efforts. The contract was subject to substantial claims and finally settled in 2000. The Chairman, in the year 2000 report, stated that the reduction in turnover (in the manufacturing division) was predominantly due to the decision 'to withdraw from installing its own products'. This was solely a reference to Durasteel's Jubilee Line contract – the Division had never really been in the business of installing its own products. The reality was that losses of the order of £2-£3 million had been incurred on the contract and in moving production to Uxbridge, all hidden within asset write offs and rationalisation costs declared in the accounts.

Industrial Products

The Washington factory was still manufacturing low density calcium silicate insulation and had been able to resurrect a product – phenolic foam – which had been introduced by Cape Insulation at Stirling ahead of its time. It was now attracting attention given the unease surrounding the fire properties of polyurethane and polyisocyanurate foam. The factory was to be the subject of a great deal of investment at a time when it could be hardly afforded. An exceptional charge of £2.2 million in 1996 covered the cost of the work of modernisation and re-equipping. The market for its main line 'Newtherm' calcium silicate insulation was very confined and being mainly export, transport costs were high. Calcium silicate insulation was being used less and less in Europe featuring more prominently in US and Japanese specifications. Its attempts to introduce new products such as phenolic foam were modest when compared with the investment being made by market leader Kingspan. An enthusiastic and sound management team deserved a better portfolio.

In the previous chapter we learnt of the acquisition of Siborit in Germany and the transfer of some of the production of high density calcium silicate products from Germiston to Luneberg. In 1995 sales are recorded as being 35% up on the previous year given demand in the aluminium industry. There was clearly rivalry between the Siborit and Germiston management and this reflected a belief that the Germiston product was superior to the equivalent sold by Siborit, which was only sustained by its nomination in German specifications. As soon as the Germiston product secured the necessary approvals it was clear that the Company could no longer support two production centres and Luneborg lost out. Within two years the Luneburg plant was to be closed and sold with the low density calcium silicate production going to Washington and the high density to Germiston, which is where it would have stayed, had the Siborit venture not taken place. Closing the German business was an expensive affair and closure involved prolonged negotiations with the workforce. A further £2.5 million exceptional costs were incurred in 1997. The one bright spot was the performance of Germiston over the last years of the decade; maybe it had taken the Siborit fiasco to shake the business up.

Manufacturing Implodes

By the year 2000 the sales of the Manufacturing Division were down from £85 million in 1995 to £50 million. The business had swung from a profit of £8.6 million to a loss. In 2000 there was an asset write down of £3.3 million and redundancy and related costs came in at £5.4 million. How could the business collapse so rapidly? The Boards business in the 1980's boasted a premium product, favourable market conditions in Europe and the Far East and a proactive sales force. Complacency crept in, innovation and new product development fell behind and production efficiency began to drop off. Investment in the plant was constrained by a lack of funds and a lack of ideas. Few of their acquisitions had been successful and in some cases misguided. Too frequent management changes and some poor production management at all levels played its part.

Industrial Services

To the management of Cape Industrial Services (CIS) the demise of the manufacturing businesses came as a shock, and if truth be known an element of schadenfreude. From its beginnings as the Outworks Department at Barking, Cape Contracts (as it was) had been the poor cousin. Cape had been a reluctant contractor and the business was considered as the rough end of the industry and its practitioners a sharp lot! The business had always managed its working capital well, and there was a sense, amongst its managers, that it only generated cash for it to be then squandered on some of the Manufacturing Division's poorer investment decisions. The hitherto superior performance of Cape Boards and Panels had placed it on a pedestal and the collapse had been sudden. By the year 2000 Industrial Services was earning £11 million operating profit on sales of £186 million. This compares with £4 million and £85 million a decade earlier.

In the Industrial sector the UK had seen a recession in the first few years of the decade and investment by the oil majors was held back as the oil price stagnated around the US$40-$50 range, but growth in international sales throughout the decade helped to maintain momentum. Whilst a picture of solid growth, CIS was not sufficiently attractive to excite the City when pitching for flotation. For the managers of the business its flotation would have been a distraction, and they prospered without it. The success of the business was attributable to three major strategic features of its marketing proposition. Firstly, it had assembled a platform of services or trades such that clients could now employ a single industrial services contractor, avoiding the administration and management of a number of subcontractors. This allowed them to pass on interface issues, reduce administration, and control projects better. Secondly Cape had secured the confidence of major international end users and contractors in their demand for world class standards of safety and quality. And finally a focus on maintenance, which was lower risk and involved longer term repetitive contracts. These features served to increase the barriers to entry and few of its competitors could match this capability. By the end of the decade Cape was the leading contractor in its field not only in the UK but internationally beyond Europe and the USA.

United Kingdom

UK sales still comprised the larger share of Industrial Services turnover there being a simple reason this – the higher cost of labour. Typically labour cost could comprise 60-70% of the cost of a project, materials and equipment comprising the balance, whereas in the Middle East, for example, the percentages were the reverse, due to the lower manhour cost. A key performance consideration in the business, particularly in the UK was the importance of estimating labour costs accurately, or alternatively having adequate contingencies in the price to cover the risk of a cost overrun. Competitive pricing rarely, if ever, allowed the latter. A development over the decade in which Cape played a part was the evolution of alternative performance-driven forms of contract. The acronym 'KPI' – Key

Performance Indicator, came into use as a measure of performance, whether quantitative or qualitative. As opposed to the old lump sum or schedule of rates contracts more collaborative forms of contract emerged. The holy grail being 'open book' contracts, the aim of which was for each party to the contract to be seen to achieve an agreed budget for a given scope of work. For the contractor the aim would be to have its costs plus an agreed profit reimbursed, the KPI's then determining the extent to which it could receive a bonus (or have a penalty applied).

This form of contract was common in the UK Offshore industry from the start, given the nature of the work. Offshore work also displayed a further feature - client pressure ensured that a level of multi-discipline working was established. This was less easy onshore where trade demarcation still dominated. Cape Offshore quickly adopted the NVQ (National Vocational Qualifications) system of skills enhancement training, after its introduction in the UK in 1987, and boasted of men with upwards of ten trade skills. (On an offshore rig a scaffolder may be required to take his turn in the cookhouse amongst other activities - Cape's 'integrated support services' contract for British Gas on the Armada field in 1997 included catering services). Among the other skills was abseiling, and with the new forms of contract providing incentives to effect savings for the client, a proposal might be put forward involving abseiling to deal with an access problem rather than elaborate scaffolding. One of Cape Offshore's major contracts was for BP's terminal at Sullom Voe on the Shetland Islands where, as the incumbent contractor, it employed over one hundred men. In 1997 it recorded four years under the contract without a single safety incident involving lost time. In the same year it managed to re-secure the five year multi-discipline fabric maintenance contract based at Shell's Mossmoran and St Fergus terminals. A similar capability was deployed at Cape's North East Depot providing for module and offshore services in the southern sector of the North Sea. In 1999 the North East operation was enhanced by the acquisition of Duffy and McGovern Maintenance Services for £400,000 which gave it a presence in Yarmouth.

Cape Industrial Services was beginning to benefit from its ability to provide a platform of services and from now on we see local depots combining under the label 'Cape Industrial Services.' A model regional depot such would provide a sheet metal shop for insulation, a scaffold yard and shop for corrosion control plant and equipment – the key centres being Glasgow, Warrington (North West), Nouth Shields (North East), Cardiff (Wales) and Southampton (South). Each region was a profit centre, employing its own operational staff. In all, eleven depots employed over 2000 people. A multi-discipline contract for National Power at Eggborough in 1996 included industrial cleaning for the first time as a service. Whilst this initially involved little more than hiring in industrial scale vacuum cleaners and dustcarts, it was to develop into a business embracing more complex cleaning processes on oil refining and petrochemical installations.

The scaffolding activity continued to have a hire and sale division. This was an attractive business but was capital intensive. Key to it was the control of assets and Cape had good systems in place. Money was made when hire was inevitably extended and compensation secured for non-returns. It was however a different business from the mainstream scaffolding activity which involved design and erection, and demanded a different management structure. An attractive capex proposal could always be put forward for a hire and sales depot, but the reality was that the opportunity cost of the investment did not always add up given the greater added value generated on labour, in addition to hire, with a typical industrial services contract. It also involved a higher risk debtor profile. The number of hire depots was up to eight in 1996 but this peaked in the next few years as it became increasingly difficult to make the capex case to the Main Board and there being a greater need in the mainstream business.

Some of the major oil related, petrochemical and power plants constructed after the war were now requiring substantial maintenance and this might involve s shutdown or 'turnaround.' Given the need to minimise downtime these might extend to only 30 or 60 days and involve a large labour force, two shift working and an uncertain scope – a massive task in terms of logistics, manpower and equipment. Cape were uniquely equipped to handle this type of project and contracts would provide for incentives to meet deadlines and safety targets. These were the dying days of the big coal fired power stations and a major site was Drax where in 1992 a shutdown involved seventy scaffolders for twelve hours, twenty four seven, 500,000 ft. of scaffold tube and 380,000 ft. of boards. (See illustration page 127). To maintain utilisation of equipment against such a variable activity profile was some challenge.

The first contractor in its field to achieve the latest quality and safety accreditations for each of its areas of activity, Cape went further and established its own Management Information System ('The IMS'). This covered all its operational procedures and was a further enhancement of its services, as it demonstrated to clients how work was efficiently carried out, quality assured and safely. The system was also designed such that it could be integrated within client's systems when operating an open book type contract. Given that major clients operated sophisticated IT systems, many using SAP Technology software, Cape too installed SAP systems – again ahead of any of its competitors. By this time the Industrial Services business was headquartered at Wakefield, South Yorks, which was where the scaffolding business had historically been located; it was also the base for Managing Director Paul Ainley.

Paul Ainley was a scaffolding man by background and had progressed through site, project and depot management to his present position. Commercially very astute he had a good eye for management talent and lead his team from the front. Scaffolding is to a large extent about logistics and the control of assets – and requires a hands-on disciplined approach. Having these attributes Ainley was the ideal man for the task, and was given a free hand by Rutland. He had a clear strategy for the business which had the support of the shareholders. A proud Yorkshireman he had the self-confidence to risk unpopularity when tough decisions had to be made. Two events characterised his style. On one occasion head office staff were each, including Directors, subject to an unannounced drugs test, without warning. This was resented but it was a discipline observed on sites under the IMS, so as far as Ainley was concerned head office staff should be subject to the same procedures. Fortunately they all passed! The other - when it came to Christmas parties at Head Office, staff had to pay for it themselves!

Mainland Europe

Mainland Europe was now part of the international business under Peter Gartside, and having disposed of Hessische, Entsorgungstechnik and Socap the business comprised Cleton Insulation. Gartside appointed Jannie Schokkenbroek-Vos as Managing Director – a woman in very much a man's world was quite a novelty. Jannie had risen from a clerical roll in the company to head up the branch at Klazienaveen in the North. The business was structured in a way that mirrored the geography of the Low Countries, with depots in the North, Central (Vlaadingen, near Rotterdam), the South and West. There were nameplate offices in Germany (Meppen) and Belgium (Antwerp). Jannie was true to the perceived stereo type of those from the North – serious, industrious, forceful in her views. She formed a good if not like minded management team, ran a tight ship and understood the business well. As revealed in previous chapters, shareholders had not served them well prior to Cape and there was still defensive barriers erected against the shareholder. The insulation industry in Holland was highly structured with a well unionised workforce, a common manhour estimating and productivity platform and a functioning cartel. The lack of competitive pressure made for a low margin business relative to the rest of Cape's Industrial Services activities and difficulty in seeking and effecting change in the business. The decade however was good for the Company, with its main accounts – Shell Pernis – the largest oil refining complex in the world – and GasUnie in the North investing heavily. There was the first signs however of one development which was to rock this boat – smaller companies were beginning to bring in labour from new EEC entrants. Poland was initially the main source and migrant labour could be paid in their home country at significantly lower rates. Even Cleton found it cheaper to bring in and house UK laggers in times of need. However Cleton had a large and ageing permanent workforce to accommodate and the facility to bring in East European labour was not really an option. The business was firmly embedded in thermal insulation which had always involved lofty standards (probably better than the UK) and there was a certain prejudice displayed towards ancillary activities such as painting and scaffolding, so it was proving difficult to drive the business towards the multi-discipline UK model.

International - LNG

This was the decade when Cape established a position of world leadership in the LNG sector. Natural Gas was now beginning to power the grids of Japan, Europe and the USA. An effective means of tapping the enormous resources in the Middle East, S E Asia and Australia was to liquify and transport it. Cape had earned its reputation for the sophisticated type of thermal insulation required in LNG gas plants in the Gulf States. On Qatargas it had introduced the concept of a common user scaffolding contract. Hitherto the provision of access scaffolding was left to individual contractors. Exxon Mobil was an investor and Project Manager on Qatargas and insistent on the very highest safety standards. The provision of scaffolding by just one contractor meant safety standards would be common and use of scaffold optimised. Qatargas LNG Train 4 was now proceeding and neighbouring Rasgas building two trains. Qatargas eventually grew to fourteen LNG trains.

These were large and potentially high risk contracts. Owners and client Chiyoda Corporation needed to be convinced that Cape was financially strong enough to support them. Cape's exposure to asbestos liabilities was the subject of more than one defensive presentation in Yokohama. Typically such contracts involved 'On demand' bank guarantees of up to 20% of contract value together with work in progress financing, exacerbated in the event of delay. The terms of contract could be very onerous including liquidated damages penalties for delay or non-performance, and be subject to Japanese or local law. As we saw in the last chapter projects were often delayed which would cause 'tail-end' contractors such as Cape to be faced with a completion scenario which would involve considerable extra cost. Strong commercial management and its operational strengths generally enabled Cape to recover costs outside its control and achieve completion bonuses. The incorporation of scaffolding also provided a compensating bonus at the end of projects, as inevitably more scaffolding was required to finish the project and this provided the opportunity to increase hire rates such as to enable new capex to be partly amortised on the project.

It followed that when Oman followed Qatar's example, Cape would be in pole position when Oman LNG built its first LNG Train in 1994. To position itself for the project it was necessary to form a local company, and engage in the process of employing Omani nationals wherever possible. An Omani Manager was appointed and a local partner sought in order to meet the requirement for 51% Omani participation. Cape was able to incorporate Cape East & Partners WLL in partnership with the Chairman of Oman LNG (such a transparent potential conflict of interest was not unusual!). Main Contractor Chiyoda Corporation had already decided in favour of Cape given its performance on Qatargas, so it was not necessary to draw upon the connection. For the Oman work Cape was able to add painting and refractory to its work scope. Painting involved the setting up of a complete spray painting shop to coat all incoming pipe spools as well as final touch-up on site. Oman LNG introduced a further dimension to Cape's capability - training of nationals. Incentives were provided under the contract to employ Omani nationals. This was a challenging task in that Omanis, or for that fact other Gulf nationals, were not necessarily used to manual labour and many were able to earn a living without the need to work on a site. All Cape personnel worked a 60 hour week – unknown in the local economy. Cape set up training schools and met its objective. By then it had setup a training capability in Abu Dhabi utilising the UK's NVQ system which had set the training modules. This proved very successful with its TCN labour force since there were no trade demarcation issues and personnel were keen to learn additional skills. When it came to Oman LNG adding a further LNG train the requirement was for contractors to employ 30% Omanis. This was achieved leaving at the end of the contract sufficient skill to enable maintenance to be carried out utilising local labour. (See illustration page 155).

At the end of the decade Chiyoda's major competitor, Japanese Gas Corporation (JGC) in joint venture with M W Kellogg, with whom Cape had contracted in Australia, was awarded an expansion of the Bintulu LNG site in Sarawak, Malaysia. A local company, Cape East Malaysia Sdn. Bhd., was set up and secured contracts for thermal insulation and scaffolding. Cape had cut its teeth on the rejuvenation of the cryogenic heat exchanger at Brunei LNG and its performance had come to the attention of the Bintulu LNG owners, Shell and Petronas. The long rundown lines to the export jetty were pre-insulated in a purpose built factory near the job site. This proved a challenging task and necessitated completely re-building the production line to meet a tight schedule. Any losses were made up on the scaffolding work where Cape trained eight hundred Malaysian scaffolders. Shell demanded a state of the art safety regime and in excess of five million manhours were expended without lost time incident.

In Australia, a further expansion was carried out on the N W Shelf LNG terminal at Karratha, again in JV with local companies. Labour relations were problematic – UK supervisors, seconded to the project, were surprised to find themselves dealing with ex UK trade union activists who had moved on to more fertile Australian pasture, following the Thatcher era! Again contracts were let on a cost reimbursable basis - target manhours and material utilisation factors would be agreed and govern the bonus or penalty applied to the final contract value. A uniform site rate of pay was imposed on the contractor and the cost of strikes other than those clearly of its own making, were reimbursed. This meant for a given work content, contract values were substantially greater than in the Middle East where labour costs were low, utilising third country labour.

Cape secured most of the major contracts on Export LNG terminals let during the decade save one – Nigeria LNG. This was step too far for Cape PLC who baulked at the risks, Cape having had no experience in West Africa. Ironically its old South African subsidiary played a small part in the execution of the project. For Cape PLC one of these projects could generate returns equivalent to 10% or more of Industrial Services overall profits so it made forecasting difficult and gave rise to a lumpy pattern of profit, but what it did was enable the business to establish an ongoing presence in the countries where these projects arose, which in turn would lead to sustainable future revenues. A primary objective in each case was to pick up the maintenance activity beyond project completion.

It could have been easy for Rutland to fight shy of the risks involved in these contracts and their locations, at a time when Cape was under threat again. It is very much to their credit (and the company's bankers) that they gave their support in seizing such opportunities.

South East Asia.

This was a decade when Cape established firm roots in South East Asia. The Brunei and Malaysia LNG contracts helped to make its name. One of the most successful operations was in Thailand as recounted in the last chapter. In the Philippines Cape East continued to carry out work at the Batangas refineries where Shell and Caltex were finding trading conditions difficult as the oil price drifted and refining margins tightened. They were looking to Cape to reduce their cost by putting forward innovative maintenance procedures and disciplines. This gave Cape the opportunity to develop a trained Filipino labour force. Whereas Thai's were reluctant migrant workers, many Filipinos needed to seek out overseas work, and their training proved a worthwhile investment in the years to come. Operation in the Philippines had its own challenges not least of which was dealing with Barangay local Mayors and, over the years, more than one wayward expatriate secondee!

Industrial Disease Compensation

Earlier in the chapter the arrival of a further geographical dimension to Cape's asbestos legacy - South Africa - was daunting enough, but alongside this event claims continued in the UK and the decade saw further significant developments in litigation and compensation. No more so was this evident than with Turner & Newall (T&N) which had been responsible for 60% by value of the asbestos products supplied in the UK. Unlike Cape, T&N was still mining and producing asbestos based products in 1989 and it was not until 1995 that it had relinquished residual interests in India and Africa. In 1998 it succumbed to an unconditional takeover by Federal-Mogul Corporation (FM) of the USA. For FM it looked a good fit as it enabled them to provide a full range of automotive parts for engines and transmissions and in this line T&N had a successful business. T&N had taken an exceptional charge of £515 million in its 1996 accounts, and it had bought insurance and provided for a total £1.2 billion to cover asbestos related disease. FM had existing asbestos claims against them in the USA and in providing $2.1 billion to cover asbestos claims, after the purchase of T&N, must have thought they were well covered. But by 2001 the company was filing for Chapter II reorganisation in the USA, and administration in the UK, faced with 263,000 personal injury claims in the USA and 91,000 in the UK. This in due course lead to the setting up of the Turner and Newall Asbestos Trust. This whole sequence of events could only draw attention to Cape.

During the decade there were a number of industrial disease court cases in the UK, from those that had suffered from asbestosis, cancer and mesothelioma. Whilst defended rigorously by the employers, they achieved the purpose of clarifying the legal grounds under which claims could be successfully made. There was the question of apportionment where more than one employer was involved, with contributory negligence, void periods of cover, deductibility of previous awards and one in particular – the extent to which a reasonable employer could and should have been aware of the dangers of asbestos[8] - the conclusion of which was that a prudent employer would have taken precautions, or have made himself aware of the precautions necessary. The publication of the Judicial Studies Board Guidelines brought structure to the level of compensation for each category of disease[9]. All of this broadened the scope and raised the quantum associated with potential IDC claims against Cape.

Against this background Cape felt it necessary to clarify its position in its year end annual report. It reported that in 2000 the IDC charge against the P&L was £5.5 million, £4.4 million net of insurance recoveries. In the notes to the accounts a long statement ended with the comment:-

'If it were possible to assess reliably the present value of amounts that might be paid in future… there could be a materially adverse effect on the group's financial position. There is great uncertainty over the net present value of the future claim settlements which could occur in excess of twenty years, but they may exceed the amount of the net assets included in the current balance sheet. …Based on the recent history of settlements, Directors anticipate that claims can be made from future cashflows… Should the future pattern as regard timing and quantum prove inaccurate there could be a material adverse impact on the group's financial position.'

The composition of the statement suggested it had the input of many and the lucidity of none. To the alert shareholder it must have rung alarm bells. Apart from being inconclusive, it suggested that attempts had been made to make an actuarial assessment of potential liability but that it was found to be too unpalatable to be put into clear words.

In Conclusion

This was the time when the Industrial Services business, hitherto the poor cousin, emerged as the only hope of a future for shareholders and UK claimants. But first Cape had to deal with the legacy from its mining days – one which it had never bargained for, but one that had to be addressed.

CAPE NEWS

The newspaper for employees of Cape PLC   July 1996

Rising star of the East

■ Focus on Cape Asia Pacific

TURN TO PAGE 5

Left to right: Christopher Dowling, Michael Langdon and Paul Cartwright

Rutland Trust takes major stake in Cape

RUTLAND Trust PLC has bought a 25 per cent shareholding in Cape from Charter plc, previously Cape's largest shareholder with 65 per cent of the company's shares.

Charter has sold its entire shareholding in Cape, allowing it to invest in other engineering-based businesses, and the balance of the shares that Charter owned has been sold to institutional investors. Cape will remain an indepen-

dent quoted company.

Rutland is providing a senior management team to run Cape, with Michael Langdon the Chief Executive of Rutland as Chairman of Cape, Christopher Dowling Deputy Chief Executive of

Rutland appointed Chief Executive of Cape, and Paul Cartwright, a Director of the Rutland corporate finance team, as Group Finance Director. Michael Farebrother, Chief Executive of Cape since 1989, and

Cape News welcoming Shareholders Rutland Trust

(Illustrations, courtesy of publishers Key Communications)

CAPE NEWS

The newspaper for employees of Cape PLC   April 1997

Anyone for tennis?

■ Game set and match for Cape Boards at Wimbledon

TURN TO PAGE 4

Strong outlook for Cape's businesses

THE future is looking strong for Cape's core businesses with further expansion in the pipeline following the successful reorganisation of the business.

Chris Dowling, Cape's chief executive, predicted many opportunities for the company as it concentrates on developing its two core businesses in manufacturing and industrial services.

"I see a strong future for both sides of the company, both here and abroad, and we'll be expanding both within the UK and internationally. We are world leaders in calcium silicate technology and I firmly believe this technology will continue to give Cape many opportunities."

On the manufacturing side, Chris said market conditions in the UK and Europe were at last improving after a period of severe recession in the construction industry. The Far East remains, and will continue to be, a buoyant market for Cape products.

To illustrate this, Chris highlighted the changing trends, especially in the Asian markets where the authorities were laying down stricter

guidelines on fire protection, and where the moisture resistant nature of our products made them all suited to the climatic conditions.

Market Leader

The other half of the business, industrial services, is maintaining its position as market leader in the UK and internationally, particularly in the area multi-discipline services. Said Chris: "We have an unrivalled ability to offer multi-discipline services – a sort of one-stop shop – to our customers."

As for the company's future in Europe, he predicted an upturn in the construction industry as the business emerges from the recession. However the market still remains competitive and affected by the strong pound.

Said Chris: "Many of Cape's businesses are outside the UK so inevitably the stronger pound will affect our ability to compete. However, I'm confi-

dent we have the products, services and cost base to continue to do so effectively."

Reflecting on the Cape's progress since he joined the company last year, Chris said: "In terms of our original objectives when we came into the business, we are very much on line with the implementation of our plans to date in terms of timing and costs.

Strategy

"As part of our strategy to concentrate on our core business, we have now exited from our German, French and Norwegian contracting businesses and sold our Architectural Division to mangement – a decision which best protected the interests of employees there.

"Inevitably, the reorganisation, which was completed last December, may have caused some concern among our employees, but I feel we can now look forward to the future with optimism," he continued.

In 1997 a public flotation proposal covering Cape Industrial Services included this photograph of the management team.

(Top Row Mike Reynolds, Paul Ainley, Chris Dowling, Paul Gratton, Next Peter Gartside, Klaus Versteegh, Lejn Emmerzaal, Gordon Verity Next Nigel Hughes, Guy Rackham, Jannie Schokkenbroek, Ian Nickerson, Arie Bouma Next Bill Harding, Paul Richards, Brian Duxbury Bottom Bill Craig, John Hockin, Julian Gammage, Mike Wilkes)

By the end of the decade Cape's business in the Gulf States was the largest contributor to Cape's profits. The foundations were laid in the 1990's by key unit managers - **Top left across** - *Hemachandran* (UAE) *Frank McCoy* (Saudi Arabia), *John Hockin*, (Cape East Regional Director)- Middle row *Samir Chopra* (Qatar), *The Author* - Front row *Nigel Hughes* (R B Hilton Regional Director*)*, *Sanjay Ganguly* (Bahrain).

Cape solved the problem of transporting over 1000 man from camp to jobsite at **Qatargas LNG** by importing four retired Birmingham City Corporation busses. *(Photographs by MEBD)*

LNG. Cape East & Partners LLC (CEPL) provided insulation, scaffolding, painting and refractory services on all phases of the Oman LNG Development at Qalhat.

(Illustrations from CFW Close-out Review)

Cape East & Partners LLC

Safety Contractor of the Month

May 2004, February 2005, April 2005, June 2005, July 2005, September 2005. CEPL have received this award more times than any other Contractor on site.

Quality Audit Awards

June 2005, August 2005, October 2005

Omanisation Contractor of the Month

October 2004, April 2005, September 2005

A total 19 million Manhours have been worked on site without Lost Time Incident, of which CEPL have worked 2.7 million Manhours

Chapter 8

A Shift in the Weighting

"This Company has been brought to its knees."
Richard Meeran. ITV Documentary. You Will Know Them by Their Trail of Death .2004

Rutland Trust's May 2000 accounts show a market value of £5.5 million for its 25% equity share in Cape which had cost it £17.66 million in 1996. It was the one black spot in an otherwise successful decade – in the same year it made an exceptional gain of £17 million on its investment in Castle Music. Private Equity was boosted by the introduction of Venture Capital Trusts in 1995 and by May 2001, Rutland closed its first fund, raising £210 million, taking care to isolate legacy assets such as Cape away from its new funds. It had earned no return on its investment in Cape despite tying up the time of its top executives. For shareholders, Cape was proving to be a disastrous investment, and they were now staring into the abyss of the outstanding South African litigation.

Since the initial action in 1997, senior Cape personnel had visited South Africa, interviewed old members of staff, including former Managing Director, Justin Mackuertan, and experts, in an endeavour to establish a line of defence against the South African Group of Five. Few records were available, and the old Cape management had moved on or did not want to engage. Arguments such as the suggestion of dust arising from natural erosion certainly did not fly. Their evidence must have been underwhelming to the top legal team that Cape and Rutland had gathered in London. The Lawyers, though, would have recognised that weaknesses in regulations, the oscillating nature of employment, and the Government support given to the South African mining industry, could feed an element of casuistry in dealing with the causal link back to Cape. Whilst they had made it clear that they would fight the case on the accusation of the negligence and medical condition of the plaintiffs, they soon concluded that Cape's first line of defence had to be based on 'forum non conveniens' – the jurisdiction in which the case should be heard. Clearly if it could be heard in South Africa the level of compensation would be far less and the possibility of putting together a line of defence possibly easier. As we learnt in 1998, Cape's application that the trial should take place in South Africa had been granted, but this had subsequently been reversed in the Court of Appeal. In 1999 another two thousand claimants had entered cases, being submitted alongside the existing claim and Cape was granted a stay of execution. However, on the Plaintiff's Appeal to the House of Lords in 2000[1], the Law Lords found that South African courts would not be a viable alternative forum for a case of such complexity because legal aid in South Africa had been withdrawn for personal injury claims, and there was no reasonable likelihood of effective legal representation on a contingency fee basis. By 2001 there were a further 7,500 claimants and UK legal aid was at the Plaintiff's disposal. A date had been set for the Court Hearing in March 2001. Cape's share price dropped from £1.50 before the litigation commenced, to a low of 6p in November 2002.

Not surprisingly, from 1999 onwards Cape and Rutland had been at the end of a targeted campaign in the press[2] and by pressure groups, exacerbated by a motion tabled in the House of Commons[3] by lead sponsor Ken Livingstone M.P., Jeremy Corbyn M.P. and others, in March of that year. This was aimed at Cape's lobbying activities the purpose of which was described in the motion as being:

'To launch a campaign aimed against the ambulance chasing activities of Leigh Day, the claimants lawyers, and to encourage the Daily Mail to embarrass the Lord Chancellor by making him to have to choose between black workers and multinationals (*such that*) the detail of the claims is likely to be of secondary interest.'

YJL/Montpellier Group enter the Scene.

A building company set up (before Cape) in 1886 by Young James Lovell, YJL PLC had in 1999 been chosen by Peter Gyllenhammar, the Swedish entrepreneur as a vehicle for buying equity in high-risk turnaround situations. After a somewhat turbulent career in his native Sweden involving bankruptcies, Gyllenhammar had taken up residence in the UK, and was the source of a flurry of corporate activity amongst medium and small UK companies[4]. Typically, he would take a 25% holding in a company with undervalued assets, secure board representation and thereby be able to resist any shareholders vote against him ('negative control'). In 1999 YJL's attention was drawn to Cape PLC, and during the year 2000 YJL built up a stake in the company, it would appear mainly drawn from Schroder Investment Management's holding, and at an average price of just over 50p. This would not necessarily have been known to Rutland, as it was not Gyllenhammar's style to engage with a target's board when building up a stake. In March 2001, a further one million shares were acquired in the market taking their shareholding up to 16.84% (*"YJL Inhales More Wheezing Cape"* – City Wire Funds Insider headlines). This was alongside a series of other acquisitions including shares in M J Gleeson, VHE, Jarvis Porter and even Lonrho. Lead by Chairman Cedric Scroggs, former Chief Executive of Fisons, Deputy Peter Gyllenhammar and Finance Director (later Managing Director) Paul Sellars, YJL then changed its name in April 2001 to Montpellier Group PLC. Chartered Accountant Paul Sellars had honed his property dealing skills in the housebuilding and land development sector under Tony Pidgley's Berkeley Group and Gerald Ronson's Heron Properties.

In common with Montpellier's approach to other predatory investments, they would have been pressing Rutland and the other shareholders for board representation. There was resistance to this - Montpellier was considered something of a maverick in the private equity business and was not entirely trusted in the City, having played hardball, with bankers and investors in some of their ventures. But by October they had persuaded Rutland to sell them 10.3% of their 25% at a price of 15p per share, giving Montpellier finally 29.9% and Rutland 14.7%. Despite their initial resistance towards Montpellier, Rutland, having already given up on their investment in Cape, saw the attractions of the spotlight being transferred from them to Montpellier, thereby reducing the risk of further reputational damage.

The speed at which Montpellier was making investments would question how far due diligence, as opposed to instinct, was guiding their decision, but certainly on the face of it Cape looked a reasonable gamble. The South African litigation was getting messy. Cape's lawyers were accusing Richard Meeran of Leigh Day of 'abuse of process' – some members of the legal establishment saw Leigh Day as disruptors - and costs were escalating. There was every chance Cape would lose the case, more likely it would drag on for years with further appeals. The uncertainty would not only undermine the interest of shareholders, but also disrupt a company that had a solid asset base and two viable businesses. Rutland was in a quandary, but pressed by the lawyers to fight on. In the light of the next set of events (but not subsequent) it perhaps should have sought an earlier settlement. Richard Meeran of Leigh Day has stated that an earlier settlement move had been anticipated by the Plaintiff's legal team[5]. But Cape would want a settlement that capped its liability and the list of claimants was mounting each day.

In gaining their 29.9% Montpellier were in a position to assume control which they did. Rutland ceased to be the Managers, Montpellier took over and Paul Sellars assumed the role of Chairman. Gyllenhammar's style had no place for an army of advisers or lawyers and he and Sellars had already made up their mind to pursue a South African settlement at all costs. They were letting it be known that Cape was in financial difficulties, and that if the case went to trial, the plaintiffs could lose either way – they could lose the case or if they won also lose in a long drawn out appeal process, during which Cape's ability to satisfy a claim would be greatly diminished. By then it would be too late for many of the suffering claimants. There was therefore an incentive on both sides to settle, and the question arose as to how much? For the Plaintiffs it had to be a worthwhile sum, for Cape it was simply a question of how much they could afford, but also there had to be finality in the settlement. The Plaintiff's lawyers, Leigh Day, who had now been joined by Manchester solicitors John Pickering and Partners, had attempted to quantify a level of compensation of the order of £3,000 to £5,000 per claimant and an all up bill approaching £50 million, but the amount was becoming academic as the numbers of claimants kept rising, and Cape's financial position kept deteriorating. Doubts as to whether Cape would deliver were expressed in the press and were beginning to creep into the minds of activists, notably ACTSA (Action South Africa) - successor to the Anti-Apartheid movement - which had maintained a consistent campaign from the beginning. They were now pressing Cape shareholders and demonstrating at court hearings. By December 19th it looked as though a deal would not be accomplished by the year end, but Sellars persevered and on Friday 21st December 2001, just before the lawyers drifted off for Christmas, an out of court settlement was reached. The settlement involved Cape making a compensation payment of £11 million (reported as £10 million by Cape, taking a different exchange rate) to a trust fund by 30th June 2002 and £1 million thereafter annually for 10 years, the money only to be forthcoming if Cape PLC remained solvent. If Cape were placed in liquidation the court case would resume. The settlement was subject to Cape's shareholders and banker's approval but more importantly subject to undertakings by the South African government that Cape would not be liable for cleanup of former sites, and that they would not fund further legal actions against the company. For Leigh Day's part, they were bound not to support any further such claims against the company. Cape also had to pay £2.25 million of Plaintiffs legal costs. A further motion in the House of Commons welcomed the settlement[6].

On the face of it and relative to Cape's assets and liabilities the settlement was unaffordable, but it had the advantage of putting a firm line under the potential for litigation from this source. Even Richard Meeran who had led the case for Leigh Day admitted it as 'quite possible that the second tranche of £10 million or part of it may not materialise'[7]. For Sellars the latter could mean that for Montpellier nothing would materialise either. It clearly suggested though that he might get a deal now at a lesser overall figure. There was however a risk that they would not obtain the South African Government approvals.

So, for Cape's stakeholders there was a shift in the weighting between them - the shareholders were now potentially dead in the water - to the benefit of claimants. Claimants were now likely to secure some meaningful compensation in South Africa as well as the UK. As for the employees, they had the security of being engaged in viable businesses that would survive. The moral case for compensating South African miners was of course unarguable, and the truth was that the industry had failed miserably to protect its employees from industrial disease. This sequence of events had not involved Cape's line management and employees, having being dealt with by Montpellier and Rutland behind closed doors. It came as something of a shock to employees, albeit tinged with an element of resentment at the use of UK legal aid. This was widely criticised - the prevalence of self interest in worker solidarity noted by Lord Elton in chapter 1 (p.12) tended to prevail. The fact that the case became so complex was due to its focus on jurisdictional legalities and the UK legal aid involved. This of course had been only encouraged by the nature of Cape's lobbying activity back in 1999. Had the plaintiffs case been dealt with on its merits, proper arguments of causation, consequence and due compensation might have been addressed. Some precedents could have been set that would have speeded up the processing of the claims in the mining industry that were to follow.

Sale of Cape Calsil

Meanwhile Sellars was going ahead with his own 'unbundling' to realise assets and calm bankers, for whom the settlement looked unaffordable. Whilst outwardly the impression was given that either one or other of Cape's Divisions was up for grabs, it is unlikely Montpellier had any intention of offloading Industrial Services (CIS). Gyllenhammar liked contracting businesses as they were capable of functioning on negative working capital. One of his first ventures – construction business Britannia Group - had proved a very successful investment as he sold the capital-intensive assets and used the negative working capital business to finance other ventures. With Cape Calsil's recent problems, he realised it was not a candidate for flotation, but it could be sold, and assets realised. The obvious buyer was Promat, part of the Belgian Etex Group (better known under the Eternit name). Promat had only just ceased using asbestos in their production, and Cape's Masterboard, Superlux, Monolux, Vermiculux and other lines were attractive additions to their portfolio and remain so today. Cape's desperation was apparent to Promat who was able to adopt a tough negotiating stance. Sellars was not going to steam roll Promat to a swift deal and negotiations were left to Chief Executive Ian Maclellan. Had Cape more time, there would have been other potential buyers prepared to pay more. Promat had been catching up with Cape's technology; they knew the business well and understood its weaknesses and strengths. The Germiston products were important but beyond that their interest was to protect their European market. Cape's Japanese competitors had been desperate for the asbestos free technology only five years previously. Cape had missed the opportunity in prior years to receive a good price for the business. By July 2002 they were able to announce a deal, stating that the proceeds were needed to pay down bank debt. It had been a long drawn out business and Promat were determined only to cherry pick what they needed and without incumbrances. The sale took in: -

- The manufacturing facilities at Germiston (the freehold of the site being retained by Cape).
- The UK marketing, finance and support activities relating to the Cape Calsil business.
- Certain items of machinery.
- The business and assets of overseas subsidiaries in France, Germany, The Netherlands, Singapore, Hong Kong and Malaysia.

The entire process must have been extremely frustrating for Sellars and the Board, as the complexity of the deal meant that it was some time before they could get the seventy five page document[8] covering the disposal out to shareholders and a result in time to deliver on the South African settlement. Moreover it was clear that the disposal proceeds were barely sufficient to fund the settlement. The consideration for the sale was £9.2 million subject to various adjustments, of which £1.5 million was to be placed in a retention account and a further £2.5 million placed in an industrial disease provision account. The book value of assets transferred was £9.9 Million, and, of the assets retained by Cape, £9.5 million. The latter involved the properties all of which had potential clean-up liabilities. Cape retained any liability for industrial disease and in any event provided Promat with warrantees. Etex knew well how to tie this up given its own asbestos legacy experience through Eternit.

Cape's 2001 annual report and accounts was not published until August 2002 and made for grim reading in that they had to make provision for the South African settlement as well as the Calsil disposal (which involved a £18.4 million impairment). The accounts were something of a mess and other than to a highly tutored eye almost unfathomable. Exceptional items totalling £32 million had to be declared covering not only the South African settlement but also the outcome of the Calsil sale. Montpellier, which had a quick eye for pension liabilities and assets, had recognised that the Cape's defined benefit pension scheme was substantially in credit. Without bringing in a pension asset of £17.5 million shareholder's funds would have been barely positive. Short-term borrowings stood at £31 million. Fortunately Cape Industrial Services was reporting a solid performance again and an encouraging outlook going forward.

Back to Litigation

Following the settlement Cape had reached an agreement with its bankers for new facilities, thus allowing it to meet the terms of the South African settlement. However, this was subject to completion of the sale of Cape Calsil to Promat and raising £30 million from the partial sale of Industrial Services (CIS). The delay in issuing the 2001 annual report allowed Cape to hold back the warning that if the partial flotation of CIS was not possible it would be necessary to renegotiate the South African settlement.

The immediate cash receipts from the sale of Calsil hardly dented the c.£31 million, and there remained remnants of the business (mainly properties) still to dispose of. The banks were nervous. Nonetheless, up until August much of the work on establishing the trust into which the South African compensation was to be paid, had been done, and the initial payment was still expected. Two extensions were given beyond the 30th of June date scheduled for the payment of the £10 million. Cape was in fact playing for time as it was clearly impossible to effect a flotation of Cape Industrial Services (CIS) in the timescale. More importantly legal advice suggested that it was impossible to do so without CIS being exposed to claims, and, anyway, the shareholders did not want to dispose

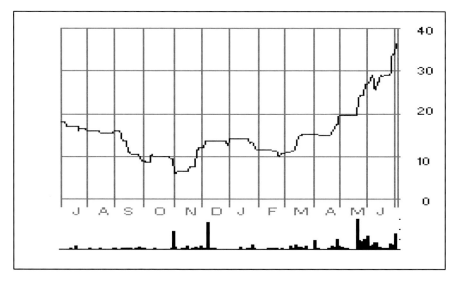

Cape PLC Share Price 2002-2003

of the business in whole or in part. Leigh Day sent a letter to Cape's Directors, to Shareholders and the Chairmen of Cape's Banks – RBS and Barclays - threatening they would hold them personally liable if there was evidence that they had induced a breach of contract. ('*Banks fingered in asbestos case payment delay*' read the *Guardian* headline). Cape was then forced to declare that the settlement funds would not be forthcoming. There were sufficient assets to provide the securities required, it claimed, but it was the banks that were resisting lending the money. The plaintiff's lawyers were becoming impatient, alleging that since the start of proceedings in 1999 some three hundred of the claimants had died.

So, in September 2002 the litigation recommenced, and the share price dropped to below 10p.

Ian Maclellan resigned as Chief Executive once the disposal of Calsil had taken place and Paul Sellars brought in a turnaround specialist, Martin May, as General Manager of the business. His task was described by Paul Sellars in the 2001 annual accounts (dated August 2002) as being to dispose of the surplus properties, complete the settlement of the South African litigation, and administer the agreed schedule of repayments to the banks. In addition, he would be responsible for day-to-day management. May was a Chartered Cost and Management Accountant and had his own turnaround consultancy business – M & J Associates. He was just the man to bulldoze through the task at hand. As soon as he got his feet under the desk in August 2002, he made it quite clear that he considered the South African settlement unaffordable. A circular was sent to shareholders explaining that the settlement was to be renegotiated. In the meantime, a further event came to Cape's rescue.

The ramifications of Cape's settlement had been sinking in within the South African mining establishment, no more so than Anglo American. Mining house Gencor, in which Anglo had a shareholding, and which owned Cape's old mining entities together with Gefco and other residual asbestos mining interests, had been following the London litigation carefully. Gencor itself was receiving asbestos related claims in the Johannesburg High Court. Given a lack of precedence, a three year statute of limitations, the fact that workers could not sue employers under the Occupational Injuries and Diseases Act, together with a lack of funding, there was little hope of success in South African courts. But the Cape precedent suggested an alternative avenue for litigants and one that would attract UK legal Aid. The first step, however, was to halt the process of unbundling of assets being undertaken by Gencor, which had the stated intention of winding up and distributing proceeds to shareholders. By May, the number of Gencor claimants was over 4000 and UK solicitors, Thompsons, had been called in to assist South African Lawyers Ntuli Noble Spoor. Given the legal moves in South Africa involving Gefco and parent Gencor, it had become apparent that many of Cape's 7,500 claimants had also worked for Gefco. In October 2002, an application was heard in the High Court for the Cape PLC summons to be amended to include Gencor as a Defendant and also Charter

PLC. (The Plaintiff's lawyers clearly felt it appropriate given Cape's precarious financial situation to enjoin Charter in the proceedings). An intervention application was then introduced in the Johannesburg High Court by Cape to intervene in the unbundling of Gencor. Cape in effect was taking action to secure a contribution from Gencor towards satisfying the claims.

Since most of the South African asbestos mines (including Cape's) had ended up in Gencor's lap and it was seeking to liquidate its assets, it was looking for a wrap up deal to cover all future liabilities. It was nervous that further liabilities could arise out of clean up operations, and the Government would now increasingly focus on the negative legacy aspects of the mining industry. This was to Cape's advantage and Martin May headed up the deal for Cape. The agreement reached between the parties involved Gencor placing £30 million in a newly established Trust - the Asbestos Relief Trust. Cape were to pay £10.6 million to its claimants, Gencor contributing £3 million towards this sum reflecting the fact that the claimants will have worked for both companies. By June 2003, the Asbestos Relief Fund was in place and payments commenced. The Trust continues to make payments of the order of £1 million per annum to claimants (2022). In 2006 a further Trust was formed – the Kgalagadi Trust – funded by Swiss Eternit who had owned the Kuraman and Danielskuil mines. As an open settlement the setting up of these Trusts was the better deal as it embraced future claimants. As a closed settlement Cape's merely addressed the needs of its 7,500 named claimants. The amounts paid (all within a year of the settlement, reflecting the speed at which some claimants were dying) varied depending on severity with mesothelioma and cancer sufferers receiving SR71,000 (c.£5,500)[9]. One good feature that differentiated the South African outcome relative to the UK was the inclusion of pleural plaque as being eligible for compensation, although the amount paid was small.

On the face of it the settlement exposed Cape to further potential claims. Other claimants could pursue the same action and there was no deal with the South African Government covering environmental remediation. That it did not receive further claims is probably explained by the fact that claimants, having most likely worked for one of the other asbestos mining companies or for Cape's successor company would have easier recourse to the Asbestos Relief or Kgalagadi Trusts, where there was money.

It turned out that with the establishment of the Trust, and the undertaking by the South African Government of most of the environmental remediation, Cape was not the subject of further claims, although the issue continued to remain as a note in the accounts as a possible contingent liability. Overall, the amount of compensation available was small in relation to the numbers employed in the industry over the years. At times as many as 80% of the workforce were migrant workers from neighbouring countries, who, having returned anonymously to their homelands, would, be afforded no relief other than any provided by their own governments. At least it could be said some compensation was paid by Cape and Gencor; similar claims in the London courts on behalf of six hundred asbestos workers employed at T&N's mines at Havelock in Swaziland, had to be abandoned on T&N's slide into bankruptcy in 2001[10]. Lonmin/Xtrata employees at Emerentia and Wandrag also lost out. Ironically, only in the same year, was South Africa's last asbestos mine, at Msauli, finally closed down.

Cape's erstwhile shareholder Anglo American Corporation would have been closely following events. As commented earlier there were those who believed that the South African mining industry deliberately allowed asbestos to act as the 'stalking horse' in the inevitable fallout that would emerge in relation to industrial disease in the other mines. Lawyers were gearing up for an onslaught on the big guns of the mining industry. The Government were getting round to focusing on some of the industry's past transgressions. The Compensation for Occupational Injuries and Diseases Act in 2003 paved the way for civil actions in addition to the existing means of compensation funded by an industry levy. By 2003 test cases were being brought on behalf of claimants from the gold mining sector who were suffering from silicosis, which affected up to 25% of the miners. Leigh Day supported local lawyers in these test cases which took nine years to conclude. In 2013 a case was won against Anglo American South Africa Ltd in support of 23 claimants which enabled an action to proceed on behalf of a total 4,365 claimants against Anglo American and Anglo Gold. The compensation awarded, amounting to £23 million, was subsequently placed in the Qhubaka Trust. Thereafter there were a number of other successful claims against the major mining companies covering compensation for silicosis (e.g. the Tchiamiso Trust in 2020) and other industrial diseases including TB and lead poisoning. The latter continues (2023) to be the subject of litigation involving Anglo. Leigh Day continue to figure in most of these actions.

On October 11th, 2002, May was appointed Group Managing Director, Maclellan resigned as a director; Sellars resigned as Chairman in favour of Gyllenhammar. Both Sellars and Gyllenhammar resigned as Directors at the end of November. The fact that Peter Gyllenhammar had to step in as Chairman in a hurry suggested there may have been a falling out. But the most likely explanation is the need for Sellars to deal with other pressures within Montpellier given the pace of acquisitions. Montpellier by now would have realised that they should cash in their chips on Cape, so why not move on, and bail out when the share price picked up, as it most likely would. Additionally, they would by now have had confidence in Martin May to deliver for them.

Conclusion

From Cape's perspective, the best that can be said of its actions was that it allowed the Company to survive. In playing for time, Cape happened to bring about an industry settlement in South Africa which otherwise might not have occurred, at least as quickly. It was certainly to Cape's benefit as its net liability had in the process been reduced to £7.5 million – a long way from the amounts that were initially agreed. The South African mining establishment, in the form of Gencor, had come to the rescue with a 'get out of jail' card. In the process

Cape PLC. Profit and Shareholders Funds. 1998-2002
£ millions

Year End	Operating Profit Industrial Services	Operating Profit Cape Calsil	Total Net Profit after Exceptionals, Recurring and Interest	Shareholders Funds
1998	9.60	6.30	8.80	53.60
1999	10.10	3.00	9.10	55.20
2000	11.00	-4.10	-14.80	38.90
2001	10.80	-5.80	-32.40	20.50
2002	9.80	-0.80	14.60	24.10

over £3 million of legal costs had been expended. It capped a record by Cape which was symptomatic of some of the worst of the charges brought against the asbestos mining industry in South Africa. Leigh Day came out with credit. They recognised the limits to which they could take Cape – if they had gone for the jugular they may have ended with nothing, or more likely as participants in long protracted litigation with a liquidator. The entire process spoke well of the UK's legal system. Across the Atlantic corporate America had decided to stand and fight the court system itself and its entrepreneurial lawyers, rather than continue to agree settlements[11]. To claimants it suggested Cape was now vulnerable as a target; to management it served as notice to seek solutions to the looming UK IDC problem; to shareholders and employees, it meant survival.

Financially, the last five years had seen the destruction of Cape's balance sheet, the contributing factors being the disposal of Cape Calsil and the South African

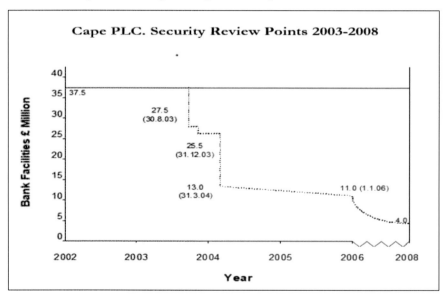

settlement. Industrial Services profits and to a degree cashflow had held the business together. Had the company had to meet the initial agreed South African settlement, its bankers may well have given up on it. Both Barclays and RBS had set strict review points covering the repayment of loans, and the reduction in debt. Martin May had a demanding target to meet but had made a good start by achieving a settlement well within provisions.

Chapter 9

Sunny Uplands?

Corporate

So, by 2003 Cape had managed to rid itself of the South African litigation, sold the deteriorating Cape Calsil business, and was under new independent management – independent as both of its shareholders 'in for the ride' were to dispose of their holdings. In the process Cape had moved from the main market to AIM reflecting its reduced status.

Rutland waited for the dust to settle before it disposed of its 14.7% holding for £3.7 million or 47p a share in the second half of 2003. Overall, it had lost £13 million on an investment that consumed too much of its time. There were institutions ready to jump on board, initially Prudential and RBS (being impressed with the speed at which the borrowings were coming down) but there was a fair amount of churn and eventually M&G and Schroder became prominent.

Rutland had earned the respect of the business managers of Cape but as soon as they found their hopes for their investment were unachievable, understandably had lost interest. To an extent Montpellier came to the rescue, took some flack, and did them a good turn in allowing them to exit quietly. But Rutland could bow out gracefully and take some credit in the survival story of Cape. Interestingly it took private equity shareholders (i.e. Rutland Trust) to look at the IDC liability squarely in the face. It was a forerunner of things to come and had it been Charter may not have been confronted in the same way, given its Anglo connections.

Subsequently Montpellier also disposed of its holding for £9.47 Million at an average 58p a share. This yielded them a profit of £4.7 million. It had been a risky venture and they may have doubled their money but the opportunity cost was great. Their 2003 accounts show a sales turnover of £425 million, and a profit before interest and tax of £5.7 million, including the Cape exceptional, so

Gyllenhammar's corporate spending spree was hardly generating large profits. Montpellier's auditors, Price Waterhouse, had resigned, as had the Company Secretary, which may suggest that all was not well. By 2004 Cedric Scroggs, Paul Sellars and Peter Gyllenhammar had resigned from the Montpellier Group Board, although Gyllenhammar's investment funds retained a 33% shareholding. The company continues to exist as Renew Holdings PLC, a successful AIM 100 company. The management of Cape were not sorry to see Montpellier go as it was clear they had no intention of staying the course.

At the end of the previous chapter, and as of the end of November 2002, Cape had no Chairman; Messrs. Sellars, first, and then Gyllenhammar having resigned. It fell to Martin May as a hired in turnaround specialist and the then non-executive directors to safeguard shareholder's investment. Initially there was no-one to step up to the Chairman role and it was left to the two remaining non-executive directors to act as Joint-Chairmen. One was John Pool who went back to the Charter days. Appointed in 1997, and a Chartered Secretary, he had spent his career working for Anglo and Charter, latterly as Managing Director of the newly acquired Esab operation in Singapore. It was his experience in Singapore that was considered of particular value to Cape at the time, but his background may also have been of some help during the South African litigation. It could not be said he was an experienced non-executive Director, but he became a loyal anchor man during a period when corporate and legal responsibilities will have weighed heavily on him. The other Non-Executive Director and Joint Chairman was Sean O'Connor. Appointed in 1996, he was a Rutland appointee having headed a Rutland business named Trillium Venture Developments. He had become Non-Executive Chairman of Stoves Group PLC and held a variety of non-executive positions. The fact that they were Joint-Chairman suggests there was reluctance on their part, and it was clearly an interim arrangement. To be a director of Cape at this time, certainly chairman, was not easy. Tough decisions on IDC issues were unlikely to enhance an incumbent's reputation, and there had been a perceived underlying risk of threatened personal liability.

This was all taking place against the background of the demise of Cape's old sparring partner, Turner & Newall. T&N, with its potential liabilities believed to have been adequately covered, was now in the hands of Federal-Mogul. Despite the *Times*[1] commenting that the extent of T&N's ring fence 'is about double the worst case prognosis for the Company', it was proving inadequate and, as we learnt in Chapter 7 Federal-Mogul filed for Chapter 11 bankruptcy in 2001. Whilst it was the extent of claims in the USA that were T&N's undoing, these background events will not have been lost on shareholders and the Directors of Cape during this period.

For Martin May the demands on him, in his capacity of Group Managing Director, were such that he needed to reduce his commitments elsewhere. The 2002 Annual Report refers to him operating on a part time basis for Cape. He appeared to have legacy commitments providing consultancy services, as a turnaround specialist, to other companies, including Connolly, Gresham Consulting and McNicholas. He had played an active role in the Society of Turnaround Professionals, and in 2004 was recognised with the 'Practitioner of the Year' award. He now had less time to give the Society at a time when it was beginning to prosper. It became the Institute for Turnaround in 2007. By 2003 he had taken on the role of Chairman of Cape from John Pool and Sean O'Connor, the latter retiring.

The only positive to be drawn from the 2002 accounts was a release of a significant element of the provision covering the previous South Africa settlement. The business otherwise still remained in the hands of Cape's bankers. The Head Office of the parent company, which had been at Cape Calsil's Uxbridge base and then Cape House, Watford, was now moved to the Head Office of the Industrial Services business at Wakefield.

Industrial Services (CIS)

Fortunately for Cape PLC, Cape Industrial Services (CIS) was continuing to perform, throwing in a consistent profit and cashflow. It was however not an easy time. The oil price did not pick up quickly from its lows in the late '90's, given 9/11 and then the Iraq war. Coupling this with a mini recession in the UK and Europe in 2001, utilities maintenance expenditure was cut back. More particularly, and given Cape's problems, capital expenditure in CIS was reduced and was below the level of depreciation. The business had substantial stocks of scaffolding and the write-off assumptions were always visited by Head Office Accountants, searching for means of enhancing profit. During this period, the amortisation rate for steel scaffolding tube and galvanized fittings was extended again to the benefit of the P&L account. In 2002 sales turnover dropped from £218 million to £189 million and operating profit from £10.8 million to £9.8 million. Whilst maybe commendable in the circumstances, this was hardly going to set the City alight in the context of a flotation, which for IDC reasons was looking highly improbable.

Employees were largely kept in the dark as to the South African litigation and the company's deteriorating financial situation, although they were aware cash and capex were tight. They would read more about it in the newspapers. This probably helped to maintain morale and it was only when clients raised questions, that subsidiary Directors were briefed such that they could deal with their concerns. In the UK there was some comprehension of Cape's situation, almost empathy, as quite a few of its major clients were also facing asbestos related claims – the shipyards, power plant operators and contractors such as Babcock Power.

In the context of the large contracts being secured overseas, clients were nervous, and further presentations had to be made to major clients such as Chiyoda Corporation and JGC in Japan. To most employees the record of Cape in the South African mines was a shock, and had a significant impact on their perception of the Company's role in the unleashing of asbestos related industrial disease. As commented earlier, the full evidence was rather submerged beneath the dominating arguments pertaining to jurisdiction and legal aid. Very few employees now had working experience of the days of asbestos, and there was no longer any great propinquity with the issue amongst employees, or so much defensiveness in the face of attack.

UK

The UK operation got off to an uneasy start in 2001 having to stomach some bad debts because of the liquidation of Enron UK. By 2003 activity was picking up underpinned by offshore work on the Golden Eye project for Shell at St. Fergus, BP's Clair Drilling Rig and its Schiehallion FPSO. The latter demonstrated the range of services now provided in the UK, the work including logistics management, insulation, scaffolding, specialist coatings, fire protection and industrial cleaning. However, the overall business seemed to have lost momentum - the distractions of the previous three years and lack of capital investment were beginning to take their toll. Management was now stretched. The CIS Finance Director, Mike Reynolds, had stepped in to assume the Group Finance Director role, then combining it with the Company Secretary position, thereby leaving a gap at the workface.

New project construction in the UK onshore Oil, Petrochemical and Power Plant sector was levelling off, the emphasis now being more on upgrading and maintenance. Cape's diverse offering and high standards brought considerable success as the decade progressed. Many of the old ICI assets in the Teesside Region had been taken over in 2005 by Huntsman and Cape secured a five-year term maintenance embracing access scaffolding, insulation, painting, cleaning and grounds maintenance throughout their plants. By 2006 Saudi Basic Industries (SABIC) had taken over the plant, and in the process became one of Cape's major international clients. At BNFL Sellafield a five year total access contract covering scaffolding, powered and rope access was secured. It had three year terms on five of British Energy's nine nuclear power plants. Contracts were becoming larger and a ten year multi-disciplinary maintenance contract for Scottish Power on Cockenzie and Longannet power stations was provisionally valued at £78 million. Workload visibility was rising annually and now at each year end some 70-80% of the next year's budgeted turnover could be in hand.

Europe

The residual activities in Mainland Europe centred on the Cleton Insulation business. This had always been a relatively low margin business and for some time Cape had been endeavouring to take it forward on the wider disciplinary basis that had proved so successful in the UK. Clients were moving in the same direction, albeit not as rapidly in the UK, as single discipline processes were deeply entrenched.

In Holland and Germany insulation had always been of a high technical standard and trades such as scaffolding and painting tended to be considered of a lower tier than thermal insulation. There was reluctance on Cleton's part to diversify beyond insulation. Scaffolding tended to be tackled differently in Holland, and as explained earlier, Cape UK's scaffold equipment was not transferable. The market was still characterised by some deeply entrenched practices. Into the nineties, for example, the expenditure of 'black money', albeit modest - was an accepted charge against the P&L account under the company's external Dutch audit. Cape had grown tired of a management and culture resistant to change, and whilst the business was not a loss-maker its profit contribution had always been modest. Sales of £30 million were barely yielding a 2-3% return and it had always been difficult to secure invoicing and cash terms similar to the UK. The decision was made to put it up for sale.

The major scaffolding company in the Netherlands at that time – SGB, a subsidiary of Harsco of the USA – was looking to add to its skills in the same way as Cape, and soon took an interest in Cleton's insulation capability. SGB or 'Scaffolding Great Britain' dated back to 1919 when it was founded on the back of the development of the universal coupler, enabling two steel scaffold tubes to be secured together at a right angle. The sale of Cleton proved to be a difficult one – for the proud management to be absorbed by a scaffolding company did not rest well. The Works Council were opposed, and some resistance was stoked up amongst clients. For Cleton though, which had only just embarked on an investment in scaffolding, it meant that it would have a joint capability that would satisfy the demands of its largest clients. At the Europort Pernis Refinery where Cleton was the incumbent insulation contractor and SGB the scaffolding contractor, Shell supported the combination. A sale was finally concluded in 2006. An immediate cash consideration of £5.4 million was followed by property sales of £2.9 million. There was a small surplus on the sale against carrying value. Cape retained any liabilities for asbestos related industrial disease, but this had always been adequately covered by insurance. Harsco/SGB struggled with integration and in the North and Germany lost much of the business in the North to a company managed by the former Managing Director of Cleton.

International

This was a period when the International business powered ahead on all fronts. In the Gulf, Cape was now the clear market leader in UAE, Qatar, Oman, Saudi Arabia and Bahrain (R B Hilton). Although National Oil Companies were shedding some of their historic links with the multinationals, they inherited and adopted the best international standards and practice. Cape was able to offer a multi-discipline platform of services and enter into term maintenance contracts with most of the leading oil, gas and petrochemical companies. Its Third Country National (TCN) workforce welcomed the opportunity of learning different skills and, relative to the UK where demarcation still existed, were now not only more versatile but also more productive. By now Cape Abu Dhabi was an accredited training centre for the UK's NVQ system of competency assessment, the first to be established overseas and served the other units in the Gulf. Whilst UK Expatriates held senior positions, middle management positions were increasingly filled from a largely Indian or local pool.

By this time the Gulf States were looking to reduce dependence on foreign companies and personnel. A growing number of educated young Nationals were in need of career opportunities. We saw how in Oman Cape was obliged to employ and train Omanis; there was a similar movement in Saudi where to get work visas, a quota of Saudi Nationals had to be employed. Cape welcomed this in that it had the training skills and personnel able to meet these demands. However, it was not easy – Nationals were not used to manual work or to the working hours involved, and employment tended to be confined to drivers and those involved in government affairs. Similarly, 'Anti-Fronting' Laws were being adopted which sought to encourage the genuine equity and management participation of Nationals. This represented a threat to the arrangements Cape had in paying a majority partner a fee, in lieu of participation in the risk of profit and loss and funding. Implementation of the law was slow and it did mean the renegotiation and restructuring of some of the entities, including some local risk participation, most of the companies remaining in place today. Cape had set up a holding company in Bahrain for its minority shareholdings – Cape East EC. This was considered a local Gulf Cooperation Council company and in at least one country - Saudi Arabia – it was possible for this to be the local shareholder giving Cape (trading as R B Hilton Saudi Arabia Ltd) in effect 100% ownership.

The company's domination of the LNG sector continued. Cape secured the insulation and scaffolding contract on the Damietta Export LNG terminal being constructed in Egypt from Engineer MW Kellogg, forming a joint venture with local contractor, Orascom. A second LNG train was built at Oman LNG and work secured on the Rasgas LNG expansion in Qatar.

Given that Cape's sources of labour in the Gulf were largely from the Indian subcontinent, it had set up a company in India for recruitment and operational purposes and completed work on the Daheej LNG import terminal. In the Far East the primary source of labour was the Philippines. The oil refineries on which Cape had depended on maintenance work in the Philippines were beginning to lose their competitiveness and Cape had focused its efforts on the training and provision of labour for both on and offshore work, again to British and International standards. This soon enabled it to acquire offshore maintenance work on Shell's Malampaya platform, the Bayu Undan field off Timor/Northwest Australia for Conoco, and scaffolding for the Inco Goro Nickel-Cobalt development in New Caledonia. It also enabled Cape's UK Offshore business to offer a worldwide servicing capability. This extended to the provision of Filipino planning, safety and IT blue collar staff. Cape was now completing the Bintulu LNG project in Malaysia, employing over one thousand scaffolders.

In 1999, through its Aberdeen connections, Cape had the opportunity to tender for offshore maintenance services on the BP installations in the Caspian Sea at Baku, Azerbaijan. Azerbaijan had been a pioneer in the development of the oil industry, but was now being opened up after a period of inactivity under Soviet control. The contract was won, and a business set up. This involved training Azeri Nationals and establishing a presence under an Iranian Manager who had worked with Cape in pre-revolution days. At the same time British Gas were participating in the development of the gas fields at Karachaganak in Kazakhstan. Cape won the contract for insulation work and subsequently scaffolding. Initially access to the site for personnel was overland via Moscow. A local workforce had to be trained, supplemented by Azeri workers; productivity being a particular problem. Cape remained on project completion, carrying out maintenance. Cape's experience in Azerbaijan and Kazakhstan gave Regional Director Guy Rackham the confidence to pursue further work in the Eastern bloc culminating in prequalifying for the Sakhalin II LNG project. This was located on Sakhalin Island off the far eastern coast of Russia and involved Shell as a participant. Again, Cape was dealing with Japanese Main Contractors, including its old friend Chiyoda Corporation. Winning the project against Japanese competitors, the work involved insulation to a new specification and the provision of common user scaffolding. Having hired Russian speakers in

Azerbaijan and Kazakhstan there were personnel available to head a taskforce set up for the project which presented major logistical challenges. Particular precautions had to be taken to counter the effect of low temperatures - the embrittlement of scaffold fittings and curing of the resins involved in cladding pipe and vessel surfaces. A Russian workforce was recruited and trained, supplemented by UK supervision and Azeri and Filipino administrators. This project had a high-risk profile, and it was a measure of the Board's and Cape's bankers' confidence in its execution capabilities that it provided the necessary on demand bank guarantees covering performance and downpayments. Political issues delayed construction, but eventually the contract was completed profitably in 2009, the value exceeding US$110 million.

The International business still retained a small UK head office which also carried out work on an opportunistic basis, in Malta, Spain, Trinidad for Trinidad LNG and Argentina. Twenty years after its first Queens Award Cape International won its second Queen's Award for Export/Enterprise in 2008.

Tackling the UK Industrial Disease Legacy

Cape continued to be a target for media attention and TV documentaries. In August 2004, ITV broadcast 'Real Life: You will Know Them by Their Trail of Death,' in which Pauline Bonney and Joan Baird followed 'the toxic trail left by the deadly mineral from the workplaces and homes in Great Britain to its origins in South Africa.' On BBC2 in November Julie Burchill highlighted the fate of her father and a generation of men who died from mesothelioma[2]. There was a difference this time, as against the earlier documentaries in the eighties and nineties, Cape Directors and senior staff were now circulated with video copies, and encouraged to see the record for themselves. Martin May, having dealt with the South African Settlement, was more than aware that there remained an elephant in the room which could also be an existential threat – UK industrial disease compensation (IDC). His focus on this suggests that he was looking beyond the 'turnaround' and to a longer term future with Cape. The South African outcome had drawn attention to the desirability of setting up a fund rather than the closed settlement that transpired for Cape's plaintiffs, as in the case of the T&N UK Asbestos Trust arising out of the demise of T&N. This could also have the effect of de-risking Cape when it came to bank finance.

The net UK IDC charge against the P&L account had amounted to £4.4 million in 2000, then £3.7 million, £2.4 million, £3.8 million and in 2004 £3.7 million. Whilst not increasing substantially, the peak of claims, given the latency effect, was believed still to come. In 2004 May announced that Cape was looking at various funding options to introduce 'proposals for the long-term financing of a significant element of the Group's asbestos related claims in the UK'. This was against a backcloth of rapid progress towards the reduction in debt demanded by its bankers. Against the target reduction to a figure of £13 million (illustrated on Page 168) 2004 Group debt reduced to £2.4 million. With earnings per share standing at 10.7p, those shareholders who had picked up the Rutland and Montpellier holdings were showing a return in excess of 100% in a matter of year, so this was potentially the time to tap them for additional funding. The purpose of the additional funding was to enable a scheme to be set up under which the cost of future UK asbestos industrial disease claims could be met[3]. Thereby the ongoing business could develop freely without the constant burden of satisfying claims for compensation. To do this it was necessary to quantify the potential future liabilities. This was no easy task as the boundaries for claim were constantly changing as individual cases tested the courts. One that caught public attention was the claim brought by the widow of Arthur Fairchild and others against more than one employer in 2002, seeking compensation for mesothelioma, where more than one employer may have been responsible and where the period of critical exposure was unknown[4]. This was of particular interest to insurers and the initial decision meant the claimant could only secure full compensation by proving causation from a single employer - the action of the insurers being described by the TUC as 'chicanery'. After further cases and appeals it was finally held that all the relevant employers were jointly and severally liable for the claim and confirmed in the Compensation Act of 2006.

Cape looked to the independent actuaries Tillinghast to come up with an assessment of its likely liabilities for asbestos related claims in the UK. By now there were established precedents for the calculation of compensation due to each category of claimant, ranging from the most life threatening (mesothelioma) through lung cancer, asbestosis to pleural plaque. (A House of Lords decision in 2007, upholding an Appeal, subsequently precluded pleural plaque as a qualifying condition)[5]. The analysis included the shipyard claims, amounting to £10.7 million, where Cape had agreed in 2003 to meet an element of the claims received by participating shipyards. In relation to some of the acquired companies such as Darchem Contracting, the company had recourse to the vendors in which case such claimants were excluded. A particularly difficult area was assessing insurance recoveries where the record of cover was not sufficiently known or the exclusion clauses had not been legally scrutinised. A portion of the claims would relate to the period prior to the need for compulsory employers' liability insurance (1972). Many policies after 1984 excluded asbestos claims and some precluded claims beyond the period of cover. To understand fully the insurance picture was going to take time.

Tillinghast concluded that claims would continue for 46 years, and peak between the years 2025 and 2030. Their best estimate of the aggregate projected discounted value, net of insurance recoveries, of all the Group's unpaid UK asbestos related claims was £81 million, the highest estimate being £160 million and the lowest £49.5 million. Based on these figures Cape proposed to its shareholders that it set up a fund amounting to £40 million, the amount of which would be reviewed every three years, with an obligation on Cape to top up any projected shortfall, subject to a cap of 70% of its consolidated adjusted operational cashflow. The figure of £40 million was acknowledged to cover potentially only twelve years of Tillinghast's estimate and to have been calculated substantially on the basis of affordability.

In June 2005 Cape proceeded with a placing of twenty-nine million ordinary shares at a price of 110p to raise £32 million. Of this amount, £7 million was required to meet the cost of the placing (£1.5 million) and the setting up of the fund (£5.5 million). £3 million would go towards working capital leaving £22 million for the fund. The fund would then draw on £15 million of bank facilities and £3 million from the proceeds of property sales. The offer document acknowledged that it might not be possible to set up the fund, in which event the proceeds would be added to working and investment capital, and ongoing claims met out of profits. The programme for providing details of the Scheme arrangements, creditors meetings and court approvals, was set as commencing in October of the same year.

To the shareholders it offered the opportunity to de-risk their holding and the prospect of dividends in the future. They were somewhat taken aback by the

£5.5 million cost of setting up the scheme but this reflected its administrative complexity. They were also surprised to see in the placing document that Martin May had forty-one current directorships or partnerships outside the Group listed, reflecting activity in his turnaround business.

Over 50% of the shares were owned by just six fund managers, the largest being M&G at 15% and Schroder at 10%, both of whom for the purposes of the placing were defined as related parties. Given that the proposal did not offer a total ring-fenced solution to the asbestos disease problem in the UK, it is surprising that the placement was so readily taken up, but Martin May had shareholder's confidence, perceived as bringing the company back from the brink. Shareholders had limited time to analyse the proposal but liked the concept and the money came in.

The Scheme

Funding proved to be the easy bit and by the promised date of October 2005 Cape and its advisers were nowhere near ready with the Scheme of Arrangement. In the same month Paul Ainley, the Managing Director of CIS had a serious accident and was to be absent from work for the coming months. Mike Reynolds, the Finance Director of both CIS and Cape PLC had to perform the role of Acting Managing Director, supported by longstanding and experienced CIS Director, Julian Gammage. Management resources at Board level were seriously stretched which all contributed to the delay. In addition several points of issue were raised relating to some of the provisions of the proposed Scheme; it was soon realised that, given its complexity, the timetable for implementation had to be extended. Furthermore in November it was admitted Tillinghast's review at the time of the share placing had not 'taken full account of all the claims that may be made against the Companies included in the Scheme.' The review now looked to liability ranging from £70 million to £240 million, the mid point (best estimate) now being £119 million, a substantial variance relative to the amount declared at the time of the share placing (£81 million).

The mechanics involved identifying and listing all the Cape companies and factories having a potential liability, and over what period. In total these numbered nearly one hundred and had involved frequent name changes and reorganisations, some of which probably represented attempts to distance the subsidiary from exposure to claims. It was possible to reduce the number by consolidating subsidiaries into 25 Scheme Companies. Their history, activities, latest accounts, locations and relevant insurance cover were outlined in the proposal circular, the document running to 233 pages[6]. Their employees and/or potential claimants were defined as Scheme Creditors. Apart from shareholder's and lenders approval it was required that the implementation on the part of each Scheme Company was sanctioned by the High Court.

The £40 million was to be provided to the Scheme fund as a loan from Cape PLC repayable when and if the scheme terminated in accordance with its terms (i.e., in effect when all claims were satisfied). It was to be administered by a company set up for the purpose – Cape Claims Services Ltd (CCS) – a subsidiary of Cape and the funds ring fenced in this entity. There would be two independent Scheme Directors – the first to be appointed being Lord Desai. There were to be special voting shares in CCS (Scheme Shares) held by an independent third party (initially Law Debenture Trust Corporation) to ensure that the interests of the Scheme Creditors were protected.

Advertisements were placed in the national press inviting potential claimants ('Scheme Creditors') to come forward and vote for the Scheme. They were invited to secure a voting form and enter details as to their employment. Since inaction would not prejudice an individual's right to submit a claim, and the form required information which may not have been at hand, there was in fact a limited response. Current employees were pressed however to complete the forms and vote in favour of the Scheme, with some encouraged to attend the court hearing. In this respect, therefore, it was staged, but without it the Scheme would not have gone ahead. There had been a lot of pressure on those concerned to complete the process in view of the associated banking arrangements.

By June 2006 the individual company schemes had been sanctioned by the Court in Chancery, and implementation commenced. It was not necessary to go back to shareholders as authority had been given at the time of the share placing. The appointment of Lord Meghnad Desai, who had a distinguished academic and public service career, as Chairman was widely welcomed. He has since served the Scheme loyally over the years, remaining in post today (2022). For claimants the setting up of the Scheme had a particularly beneficial aspect. In the knowledge that there was an available fund and one that specified a range of compensation for each category of disease, the Cape Head Office team set up to deal with the claims had clear guidelines, and this enabled them to settle claims quickly without administrative delay or seeking to find legal loopholes. The attitude within the company towards claims changed, from being defensive and often confrontational to one which acknowledged a right to compensation, and, in consequence, a certain sense of pride crept in amongst staff. The one difficulty was in verifying a claimant's employment record with the company. Many claimants had worked for more than one company, so arrangements were made with other corporate/trust sources of compensation, where they existed. Cape had spent a number of years assembling in a discreet archive all its employment and insurance records, but these were not always comprehensive. One effect of setting up the scheme was that, in the knowledge of the existence of the fund, claimants might falsely claim they had worked for Cape rather than another company from whom no compensation could be readily obtained. There were also claims involving products that did not contain asbestos that also required defending.

Had, at the time of the capital raising, shareholders seen the new Tillinghast figures and detail of the Scheme outlined in the Scheme Creditors Proposal dated March 2006, more questions would probably have been asked. It had been stage managed to give the impression that it went further than it did in embracing the IDC liability. Even if so, the outcome still represented a major step forward and the means was justified. The reality was that it was just the first bite.

Growth

For Martin May it was one mission accomplished, and on to the next stage of development, but pressed by shareholders, there needed first to be corporate reinforcements. At this time, as a turnaround specialist he could have moved on, on the basis of 'job done.' However, he was clearly attracted to the operational side of Cape, and, partly by necessity because of Paul Ainley's absence, he dropped down to the position of Chief Executive. This meant a new Chairman and Non–Executive Directors. To attract strong candidates was not easy. Cape had acquired some notoriety over the litigation and would continue to be identified with industrial disease. Elsewhere, in Europe, Directors of asbestos companies were being called to account (the last Managing Director of Cape's old company - Capamiento - in Italy had been prosecuted as we saw in the previous chapter). Whilst there was no serious danger of a new appointee to Cape's board having to assume such a risk, the reputation of the industry did make candidates wary.

In 2004, David McManus had joined the Board. David was an oil industry man having worked for ARCO before it was taken over by BG Group in 2001. At BG he was on the Group Executive, a Vice President and Managing Director of BP Advance, a head office role. He then left BG and was in November 2004 appointed a Non-Executive Director of Cape. In January 2005 he was appointed to a position with a relatively young oil & gas company, Texas-based Pioneer Natural Resources, as Vice President of International Operations. Pioneer was an exploration company with assets mainly in the North American continent but had some interests in Africa, and he was tasked with developing these from a new London office. The idea was presumably to have a non-executive Director on Cape's Board who could guide and assist the company in its dealings in the oil and gas sector. His role at Pioneer was a demanding one and was somewhat removed both operationally and geographically from Cape's activities. Despite this full-time commitment to Pioneer, McManus became a valuable member of Cape's Board, and when Martin May stepped down to the position of Chief Executive in 2006, he became Chairman.

It was time for the ever-faithful John Pool to retire and the Board appointed David Robins as a Director. A Solicitor, David was a member of the newly formed Brewin Leighton Paisner LLP practice. The practice had particular engagement with insurance companies which would have been useful. The Board also welcomed back Sean O'Connor to the Board. Paul Ainley, the Managing Director of Cape Industrial Services, resigned having reached retiring age leaving Martin May in effect to assume his role.

A first step in Martin May's direction of the operating business was to acquire the business and assets of the DBI Group in 2006. Established in 1988, this was an industrial cleaning company having onshore and offshore based activities directed from its Paisley head office in Scotland. Whereas Cape's then activities in industrial cleaning were confined to simple site cleaning activities, DBI was into some serious industrial cleaning applications – high pressure water jetting, process pipe descaling, tank/reactor vessel cleaning, catalyst handling and chemical cleaning. It extended Cape's offering to many of its existing clients as well as some new clients in the pharmaceutical and process industries. It tended to be more capital intensive and required particular technical expertise. The initial consideration for the acquisition was £11 million with a two year earn out of £7.5 million. It made an immediate contribution to Group profit but did need both capital investment and some strengthening of the management.

At the same time Martin May introduced a new house style for Cape with blue displacing the old bright red as the colour motif, and a simple lower-case rendering of the name as a logo. It was more in keeping with the times. In 2006 he spelt out an acquisition strategy defining the circumstances where the Group would make acquisitions. Firstly, where it could establish another discipline which could not readily be created through organic growth. And secondly, to add businesses which could be 'bolted on' to existing operations, or consolidate an existing market, or extend the company's footprint in an existing market. In the 2007 he further sought to define potential acquisitions – 'a mechanical and electrical business which would increase bundling capacity, a business with existing contracts in nuclear de-commissioning and a high-end business in industrial cleaning'. Much discussion took place as to potential activities of 'bolt on' acquisitions and for many years a view had been expressed that an obvious bolt on activity was mechanical and electrical services. Historically Cape would have frequently been contracted to a Mechanical and Electrical (M&E) contractor, but once it developed its multi discipline capability its clients began to rank Cape alongside their M&E contractor, and contract with Cape separately. To acquire an M&E contractor would enable Cape to offer an even wider platform of services. One of Cape's leading competitors – Hertel – opted to do so, but was struggling to integrate it with its existing activities. Such a move would represent a major step and the arguments against included the possibility of losing work (as a competitor) where the company was still obliged to work for an M&E contractor, and the question of whether the technology and work practices represented a step too far for Cape's management. The DBI business however seemed to meet the acquisition criteria and looked a good starter for one, thus the intention of adding to it.

But first Cape needed the wherewithal to afford an acquisition strategy. 2006 marked the third consecutive year that Cape recorded an increase in sales and underlying profitability. Earnings per share was approaching 15p and the share price topping £2. Cleton had been sold and the Scheme of Arrangement was in place. The institutional shareholders were impressed with the way Martin May had turned the business round, and were prepared to participate in a further placement of shares. The stock market was approaching a peak and the timing. ideal. In April 2007 a total 26.9 million shares were placed at £2.60 per share raising £70 million. At the end of the year Barclays too had joined the cause, providing a new five-year banking facility amounting to a massive £220 million. Investors would have seen the 2007 projections for the business, which were for substantial growth in all areas. They were not disappointed. In the UK Sales forged ahead totalling £270 million and more significantly margins, making for an operating profit of £21 million. The Middle East sales topped £66 million with an exceptional 18% margin. In the CIS/Caspian region Sakhalin LNG tipped in US$6 million operating profit while the Far East, whilst profitable, was yet to deliver. Notably, work overseas was becoming more highly valued as TCN skills improved and wages rose. Given Cape's strong market position and offering, it was able to raise margins. Earnings per share would end up at 25p and the share price rose above the placement price.

Martin May stated in the 2006 annual report dated 22 May 2007 that there were 'no current negotiations in respect of any of the alternative acquisition opportunities'. It was a surprise to shareholders that within a matter of months the following acquisitions were made, for a total consideration of £194 million and cash outflow of £183 Million.(December 31st 2007 exchange rates)

21 June	Total Rope Access Intnl. Ltd. UK	£0.9 Million
21 June	Endecon Ltd, UK	£3.3 Million
31 August	TCC Group, Australia	£34.9 Million
16 October	Concept Hire, Australia	£46.2 Million
26 November	PCH Group Ltd, Australia	£108.5 Million

If in May there were 'no current negotiations,' the speed at which this took place raises the question as to whether there was sufficient time for detailed due diligence. The reality was that negotiations were well in hand in the case of PCH

Group, as Cape was confirming publicly in Australia that discussions were taking place with a view to acquiring the business as early as February 2007.

Given this M&A activity it was thought appropriate to bring on board a Chief Financial Officer (CFO) with City experience, Mike Reynolds, the Finance Director, reverting to his Industrial Services role. Martin May knew Richard Bingham as a fellow interim and turnaround specialist and took him on initially to deal with the acquisition programme. A chartered accountant, Bingham had worked for PWC and Deloittes and was appointed CFO in June.

The first two acquisitions, although small, met the criteria that had been articulated well. Total Rope Access, a small but skilled team, added to Cape's abseiling capability, enabling it to enhance its offering in access solutions. Endecon, having expertise in decontamination processes in oil refineries and petrochemical plants, was a perfect fit with DBI and again satisfied the target company criteria as a high-end cleaning business; the two operations were merged as DBI-Endecon. The extent to which the three acquisitions in Australia however met the acquisition criteria was not so clear. They were certainly large in the context of the overall business and overnight changed its geographical balance. They came as both a surprise and as something of a shock to operating management. Having spent the proceeds of the capital raising, there was no capacity left to deal with the two other areas listed by Martin May for acquisition – mechanical and electrical services and nuclear decommissioning.

This step change in the size of Cape coincided with the retirement of several executives (described by a colleague as 'the big beasts') who had grown up with the development of the industrial services business. Martin May recognised this and in 2007 with outside help made a detailed assessment of current managerial competence. The business was organised into four regions – UK, Gulf/Middle East, CIS/Caspian and Pacific/ Far East. Recruitment was necessary as there were no obvious candidates to run each of the four regions. It was not the best of times, given the acquisitions, to 'bed' in new candidates. Furthermore, the businesses were now large and the hands-on style of management that had characterised the business in the past was no longer practical. As a result, Martin May was heavily involved in day-to-day management of the businesses at a time when the acquisitions needed integrating. To cap it all, Chairman David

McManus notified the Board that he would be resigning – with the admission that the demands of an operational role at Pioneer Resources whilst dealing with developments at Cape was proving too much. Sean O'Connor stepped up to fill the gap. What was clear by reference to the geographical spread of assets in 2008 was that the Far East was to be the focus for the future.

LNG and Australia

The worldwide expansion of the LNG market was gathering pace with Japan, South Korea and China now looking to tie up more long term supply contracts. In Europe needs were increasingly being met by Russian and East European pipelines. The obvious sources of LNG supply were in South East Asia and Australia with the potential for significant investments in additional export capacity in Indonesia, later in Papua New Guinea but mainly in Australia. Given Cape's track record it was logical that Martin May and Cape should look to these markets for the next phase of growth. Japanese competitors had always had a strong presence in Indonesia at the Bontang and Arun terminals, but in Australia the Japanese contractors fought shy of labour relation issues and tended to leave the market alone. There was the prospect of substantial investment in export LNG facilities – an expansion at Karratha, Gorgon and Wheatstone LNG in WA, Ichthys at Darwin, Curtis and APLNG in Queensland and Prelude Floating LNG offshore. These were at an early stage and whilst it made sense to get in early, there was over-optimism in the company's market projections.

As outlined in previous chapters, for Cape an attraction of the Australian market was the value added given the high labour costs and the contract methodology in the LNG sector (normally cost reimbursable). The combination of this feature and an outlook of rapid LNG expansion suggested that the acquisition of a substantial presence would be a smart move. However, closer analysis of the market would have revealed a move away from in-country construction. When major client Woodside Energy commenced the Pluto LNG expansion at Karratha WA in 2007, the design of the plant involved as much offshore modular construction as possible. This represented an opportunity for Cape in S E Asia yards where the modules were built. Cape East Thailand and Cape East Philippines were already active in the local module yards, later followed by a presence in South Korea. But in Australia it reduced the onshore workload to hook up work; although given the high incidence of damage there was rectification work on site, involving paint touch-up and re-insulation.

Cape no longer had an onshore presence in Australia despite having been involved in each of the N.W. Shelf LNG terminal expansions at Karratha. It could have opted for re-mobilising and seeking organic growth, but given the prospects the case for acquisition was strong, though not without its risks. Cape had learnt that it was a regional market and that beyond the major projects both competitive and logistically challenging. Businesses tended to be family owned and, where they had expanded beyond their home state, had been failures – examples being Bestobell Australia and Bains Harding Industries. The industry was a close knit community and there had been instances of intimidation and corruption. It was into this market scenario that Cape was to make a bold and controversial entrance.

The Australian Acquisitions

The first acquisition was Western Australian based company Total Corrosion Control Group Pty. (TCC). This was a successful blasting and painting company built up by the Iannello brothers. The consideration comprised £25 million in cash and £8 million in Cape shares. A further £5.1 million would arise on TCC achieving its budget in the current year. Prior year sales of £46 million and profit before interest and tax of £5.6 million suggested a fair price which was considered earnings enhancing. The main asset of the business was its blasting and painting workshop in Kwinana which was claimed to be 'the largest in the Southern hemisphere.' The workshop had been set up originally to service the N.W. Shelf LNG development in 1988, fabricated steel imported through Freemantle being blasted and painted prior to onward shipment to the Karratha job site. With the onset of modularisation and the location of the other LNG projects outside WA there had to be doubt as to whether utilisation of the asset could be sustained. But in the short term there were opportunities in the mining industry and the acquisition proceeded smoothly.

The second acquisition was Concept Hire. This took place before the PCH acquisition, but discussions had been taking place with PCH since the beginning of the year and before the Concept Hire acquisition was being considered (see below). Press speculation suggested the approach to and acquisition of Concept Hire, being a competitor to PCH, was designed to bring pressure on PCH. The business was based in Melbourne although it had just acquired a Perth based scaffolding business - Blackadder - on PCH's doorstep in Perth (later closed down by Cape). Concept was listed on the Australian Securities Exchange and Cape's all share offer came in at £52 million including debt. Profit before tax and interest of £3.6 million on sales of £31 million suggested a full price. The business had been founded in 1985 and a minority shareholder – the Adshead family had competing interests in scaffolding. Whether this acquisition met Martin May's criteria was doubtful. Firstly, it's main activity was in the commercial sector. Throughout the evolution of Cape's scaffolding business, it had kept well away from what was called 'town work.' This was an activity best undertaken by small local often family companies. It did not involve added value design, and safety standards tended to be different from those prevailing in the industrial sector. Control of assets could be problematic. Secondly the business was based in Melbourne, Victoria – a State in which Cape had no knowledge and a considerable distance away from its new Regional Head Office in Perth.

As noted above, the approach to the PCH Group, also quoted on the Australian Securities Exchange, had been made back in February 2007. Founded in 1985, it had come to Cape's attention as it had rather enterprisingly secured work on Cape's doorstep in the lower Gulf, in Azerbaijan and in Thailand. Given the peaks and troughs of activity in Western Australia (WA) it was a means of deploying surplus equipment. It was the clear market leader in WA and had a strong presence on the N.W. Shelf LNG site at Karratha. Under Managing Director Jamie Cullen it had acquired activities alongside scaffolding, in painting and blasting, and mine maintenance. Cullen was a chartered accountant and had built up a good track record. Chairman Bill Ryan had warned of a weak first half in 2007 which Martin May sought to take advantage of in making an approach, and in February 2007 PCH confirmed that it had received an indicative offer from an unconfirmed source at Aus$90 cents per share (a 32% premium). Cape hurriedly had to reveal its identity and seemed to recoil from the description of its approach as an offer. This must have been a source of embarrassment to the Cape Board as this was before the capital raising was finalised. The PCH Board could not take it as a serious offer, Cape not having, at that time, the wherewithal to go through with the proposed acquisition. By April the two parties were at loggerheads. PCH claimed it had provided Cape with tier one due diligence but was not prepared to provide tier two due diligence unless Cape confirmed an offer. Cape were looking for a recommended offer by the PCH Board and complained that PCH were not prepared to 'engage in meaningful discussion;' talks were called off. In May PCH announced small scaffolding acquisitions outside WA and forecast an improving profit outlook for the year. In June the two were talking again and in August Cape tabled a revised offer of Aus$1.30 per share which was rejected by the PCH Board. Cape, despite a standstill agreement, turned hostile seeking to appeal to shareholders. Having by then acquired TCC and Concept Hire, Cape sought to give the impression that this move represented a threat to PCH's competitiveness. This did not go down well - Cape failed to recognise that in the Perth 'village' the leaders of these, albeit competing, companies tended to have more loyalty to each other than to an outsider like Cape. Cape raised its offer to Aus$1.40 per share valuing the business at Aus$247 million (£110 million) and the PCH Board caved in, but its members promptly resigned.

Whilst there was a small element of deferred consideration in the case of Total Rope Access, Endecon and TCC, the two larger acquisitions were share offers and there was little incentive left for incumbent management. But Martin May believed a new management team was required to lead the process of integrating the Australian acquisitions. There were no immediate candidates for the lead roles and the team put in place comprised local Perth-based Consultant Peter Harley as Non-Executive Chairman and non-executive senior Cape secondees, executive appointments being limited to finance and human resources.

Chapter 10

The Move East

Corporate

In December 2008 Cape announced that it had received 'expressions of interest in the Company from a number of Private Equity houses.' It is likely that the Board solicited this interest as there would be attractions, not the least of which would be Cape's legacy issues being less subject to public scrutiny. Potential investors balked at the likely buyout price and uncertainty over the limits of protection against industrial disease liabilities afforded by the Scheme of Arrangement. In February 2009 Shareholders were told discussions had ceased. Sean O'Connor stated in the 2008 report that the Company did not propose to move from AIM to the main market. By 2010 the Board had changed its mind and an application to move to the main market was made. This was assisted by the fact that Cape was now able to satisfy the provisions of the Scheme of Arrangement and start paying dividends.

At the same time a new corporate structure was to be set up. Arguing that two thirds of the profit was now earned outside the UK, and the geographical centre of gravity was moving eastwards, it opted for a new holding company – Cape PLC, incorporated in Jersey but UK listed, and with its tax residence in Singapore. An additional new holding company, and subsidiary of Cape PLC Jersey, was incorporated in Singapore - Cape International Holdings Pte Ltd. This in turn held all the interests of the Cape Industrial Services Group through a further holding company Cape UK Holdings Newco Ltd. This was at a time when South East Asia was the market focus of many international companies. Notions of floating part of the Company in Singapore were in the Board's mind. There was an element of *folie de grandeur* in this and by 2015 the UK holdings had become subsidiaries of Cape PLC again. There was a network of holding companies, in part designed to distance operational subsidiaries from potential litigation. The 'down the line' holding company which became the target for litigation was the old UK registered Cape PLC (originally Cape Asbestos and then Cape Industries) which was now renamed Cape Intermediate Holdings Ltd.

At the same time Sean O'Connor, as Chairman, did what every good Chairman should do, and provide for succession. Tim Eggar, appointed as his successor, a barrister and investment banker by background, was a Conservative MP who had held the position of Minister of Energy in John Major's government. After retiring from the Commons in 1996 he pursued a business career in the resources sector. By the time he was appointed to the Cape position he held a number of key non -executive directorships relevant to Cape's marketplace. (As an example, in 1998 he had become Chairman of Engineers M W Kellogg Ltd, a participant in many of the LNG project construction groups). Cape was extremely fortunate in securing his services. A further addition to the Board – Michael Merton - had worked for RTZ throughout the Far East and brought appropriate experience to the Board.

Industrial Services

With the new funding, the acquisitions and IDC under apparent control the outlook for growth looked very promising in 2008. It was to stretch management - no more so than Martin May. It will be remembered he was a turnaround specialist and had responsibilities outside Cape. In 2004 whilst Chairman of Cape he was also Chief Executive of McNicholas Construction, having, at the time, to deal with a claim for unfair dismissal brought by the company's former Managing Director Colin McNicholas and his Finance Director. By 2006 he was withdrawing from other activities enabling him to give more time to Cape as Chief Executive. This coincided with the loss, through retirement, of some of the old guard who had managed the growth of the Industrial Services business from the beginning. When it came to the Australian acquisitions the initial management integration plan was not delivering and diverting executives from elsewhere in the organisation, to the detriment of their operations. Martin May introduced a Leaders Development Programme which was designed to raise the competence of management and bring in recruits. For probably the first time Cape was sufficiently attractive as an employer to take on graduates, both male and female. This all did little to solve the immediate problem.

2007 was an excellent year for the UK and DBI was proving a valuable addition to the portfolio, now enhanced considerably by the addition of Endecon . CIS had twenty-eight facilities throughout the UK and 4,500 employees. With the

UK financial crash and recession, it was not surprising that revenue was flat over the next three years, but margins held up well. Maintenance now comprised over 90% of sales turnover so this was a very stable and sustainable business. Cape's platform of services, and safety and performance culture, meant that it had a very strong position in the non-mechanical industrial services sector. In power generation it maintained 70% of the coal and oil-fired installations and 87% of the nuclear. It serviced forty-six offshore installations and in shipbuilding was a co-venturer in the Ship Support Services JV providing a whole range of services in the building of the UK's new aircraft carriers. Even LNG entered the scene in the UK with import terminals being constructed at the Isle of Grain and South Hook, Milford Haven.

Sales revenue in the Middle East (now referred to as the Gulf Region) increased at a spectacular rate – from £40 million in 2006 to £170 million in 2009 dropping back to £137 million in 2010. Margins were coming through at 20%. Abu Dhabi, Qatar and Saudi Arabia were the main contributors with investment in Qatar in particular booming. Supported by heavy capex, particularly in scaffolding equipment, the business was able to take advantage of an expanding marketplace. Maintenance and shutdowns were now exceeding 50 % of the business. At the heart of this success was the strength of Cape's TCN workforce - long standing employees with a wide range of skills were now receiving 25 year service awards. Management and staff were mainly of Indian nationality with two – Samir Chopra, Regional Director Qatar and Hemachandran, Operations Director, UAE enjoying remarkable careers; operationally, Cape in Oman and Bahrain was headed by Nationals. Cape's ability over the years to establish a truly multi-cultural business, involving local partners, distinguished the Gulf business from some of the other overseas business units where UK Expatriate management still tended to prevail. Wages and salaries were now rising rapidly and Cape's reputation as an employer in India and Nepal was such that it was readily able to top up manpower resources to support the growth in activity. Territorially Cape re-entered Kuwait and Iraq. By 2009 the Gulf Region was the largest profit earner in Cape.

The third region was CIS/Caspian, CIS standing for the Commonwealth of Independent States, or those bordering Russia that became independent on the collapse of communism. The business was also looking for opportunities in the

Mediterranean having initially secured a contract involving maintenance services in Malta's Dockyard. Further areas for focus were the LNG import receiving terminals under construction in Italy and Spain and the anticipated expansion of the LNG facilities at Arzew in Algeria. Here Cape secured a contract in 2010 valued at in excess of £27 million for the Sonatrach GL3-Z LNG expansion.

Operations in Azerbaijan and Kazakhstan continued but operationally the next few years were all about Sakhalin LNG as the contract drew to a conclusion. It was successful commercially, and Cape was able to continue its presence on the island carrying out maintenance under a four year term contract. To carry out such a large US$110 million plus contract in such a remote and harsh location was a remarkable achievement.

The fourth business unit was the Far East and Pacific which now represented over 50% of the capital employed in the Company. Thailand continued to be a core earner as did Philippines. The benefit of the Philippines operation was the stock of trained manpower totalling over 700 - multi disciplined and trained by Cape – built up by Regional Director Mike Harding. With the modular approach to work, skid mounted units were being fabricated in Thailand, Singapore, Philippines and Korean yards. Whether Cape had the contract or not, it was more often the case that clients drew on Cape's manpower to speed up or complete work. It could be more attractive for Cape to lose the initial contract and be available when, under pressure, the client would let out work on a cost reimbursable basis. Filipino blue collar personnel had considerable IT skills and were employed throughout Cape's international operations. Offshore Australia was a particularly fruitful hunting ground as clients were anxious to avoid the cost and potential union difficulties employing Australian personnel.

Singapore had become the regional headquarters and by 2011 certain operational and administrative functions, including the 'management and development of the Group's non-UK intellectual property' were housed here. A 'franchise fee' was charged to business units. Whilst having certain tax advantages, this proved very expensive; Cape having in the past abandoned Singapore more than once in view of its high cost as a Regional centre. This gave rise to a further drive towards securing work in the marketplace and a major contract was secured for Exxon on the Parallel Train Project at Jurong Island.

The acquisitions in Australia got off to a bad start owing to the drawn out and hostile PCH bid. Cape started off with an imperious reputation and now had a task on its hands. The initial management task force put together lacked leadership, accountability and local relationships, and in each of the acquired companies – TCC, Concept Hire and PCH the respective Managers of the businesses left and set up in competition. Within a year Bob Overstar of Concept Hire had setup Smartscaff in competition, and Jamie Cullen and Bill Ryan of PCH set up Resource Equipment Ltd of Perth; TCC's Manager Darren Iannello opened a Perth office for East Coast leader Giovenco Industries. UK staff were drafted in by Cape but this could not halt the departures amongst PCH senior management. Modern Industries, Cape's former partner in 1988 took on ten of PCH's senior managers including the well-regarded Jim Anderson, Director of Major Projects. Cape went to court twice; cases were dismissed, and Cape had to meet the costs. The effect was disastrous and the loss of key management in the acquired business weakened the controls placed on the security of assets. But fortunately, the businesses had assets (the largest stock of scaffolding in Australia) which the market could not do without. Apart from Concept Hire, the business was largely project driven and the market was flat for the first two years. By 2010 Woodside's Pluto LNG project was approaching peak activity and revenue started to pick up. The work was very profitable since incoming modules suffered damage, or had design defects, giving rise to a lot of remedial work on site, in addition to extended scaffold hire. Weather and design issues pushed the completion date out which was to Cape's benefit. The manhour costs in Australia on these remote sites was amongst the highest in the world, so work carried out on a time and material basis yielded a handsome return and concealed weak performance elsewhere. In the first quarter of 2012 the project was finished, and the extent of the business's dependency on it was apparent.

Strategy wended a slightly wayward path during these years. Cape's success in the industrial services field was down to its focus on high end work for international and national oil and petrochemical companies where safety and quality standards were sufficiently high as to create high barriers of entry. Apart from safety and quality, it's unique selling point was its highly trained directly employed workforce, competence in technically difficult processes (such as refractories and cryogenic insulation), and performance on site. Attempts were being made to enter markets which did not fit this profile or where Cape's offering did not carry a premium. Country examples include Turkmenistan, Iraq, Hong Kong, Japan, India and Algeria. Activity examples – Concept Hire's scaffolding. Whilst there was opportunist work available management was stretched and needed to focus on core strengths and markets.

The newer acquisitions at this time were however well aligned in terms of strategic fit. In the UK Cape acquired York Linings, a long established refractory business with a wide international client base to supplement its old R B Hilton business. For a total consideration of £5 million, a business with sales of £14 million annually and operating profits approaching £2 million, this was a good deal. Shoreguard Pty. Ltd. in Australia only involved an investment of up to £2 million, dependent on performance, again was a good fit, providing Cape Australia with access to the corrosion protection market in the marine and naval sectors.

The Oriental Dream falling apart.

Back in 2008 the vision for the Company was one focused on Singapore where it would have its headquarters and the prospect of a local share placing. Sales volumes in the Far East/Pacific relative to the other three units in the years 2008- 2011 suggested the strategy was well conceived – particularly as there was a downturn in revenue elsewhere. However, looking at the breakdown of revenue, in the Far East projects comprised over 50% of sales, maintenance and shutdowns barely 30%, and the balance comprised Concept's commercial and residential hire and sale in Australia. This hardly aligned with the model in the UK and Gulf where maintenance was the larger element of work. Margins were poor relative to UK and Gulf and given the high capital investment involved, returns inadequate. Although Martin May was forecasting 10% revenue growth in 2012 this was not going to happen as Pluto LNG tailed off and new LNG projects were still distant. An over optimistic view of the timing of these projects and inadequate front end marketing analytics made for poor forecasting.

May could point to a remarkable record; for a time he had been a stock market darling. Expectations were high but beneath the surface all was not well. Sales and earnings momentum was slowing and by now shareholders were expecting the Australian acquisitions, for which they had paid dearly, to deliver. Under Tim

Eggar's chairmanship he was under greater scrutiny, and by the end of 2011 there was uneasiness at Board level given the forecasts and budgets placed before them. This may have been shared by a new Non-Executive – Brendan Connolly – who joined the Board in November. Connolly had been CEO of Moody

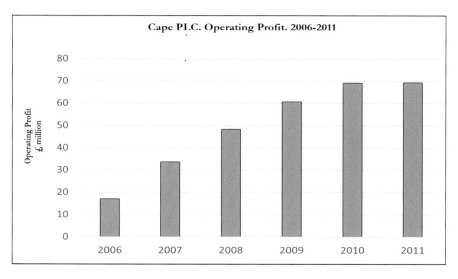

International, a quality, testing and inspection company prior to it being taken over by Intertek in March 2011. Moody specialised in the petroleum sector and had offices in the Middle and Far East. He continued with Intertek as a Vice President, which enabled him to act as a Non-Executive Director for Cape. He brought substantial oil industry experience to the role, having previously worked for Schlumberger, with a good working knowledge of the market and the timing aspect of client investment decisions.

With Eggar's contacts amongst Owners and Engineering Contractors, he will also have been made aware of Cape's goodwill issues in Australia and Connolly would have provided further insight. Action was required and this was revealed in the 2012 report, the need being ascribed to the outlook onshore Australia beyond the Pluto LNG project. The business was very project dependent and activity was grinding to a halt. Whilst the mid to long term outlook was good (it turned out that in 2013 the business booked record levels of new project work) there was a realisation that Cape had failed to deliver on its strategy of integrating the Australian businesses - the persistent low margins, the poor performance of

Concept Hire and Sale and a lack of confidence in the management and controls within the business. Receivables and debtor days had been rising, tying up working capital. Profits had been abysmal relative to the capital tied up in the business.

As can be seen from the charts below over the period 2006-2011, the Far East tied up some 55% of the Group's capital employed but generated barely 14% of its profits. The amount of goodwill attached to the Australian acquisitions could no longer be sustained.. The goodwill allocated to Australia had already been

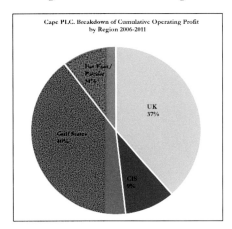
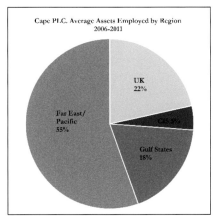

reduced from £190 million in 2009 to £154 million by means of a new method adopted in 2008 of allocating goodwill between units based on projected cash generation (GGU's). The effect of this was to shift goodwill from Australia to the UK and the Gulf Region. Despite this, the carrying value in Australia was still far too high relative to the returns being generated.

In the first quarter of 2012 it was clear changes were afoot. In March Martin May resigned, Brendan Connelly taking over as Acting Chief Executive. In June a new Chief Executive was appointed - Joe Oatley. In August David McManus, Chairman when the Australian acquisitions were made, resigned from the Board. After the inevitable profit warning, Finance Director Richard Bingham resigned. The Board came clean with the announcement that a significant write down had to be made, giving rise to a charge for exceptional items of £150 million, comprising a goodwill impairment of £111 million and asset write-downs of £13 million relating to the Australian businesses. This was hardly surprising - PCH had cost £110 million. Having net assets of £30 million at the time of acquisition, £78 million had been ascribed to goodwill. The business generated £50 million in sales with a profit after interest and tax of £3.5 million in the year of acquisition. Whilst in the intervening years sales had increased, profits stood still. Synergies in combining the business with the other acquisitions were eagerly expected, but there were few synergies with Concept Hire being in a different marketplace – commercial and residential scaffold hire. For Concept Hire the purchase cost of £46 million produced £12 million of net assets and a goodwill charge of £34 million. The business generated £32 million of sales and £3.5 million net profit in the first year of acquisition. The same picture with TCC – purchase cost £35 million, net assets £11 million and goodwill of £24 million. Sales here in the first year of acquisition were £48 million and £2 million profit. The truth was that the combined acquired businesses failed to generate the same level of net profit in any of the intervening years between 2007 and 2012. When looked at in terms of exchange rates the figures were far worse, the Australian Dollar having strengthened by some 30% since the acquisition (thereby greatly increasing the value ascribed to goodwill and the Sterling cost of writing it off).

This was a sad end to Martin May's period with Cape, given his courage and determination in driving through the South African settlement, the Scheme of Arrangement, and initiatives in expanding Cape's footprint internationally. There was little wrong with the conceptual strategy, but the Australian acquisitions were hasty, expensive and ill conceived. Due diligence had been poor. The PCH wrangle had damaged Cape's name in the market from the start. It lacked an effective management team capable of driving through the synergies, where they arose. Martin May and his finance Director Richard Bingham were turnaround specialists. Having done their job in turning around Cape, they were enthused with the business and took it on a journey which, it could be argued, was unfamiliar ground for them.

Elsewhere in the business there was evidence of management weaknesses. Complacency had been creeping in and Martin May had taken on too much himself. An example of this was the LNG contract undertaken in Algeria within the CIS/Sakhalin and Mediterranean unit. This was for insulation and scaffolding, both activities well within Cape's capability. The client was Sonatrach the Main Contractor Saipem of Italy, and the project ran into delay.

Algeria is not an easy place to do work in, presented language difficulties, and Cape had limited prior experience. A provision of the contract was to employ Algerian labour. Because of the previous phases in the construction of the Arzew terminal, there was a pool of skilled labour, employed by local companies. Cape was obliged to use them and was held to ransom. Cape did not mobilise on time, and failed to control the database, which rendered its commercial arguments weak when it came to seeking recovery of prolongation costs. When Saipem itself was losing money, it took a particularly hard line with sub-contractors. By the time Cape poured resources into the project (including Filipinos from Cape Philippines) to recover its position, it was too late. The project carried an initial value of £27 million and increased significantly in value over the course of the work, but in 2012 it was found necessary to make a loss provision of £19.8 million. This was a colossal disaster given the many LNG contracts carried out by Cape, but a measure of the risks involved if operational management was not up to the task. There were signs elsewhere of operational weaknesses. In Singapore the Parallel Trains project was approaching a peak of activity with over fifteen hundred men on site, absorbing inordinate management time for little commercial benefit. Cape had never made profits on insulation and scaffolding work in Singapore due to the difficulties in obtaining work visas and the entrenched position of local Chinese contractors. Having placed Cape's Headquarters in Singapore meant there was pressure to secure work there, and corporate aggrandisement took precedence over commercial good sense. Even in the UK there was evidence of commercial failure when there was a £4.1 million charge against losses on an offshore rig refurbishment contract in 2011. In Saudi Arabia a bad debt of £1.5 million had to be reserved. Whilst there were inherent risks in the business Cape was in, these provisions were symptomatic of operational and management weakness.

So, the 2012 accounts under a new Chief Executive were, not surprisingly, kitchen sink time. Whilst revenue increased by 7%, operating profit more than halved at £31.5 million and after exceptional costs the net loss attributable to the continuing business was £157 million, and to the discontinued business £42 million. Total equity reduced from £406 million to £178 million. The dividend was maintained barely covered by pre-exceptional earnings. This was a shock to shareholders as, in effect, the 2007 £70 million capital raising had been squandered. The banks were not impressed either. To claimants, who had been taking comfort from the steps Cape had taken to protect their interests, it caused nervousness again in terms of the security underpinning Cape's ability to meet their claims.

Industrial Disease Claims.

In the context of IDC, the inconclusive contingent liability statements in annual reports were still evasive in their language, to the extent that each year the Auditors report was qualified by an 'Emphasis of Matter' statement. The removal of this was becoming necessary in Company dealings with banks and credit agencies. The opportunity arose with the requirement under the Scheme of Arrangement to carry out a three yearly independent actuarial review starting 2008[1]. The review had to make an assessment of the projected Scheme claims against Scheme Companies over the following nine years. The initial £40 million was what Cape could merely afford and the projection was that the amount held would cover 8 years of claims. The Scheme was operating effectively with claims of the order of £4 million being dealt with annually, initially being offset by interest earned on the ring-fenced deposit. In 2007 it was considered Cape Claims Services' funds, including top-ups to date, were sufficient to cover Scheme requirements for 13 years.

In carrying out this review, it was evident that there were substantial areas of claim not covered by the Scheme. The Scheme only applied to Scheme companies, not all the subsidiaries over time, or all the companies that had been dissolved. Moreover, the grounds for compensation were broadening and the amounts involved were now increasing. It was also based on projections suggesting that claims would peak in the years 2025 to 2030 and then rapidly reduce – projections that were now considered optimistic. Projected liabilities now extended to the year 2070. Tillinghast initially in 2004 had projected a claims range of £49.5 million to £160.2 million settling for a central estimate of £80.9 million. By the time the Scheme was being formed the range had already gone up to £70.2 million to £240.3 million with a central estimate of £119.4 million. This later projection included Dissolved companies as well as Scheme Companies. The definition attached to this figure was: 'the aggregate projected discounted value, net of insurance recoveries, of all the Scheme companies unpaid UK asbestos-related claims, including the Dissolved Companies (other than the Darchem Companies)'[1]. Steps were now taken to embrace employees of any remaining Additional Companies.

In the 2008 actuarial review the range came out at £48 million to £203 million and by 2009 this had been narrowed down to £60 Million to £100 million and a central estimate of £79 million. The Board considered the analysis refined enough to allow them to take a reasonable stab at setting aside a provision to cover its full anticipated UK liability, and for this they took the £79 million. An additional provision of £70.2 million was recognised in the 2009 accounts involving a charge of £50.8 million, net of deferred tax, to the income account. This was to cover future claims over and above the funds held in the Scheme of Arrangement (£37.5 million at the end of 2008). This provision could be accommodated as, at that time, it was matched by a healthy operating profit of £71 million and the stronger balance sheet arising from the share placement and subsequent acquisitions. It was unheralded and tucked away in the accounts. The reason for this, apart from the obvious one of not drawing attention to Cape's IDC liabilities, was presumably also to avoid widening the scope of the ring-fenced Scheme of Arrangement. It also allowed the flexibility of dealing with claims either through the Scheme or by drawing on the provision. Importantly it enabled the removal of the Auditor's 'Emphasis of Matter' qualification in the accounts.

So for the first time there was a quantified provision covering the anticipated monies that would be required to feed the Scheme Fund over the years of its existence and meet any other related liability. In reality there was some looseness in definition right from the beginning and the Board would have wanted to avoid the public scrutiny had the Scheme been tinkered with. Moreover, the legal costs associated with setting up the original Scheme had been exorbitant and by simply making a provision, management time and cost was avoided. However, it would have been a matter of greater security to claimants had it been possible to expand the existing Scheme and raise the level of ring-fenced funds. As it transpired the Scheme probably would have represented a far better home for the funds than one or more of the Australian acquisitions.

Meanwhile further steps were taken to control the import and treatment of asbestos in the UK and throughout Europe. The Control of Asbestos

Regulations 2006 in the UK brought together the various strands of regulation in one document. Surprisingly it is only with the introduction of these all embracing regulations that imports were finally banned. It tightened up the HSE licensing requirements for businesses undertaking removal, and for managing asbestos at premises. Penalties were increased. A control limit of 0.1 fibres per ml. measured over four hours further narrowed down acceptable exposure limits. Asbestos removal was no longer a mainstream activity for Cape and given its history, regulatory compliance within the Company was now inbred.

Insurers Rise up.

The rise in claims in the nineties and early part of the Millennium years, particularly the incidence of mesothelioma, and the cost of claims, was clearly impacting insurers. Insurance companies looked closely at their policies and sought to tighten up the definition of boundary conditions in employer liability policies. A series of cases during the decade were heard dealing with the apportionment of liability. In the worst case Insurers had gone into liquidation because of claims (particularly in the USA). Lloyds of London was almost crippled by claims largely arising outside the UK and mainly relating to chrysotile asbestos. Lloyds 'Names' were individuals risking potentially unlimited personal liability, and there were many stories of significant losses amongst the rich and famous. The Iron Trades Employers' Association Ltd with whom Cape had policies, dumped all its asbestos related employer's liability policies into a new company Chester Street Insurance Holdings and entered into a Scheme of Arrangement, which meant that recoveries by policy holders were compromised over time.

Definitions were changing as was the scope of potential liability, as individual court cases were held in the UK and grey areas clarified. Most notably in the period 2010 an action was brought against Cape by a David Chandler, a former employee of Cape's old subsidiary the Uxbridge Flint Brick Company (later re-named Cape Distribution Ltd) in 1969, and who had contracted Asbestosis[2]. This was not a Scheme Company and there was no insurance cover in place in 1969, so the case was made against Cape as the parent company based on 'duty of care'. It attracted a great deal of attention as it raised again the extent to which the 'corporate veil' could be penetrated. Chandler won his case and Cape lost the appeal. The Court found that Cape, as the parent company, did have knowledge of the working practices and exercise direction over the safety of its employee in the subsidiary. The decision was significant, in that it in effect established that there were circumstances where an injured employee of a subsidiary company, was owed a duty of care by the parent. Its importance was not lost on Anglo American who were in the process of dealing with their silicosis claims in South Africa. The Chandler case then prompted Aviva in 2016 to test the law on the subrogation of insurance liabilities under the indemnity agreement between Cape Distribution Ltd (CDL, formerly Uxbridge Flint Brick) and Cape Intermediate Holdings (CIH) as the parent (known as the EL Claims). This involved three way litigation between the two Cape companies and Aviva, who had provided employers liability insurance cover for CDL. Aviva sought on behalf of its insured customer (CDL), to recover from CIH damages it had paid out between 1956 and 1966, and in relation to lung cancer and mesothelioma caused by exposure to asbestos. This was an important case for Cape as it could open up the possibility of several insurance companies seeking some recovery of payouts via the many indemnities existing within the Cape Group. The case was complex, getting bogged down in issues relating to the treatment of claimants straddling the key dates covering the indemnity. After two hearings, the court found that CDL was entitled to contractual indemnity from CIH without regard to insurance recoveries but did not reach a conclusion as to Aviva's right to a subrogated claim in CDL's name from CIH. The case went to appeal.

At the same time a whole new range of potential claims were unleashed by the action of a group of insurers lead by Aviva, RSA and Zurich. Insurers had paid out on Employers Liability claims, to mainly building companies sued by former employees, who had contracted mesothelioma due to occupational exposure to asbestos (known as the PL Claims). These gave rise to subrogated Product Liability claims against Cape, based on the allegation that Cape had failed to make purchasers and their employees aware of the dangers of handling the material involved, which was mainly Asbestolux and Marinite. As well as expert reports and statements, this gave rise to the production of a lot of historical evidence relating to labelling, hazard warnings and documentation covering the sale and application of the products. The core trial bundle comprised five thousand pages in seventeen lever-arch files.

The significance of these actions to Cape cannot be underestimated. From the 1931 Regulations onwards the focus of those seeking to regulate and discipline the industry, had been primarily directed towards conditions in the factories and to an extent, the mines. The handling of asbestos outside the factories had not received the same attention, either by Regulators or by Cape. This was now becoming apparent given the rise in these PL claims. These further cases potentially penetrated yet another corporate veil. Cape found itself testing well established laws and precedents. To take on the top insurers required the best legal brains. Cases and Appeals were lengthy and expensive, and involved expert witnesses and numerous reference cases. Again, Cape was faced with another potential liability that had the potential to prove terminal.

Chapter 11

Some Stability at Last

A New Management Duo

Tim Eggar did well in finding Joe Oatley to step into Martin May's shoes. Joe had previously been Managing Director of Engineers Weir, Strachan & Henshaw prior to its acquisition by Babcock International, and subsequently Chief Executive of Hamworthy. A marine engineer by background, he had a remarkable success record at Hamworthy - greatly widening its applications and product range to embrace the oil and gas industry, and through a number of acquisitions. An AIM listed company it was acquired by Wartsila in January 2012 and Joe resigned as a Director in February. He had both experience and knowledge of Cape's markets at home and abroad, and it was fortunate for Cape that he was available to take up the role of Chief Executive.

By the end of 2012, he had his own Chief Finance Officer in Michael Speakman, a rare combination of Engineer and Accountant, and who had held the same position in Expro, the oil services company, where Tim Eggar had been a Non-Executive Director. Again, he understood Cape's markets well. Between the two of them they were to prove a formidable combination in putting Cape back on the rails. They soon identified that the problem facing the business was less market driven, more the strength of management resources and operational performance. Cape's high profile in safety and quality was all very well, but for clients it had to be accompanied by operational performance.

The obvious decisions were made in short order in Australia. The Concept Hire scaffolding hire business was put up for sale as was the Kwinana shotblasting and painting shop. Cape had learnt in the UK that the commercial market for scaffolding was not its business and the detailed due diligence, so important in dealing with a scaffolding business, had been seriously deficient . TCC's 'largest painting and shotblasting workshop in the Southern Hemisphere' had been a one-off project facility and even before being acquired by Cape was unsustainable. The resulting goodwill write-offs were obvious, and thrown in for good measure were reorganisation costs as excess office and regional depot facilities were closed out. Beneath it all was a sustainable business, but from an operational standpoint there was some streamlining of the corporate structure needed. The onshore and offshore businesses in Australia were combined. Beyond Australia the build up of duplicate 'Head Office' personnel in Singapore was put on hold and the UK region was combined with the CIS/Sakhalin and Mediterranean business. The Head Office reverted to the UK and an office facility established at Drayton Hall, Middlesex.

An acquisition in Hong Kong was being finalised at the time Joe Oatley assumed the role of Chief Executive. It involved taking a stake in a Hong Kong company engaged in insulation & scaffolding for a consideration of £4.75 million. This was conceived on the assumption that the market would be receptive to Cape's standards and style of operation and at first sight the landing of a three year scaffolding contract on the power stations looked promising. Cape had made a previous attempt to enter the market in the 1980's and with the same client – China Light & Power (see p.119). But again, it came up against the stranglehold on labour exercised by local labour brokers. No doubt it was considered to be a gateway to China, but the Chinese market was not amenable to Cape's activity profile. Cape Hong Kong Fuji survived until 2016, the local management was found to be wanting, the entity was sold and the investment written off. There was probably a role for a business in Hong Kong, but only as a procurement office for materials and scaffolding equipment sourced from China.

A 'Platform for Growth.'

Unfortunately this anticipative banner had been raised too many times following some of the events and changes in Cape's history. However, Cape now had leadership in place that understood the market, and the action needed to re-invigorate what was fundamentally a very sound business. A well conceived presentation of the market, business structure and strategy was outlined in the 2013 company report. A subdued marketplace and a falling oil price meant it had to be a period for consolidation and attending to some of the operational weaknesses. The business now had 18,000 employees working across twenty one countries and the first strategic goal was to establish and embed the operational processes that were needed to upgrade performance. Alongside was a drive to raise management competence through recruitment, training and development. Some senior managers were now approaching retirement and it was a time for new ideas and a greater diversity of talent, including successfully, women.

Incoming CEO's had in the past been able to rely on the solid performance of the UK business to underpin growth opportunities elsewhere. However, over the next few years the UK market softened, competitors were catching up and management weaknesses were affecting performance. In the UK, 80-90% of revenues were maintenance driven but, on some sites, complacency had set in, and Cape was no longer coming up so readily with innovative operational initiatives. It proved hard work to conclude a further five year term contract for EDF on the nuclear sites, valued at £150 million. At the Esso Fawley oil refinery, Cape, as the incumbent maintenance contractor from its earliest days, had been under intense pressure to perform. The contract formed the backbone of the Southern Region and was under threat. Competitors had been quick to adopt Cape's multi-discipline approach and were catching up fast. Its oldest and main UK competitor, Dutch owned Hertel, had moved into mechanical services with modest success. Hertel had also followed Cape internationally with a similar footprint. The Company had been founded only two years after Cape, and had a long and distinguished history. After an upturn in the company's fortunes, its private equity owners seized an opportunity to sell the business in 2015 to a French based company, Altrad Services, of which we will hear more later. Hertel was the market leader in Holland and by this time had worldwide sales of £620 million. The transaction placed an enterprise value of £190 million on the business. Another competitor in the UK – Deborah Services (DSL) had also laid out a similar portfolio to Cape. Shortly after Martin May resigned from Cape, he became a Director of Siteserv and Chairman of its subsidiary - Deborah Services (DSL). DSL took Cape head on at several sites with aggressive pricing. Interserve Industrial Services, the old GKN Mills Scaffolding, was poaching Cape staff and chasing volume in the market, only to come to grief eventually in 2018.

The Board looked for diversification within the same end markets. In 2014 the opportunity was taken to add a further area of discipline through the acquisition of Motherwell Bridge Engineering. Motherwell Bridge dated back to 1898 and had an illustrious history in bridge building and heavy engineering. After the second world war it had developed a line in the construction of 'Town' gas holders and later storage tanks for the oil and gas industry, but with the decline of the coal gas industry had lost its way and been forced into liquidation. The business acquired had previously been bought from the receivers by Kuwaiti backed private equity and had annual sales in 2013 of £46 million with an operating profit of £4.7 million. The acquisition involved a net cash outlay of £30 million, represented by a balance sheet somewhat weighed down with intangibles. The business fitted well in terms of its international footprint and reputation. It added experience in Nigeria and other markets new to Cape. There was also significant synergy with the DBI business (now Cape Environmental) in tank cleaning, whilst insulation, painting, and scaffolding disciplines were necessary co-disciplines. There was a risk attached to the acquisition. Firstly, Cape worked with competitors of Motherwell Bridge so that might limit the degree of integration. The other risk was that the design of tanks required an elevated level of technical expertise – areas with which Cape was not overly familiar. However, in focusing the business on servicing and repairs this risk was largely offset. The business was combined with the Cape Environmental activity as Cape Specialist Services. Latterly the business has reverted to the designation Motherwell Bridge recognising the inherent goodwill in the name.

A further acquisition in 2015 – Redhall Engineering Solutions Ltd, took Cape further into mechanical work including welding services, fitting well alongside Motherwell Bridge. With annual sales of £30 million, it was loss making and purchased for a consideration of c.£6 million. Restyled Cape Engineering Services it returned to profitability under Cape's management. The business remained (as it does today) as an independent activity suggesting that mechanical services could not be meaningfully integrated with Cape's platform of services – a strategic conundrum that had exercised Cape management for many years. The market was presented with a little confusion in the different Cape labels given to the new activities. This suggested that whilst the acquired businesses welcomed the financial backing of Cape, its corporate disciplines and HSE direction, they remained largely independent and faithful to their roots.

Competitors had been forced to follow Cape in setting high standards of health, safety and welfare. Joe Oatley saw that there was a need to ratchet up standards within Cape if it were to maintain market leadership. The adoption of ISO 9001 (Quality), and OHSAS 18001 Health and Safety standards throughout the Group was being followed up with the application of ISO 14001 (environmental) standards, and audit procedures tightened up. Given the needs and care of migrant workers, the international standard for welfare, SA8000, was now adopted throughout the Group. Between fifty and sixty million manhours of work were now being recorded annually and by 2015 the 'Capesafe' initiative had resulted in the Group recording its best all time performance in the key 'Lost Time Incidence Frequency' measure. Whilst some competitors claimed better records, the integrity of Cape Industrial Services' safety statistics had always been widely respected by clients. Cape had the benefit of UK and European initiated standards being recognised and adopted internationally. Overseas businesses were now receiving some of the highest awards hitherto destined for Cape's UK businesses, examples being the R B Hilton Bahrain and Saudi Arabia units each receiving Royal Society for the Prevention of Accidents Gold Awards in 2016. The significance of this focus on safety was not only a prerequisite in a scaffolding business but essential when dealing with high profile clients.

The UK business now encompassed responsibility for the CIS and Sakhalin units, what remained of the Algeria and 'Mediterranean' activities being buried in the Gulf or 'MENA' unit. Cape had little to offer Algeria, its LNG activities being long established, and local companies provided an acceptable service. In Egypt Cape had played its part in the building of the LNG facilities, but beyond, Cape's erstwhile partner Orascom and other local companies had the capability to provide an acceptable level of service. In Azerbaijan Cape had wisely teamed up with the State Oil Company Socar in a joint venture to service the on and offshore sector, where BP remained a major investor, and this prospered, continuing today as SOCARCape. Kazakhstan proved more problematic with activity now focused on the Kashagan Gas Field development. Work was being let through contractors having only a superficial respect for Cape's standards. A level of corruption in the market did not suit Cape's model and the business was under threat. Cape had remained on the Sakhalin site and taken advantage of maintenance opportunities, but this was really the extent of the market for its services. Shell and Exxon maintained a strong influence on standards, and as long as they were in place so, most likely, was Cape. There were upcoming LNG projects elsewhere in Russia but some of the momentum had been lost as a result of the CIS businesses coming under the UK management. The Azerbaijan offshore sector had been under the influence of Aberdeen and within Cape UK's comfort zone. By 2016 Sakhalin had ended up in the Far East unit and Azerbaijan in the Gulf and this constant switching was a little disconcerting for management and clients.

By 2014 the business mix in the Gulf now involved nearly 50% maintenance, and therefore less dependent on projects. This was still a high risk environment for project work, contracts often having to be undertaken through a second tier, often third country, contractor. With a core of maintenance work, Cape could be more selective in the work it took. The focus on operational performance was needed here too, some weaknesses having been exposed in the handling of contracts. In Saudi Arabia some of the earlier infrastructure projects were now needing maintenance and shutdown expenditure, and R B Hilton Saudi Arabia was thriving. As in Qatar the company dominated the market given its command of TCN manpower resources and strength of its Indian management. The margins achieved by the business were consistently in double figures.

In the Far East, the cutting back in Australia, the streamlining and re-energising of management, proved timely as the new LNG projects were about to get under way. There were the Wheatstone and Ichthys LNG projects in Western Australia and Darwin and the Curtis Island LNG projects on the East coast. Offshore there was Shell's Prelude floating LNG production vessel offshore WA. The floating LNG production concept said everything about the difficulties and expense in getting major projects accomplished in Australia. Having been modularised and assembled in the shipyards of Korea and S E Asia it was commissioned and, beyond the reach of Australian labour unions, maintained offshore by third country nationals, offering a ready market for the deployment of Cape's Filipino workers. In addition to Cape's established presence in Thai and Philippines yards, Cape East Jusik Hoesa was formed to support its manpower presence in South Korean yards and train local workers. Cape Philippines also benefited from the offshoring of support and administrative functions in Australia.

A former Woodside Energy Executive, Samantha Tough, joined the main board at the end of 2014, having held several senior roles within the energy sector in Western Australia. Her advice would have been invaluable at the start of Cape's Australian venture, but at least now she provided some wise council as the business was re-configured. The resources sector in Australia was now less buoyant and the performance of the business suffered from singular dependence on the LNG projects, given the limited maintenance base. A bumper year on the Wheatstone LNG project in 2016 put the business back into meaningful profit but the expectations back in 2006 when Cape embarked on its Australian venture were not going to be easily realised given the difficulties in maintaining a viable national as opposed to state based business, the distances and lumpy nature of work activity. One bright spot was the submarine sector – Cape's acquisition of Perth based business Shoreguard Marine, specialising in corrosion protection services mainly for the Royal Australian Navy, was proving a success.

Cape Philippines continued to resource many offshore developments in the region with the Bayu Undan field offshore Timor as a mainstay over the years. New locations of activity included the Daewoo SHWE Natural gas project offshore Myanmar. Here Cape provided a multi-disciplinary service encompassing a number of trades, reflecting Cape Philippines wide ranging manpower and trades portfolio. Cape acquired a presence in Papua New Guinea on the back of the LNG plant under construction. Efforts were being made to penetrate the Malaysian and Indonesian markets, but the same barriers to entry presented themselves as on previous attempts, but activity was maintained in Singapore.

By 2016, Joe Oatley could at last point to significant revenue growth reflecting a turnaround in Australia. Profits had grown marginally, and the ship was heading in the right direction.

Industrial Disease Claims

In 2013 a further actuarial assessment was carried out. In the background was the insurance litigation outlined in the last chapter. It was as if history had repeated itself – the advent of new management coincided with yet another major threat from Cape's past. Both Joe Oatley and Michael Speakman would have hoped that the 2013 actuarial review and provisions would put the problem of IDC claims to bed, but the stirring of the insurance industry and their clout was such that further prolonged and expensive litigation would be the order of the day. The product liability (PL) litigation brought about by the Insurers was due a six week trial scheduled for January 2017 but in October 2016 negotiations commenced to seek a settlement. Cape's defence was not strong - the cases mainly related to the use of Asbestolux , Cape's most successful and widely used amosite based product. It had been deployed in many applications and by many installers, and the potential 'flow through' claims, should insurers have product liability recourse to Cape - whether attributable to indemnities or duty of care - were enormous. And this was only one of Cape's asbestos containing products. From the standpoint of insurers, action against Cape would be on a case by base basis, demanding evidence that would not always be easy to obtain; litigation would be long and protracted. History told litigants that a 'bird in hand' settlement was better given the financial uncertainties always surrounding Cape. 'Flow through' litigation echoed Cape's experience of dealing with the initial claims in the USA, whereas a 'bird in hand' deal was the only sensible answer in resolving the South African litigation. The Directors would have seen it as potentially an existential threat, and the shareholders yet another setback, so in November 2016 negotiations commenced, and by the first quarter of 2017 a settlement was agreed. This took the form of an immediate payment of £18 million followed by a further deferred payment of up to £34.5 million payable over a period up to 2023. This could have been quite an open ended liability and settling it probably avoided publicity that could have drawn in other areas of potential product liability claims. By April 2017, settlement too had been reached in the Aviva Employers Liability (EL) claims for which a £9.7 million provision had already been made. The disclosures in these cases presented fertile ground for lawyers and campaigners and, by April, Leigh Day were active on the part of The Asbestos Victims Support Group Forum (AVSGF) in seeking to obtain access to the evidential PL documents filed by Cape. This would have been a major worry for Cape and its lawyers, and was to be the subject of legal action and court hearings in August and October 2017(see Page 220).

In early 2017 a further triennial actuarial valuation of UK asbestos related liabilities was completed. Carried out by Willis Towers Watson, it was against a background where, in fact, the volume of the previous three years of claims had been less than expected. However, it took into account changes in case law, in payouts and the costs of settlement with insurers. The expected liability now amounted to a colossal £209 million and after discount £172.5 million, requiring a top up to the existing provision of £79 million in the 2016 year end accounts.

Whilst it wiped out profits as an exceptional charge, from shareholders view it did not affect headline earnings per share, although the final dividend was reduced. The Scheme of Arrangement ring fenced funds, designed to cover claims already in the system, now stood at £41.6 million, having been topped up by £13 million in the year. The Board was once again seeking to cap the total potential IDC liability.

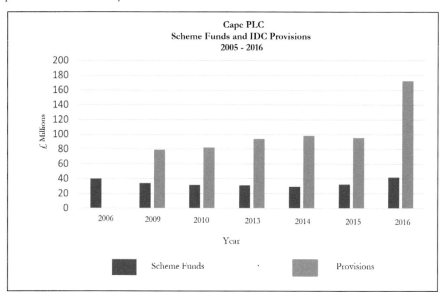

Corporate

During 2015 the corporate structure went through several changes, mainly involving bringing back the overseas subsidiaries after the offshoring attempt at consolidation under a Singapore based holding company – Cape International Holdings Pte. Ltd. There were also newly acquired companies to be housed. The effect was to put Cape Industrial Services Ltd., the UK subsidiary holding the IDC provisions, at the end of a chain of holding companies. Hitherto Cape Intermediate Holdings Ltd. (the old Cape PLC before the Jersey incorporation), which housed Cape Industrial Services Ltd., had been a direct subsidiary of Cape PLC, the Jersey registered parent company. In 2015 it became a subsidiary of a new company Cape Holdco Ltd., which in turn was a subsidiary of Cape Industrial Services Group Ltd., in turn a subsidiary of Cape UK Holdings Newco

Ltd. The latter had previously been a subsidiary of Cape International Holdings Pte, registered in Singapore but was now a direct subsidiary of Cape PLC. Having the intermediate holding companies provided a home for the overseas and newly acquired companies, leaving Cape Industrial Services, the UK business (and DBI) as operating subsidiaries of Cape Intermediate Holdings. As we have learnt, being the old Cape PLC/Cape Industries/Cape Asbestos, CIH was the focus of all IDC claims, thus it held the shares in Cape Claims Services.

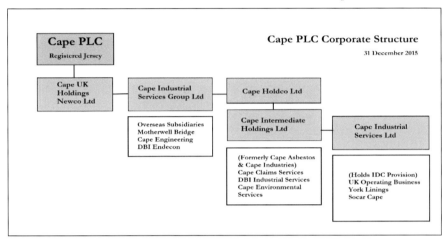

It is tempting to conclude that this somewhat complex structure derived from the stratagems of corporate lawyers, but it was probably more the result of the unravelling of the abandoned attempts at offshoring the business to Singapore. There were of course cross guarantees in place but it did have the effect of passing down the IDC liabilities firmly into the UK business.

In the 2015 Annual Report Joe Oatley anticipated the results for 2016 would be similar to 2015. The drop in the oil price was having an adverse effect on investment within Cape's market sectors. In November 2016 Cape issued a quarterly report ending 30th October stating that the year end results were expected to be slightly ahead of expectations and prospects for 2017 were encouraging. The announcement however presented a gloomy picture of the state of IDC, specifically the PL and EL claims. It spoke of threats to the Scheme of Arrangement, to the implementation of Group strategy and to the dividend, and this unsettled shareholders. The share price dropped to 150p. The litigation was obviously perceived as not going well but these rather alarmist prognostications proved (with the settlement noted above) to be unfounded. The trading optimism however was repeated in the January 5th 2017 statement '2016 full year results are likely to be materially ahead of current market expectations'. There was no further announcement until, on March 13th, settlement of the PL insurance was reported together with an update on the triennial valuation and £79 million top up in IDC provisions. Whilst a shock for shareholders these actions were to a degree comforting as they represented a cap on a liability so seemingly open ended when referred to in the October quarterly results. Two days later the preliminary statement caused more of a shock - despite the previous optimism as to the outcome for the year, earnings per share were static at 29.9p and the dividend was to be halved despite strong operating cashflow and debt reduction. Behind the figures was a serious shortfall in UK profits offset by continuing good results in the Gulf Region and a substantial improvement in Australia. The order book, up 6.5%, offered good prospects for the year ahead. Despite the disappointment, the share price which had risen from its low to 180p at Christmas now rose with the market to 246p in early April, with the help of an Investors Chronicle recommendation that forecast a forward p/e of seven. On June 5th Cape announced that it expected the 2017 results to be 'materially ahead of expectations' but warns that '2018 will be a more challenging year driven by the expected reduction in the current high level in construction activity particularly in Asia Pacific, and the effect of project delays and margin reduction in the Middle East'. The market did not like this, nor the lack of consistency in trading statements and the shares dropped by 25% and by the end of June were down to 184p.

On July 7th it was announced that 'the Boards of Directors of Altrad Investment Authority and Cape are pleased to announce they have reached agreement on the terms of a recommended cash offer for Cape by Altrad'. The price was 265p per share valuing the company at £332 million or an enterprise value of c.£400 million. Altrad would argue this represented a premium over the 180p that Cape had been trading at prior to the announcement, but looking at the chart of recent share performance there was in fact truly little premium on offer – the share had been at not far short of the same price three months earlier. Based on 2016 earnings per share the exit p/e was barely nine, when the average FTSE 350 p/e was over twenty. Altrad further declared that, as of the offer date, it had received support from shareholders to the extent of 18.2% of the equity.

Altrad Investment Authority was the vehicle built up by Mohammed Altrad, a Syrian born entrepreneur based in Montpellier, France. He had worked for the Abu Dhabi National Oil Company prior to moving to France and by chance establishing a scaffolding business based on the purchase of the bankrupt Mefran company. To this he added Plettac in Germany followed swiftly by further assets in Belgium and France and then culminating in the acquisition of Hertel of Holland. The latter took him into the UK as we noted in the previous chapter. The business took in a range of activities from concrete mixers and scaffold equipment manufacture to industrial and mechanical services. Sales revenues had grown to €1.7 billion in 2016.

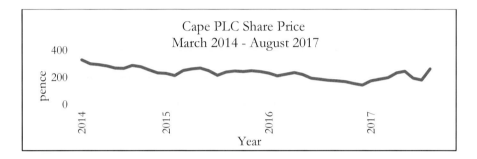

Altrad's integration of the business of Hertel had drawn its attention to the strength of Cape and its management in the international market. Altrad had a strong position in mainland Europe so Cape's mix of interests in the UK and internationally was an ideal fit and gave it market balance. Its interest in Cape was evident from early 2016 and it watched carefully as Cape's fortunes waxed and waned during the year. This was widely known and amongst those close to the Company the offer was no surprise in that there was feeling that the Board had been setting out its stall for the sale of the Company – in particular by tabling an all embracing IDC provision. If so, there may have been few potential buyers, UK private equity having had its fingers burnt on a previous occasion. What was surprising was the June 5th announcement warning of the challenges expected in 2018 which had caused the fall in the share price prior to the Altrad announcement. The announcement did not mark any particular reporting period and was a postscript to a contract award announcement, so in the context of a negotiation would appear untimely if not unwarranted. The reality was the performance of the business if anything was exceeding expectations. By the time of the interim results in August earnings per share (eps) just for the half year were up to 24.7p, not far short of the eps for the whole of 2016! Orders for the half year were up 85% compared with the same period in 2016, suggesting 2018 might not be quite so bad as suggested. Altrad appeared to be on to a bargain. It was too late for second thoughts; on the same day as the interim results were announced it was recorded that Altrad had 64% acceptances. Many shareholders were unimpressed, and the share chatrooms dreamed up conspiracy theories. But, just as the negatives in the announcements - the setting of substantial provisions, the 2018 outlook and the dividend cut - invited the charge that the Board was seeking to assist a bidder, others could take a view that the Board were seeking to deter a bidder.

So, for Altrad it looked to be a particularly good deal. The Cape business was producing more than enough cashflow to cover borrowings taken on, and on the face of it the IDC risk was well covered - if not, at this price there was contingency. It was commented that even if, in the passage of time, a further £100 million was needed to close out the IDC risk, it was still a good deal. It would be interesting to know whether Altrad gave a thought to the outcome for Federal-Mogul of its acquisition of Turner and Newall, with its bountiful provisions, back in 1998!

For Cape shareholders it was disappointing that the Board agreed to support the offer on the table without more of a fight. One explanation for this lay in the fatigue that had set in arising from Cape's history. Directors and senior management no longer had any links with the past but had been constantly sucked back into it. IDC and the insurance litigation had absorbed much of Tim Eggar's, Joe Oatley and Michael Speakman's time in 2016. And then the Triennial valuation was not expected to throw up such a notable change. 2017 in fact was now looking good, with orders trending above budget. Many of the necessary changes in performance and management resourcing were bearing fruit, but the truth was that profits had been static for three years and now the Directors foresaw pressures threatening a downturn in 2018. So somehow confidence had taken a knock. It would be surprising if Tim Eggar did not feel that every time he steered the company back on course its historic legacy knocked again on his door. Governance was now all consuming; Cape had been hard work for very little reward.

A further consideration was an ethical one, with possible legal implications. Any attempt to maximise shareholder returns at the expense of industrial disease compensation would have exposed the Board to a charge of neglecting the legitimate demands of claimants. If the company was to be sold, a low exit valuation coupled with seemingly generous provisions was a responsible outcome, and to the Board's credit. As it was, shareholders, too, were suffering from fatigue, signing up to every 'platform for growth' only to be disappointed. Cape was a favorite with the share tipsters as, with each IDC related knock, it fell in to bargain territory. Faithful investors M&G (Prudential) and Schroders, joined now by Henderson, J O Hambro and Man GLG were tired of the roller coaster ride and with the reduced dividend were happy to take the cash.

But shareholders won, as they were the only stakeholder who had a certain outcome. As to claimants, they had exchanged an owner exposed to the public gaze, and whose name rendered it a focus for redress, for the anonymity of a private company owned outside the UK. Cape by now had a record of dispensing compensation routinely, but since the pot, on which compensation depended, existed in the form of a provision, its proper disbursement was dependent on its future custodians. But there was comfort to be had in that Altrad, as the custodians, had financial strength and potentially deep pockets. For most employees there was continuity and in some cases opportunities, but for many the pride attached to working for Cape was lost.

Chapter 12

Aftermath

Rebranding

The name of Cape soon disappeared in the marketplace as Altrad sought to impose it's own house style and branding. This was consistent with the approach it had taken with other acquisitions, but in Cape's case it helped to distance the business from Cape's past. It had its limits, though, as in locations overseas some of its company structures and names were difficult to change or replicate if a loss of goodwill and reputation was to be avoided. Thus, in the Gulf States the names of Cape and R B Hilton still survive. Whilst there was a commercial advantage in some countries in maintaining the name of Cape, in Europe (essentially the UK) Cape's identity and reputation, in its field of activity, was subsumed under the name of Altrad with celerity.

IDC

In the last chapter reference was made to the efforts by Leigh Day, on behalf of Graham Dring, Chairman of the Asbestos Victims Support Group Forum (AVSGF), to gain access to Cape's files in the wake of the product liability (PL) cases, brought by insurers against Cape Intermediate Holdings (CIH). This was gathering pace during the period in which the discussions were taking place with Altrad. At the time that the takeover became final in August, a court hearing was in progress, the purpose of which was to consider the release of documents which, otherwise, under the PL settlement, would be destroyed. The conclusion of a further hearing in December, provided for the full release of the written submissions, witness statements, experts reports and other disclosed documents. CIH/Altrad appealed and a subsequent Court of Appeal hearing in 2018 and Supreme Court hearing in 2019 upheld the decision to release the written submissions, witness statements and experts reports, but referred the release of other disclosed documents, not drawn upon in the written submissions, and housed within the electronic file, back to Judge Picken, who dealt with the original PL trial. Cape/Altrad appeared to be in no hurry to conclude the matter and it was not until 2020, delayed further by the onset of the covid pandemic, that a court hearing under Judge Picken, upheld the decision but refused access to the other disclosed documents.

This had dragged on for three years and involved substantial legal fees, some of which AVSGF had to pick up (although certain Leigh Day lawyers waived their fees). There appeared to be nothing in the documentation that constituted grounds for specific legal action, but there was evidence that AVSGF could use in dealing with future claims, as it constituted a damning indictment of the failures of Cape to warn and protect users of its fibre or products. Clearly the Cape Board, when considering Altrad's offer back in 2017, would have been conscious of the possibility of these documents being made available and it could have weighed on their mind particularly if, amongst the documents not disclosed, there were matters that could lead to further potential litigation.

The acquisition of this evidence enabled AVSGF to adopt the moral high ground in the pursuit of further compensation to deal with the high incidence of mesothelioma. It chose to make the case for CIH/Altrad contributing towards investment in mesothelioma research. It was able to gain parliamentary support by means of a motion tabled on 23 May 2022, the lead sponsor for which was Ian Lavery, Chairman of the All Parliamentary Committee on Health and Safety. The motion which was supported also by the TUC called for a £10 million donation from CIH/Altrad towards the funding of mesothelioma research[4].

In Conclusion

A whole chapter could be devoted to 'what if?' speculation about Cape, and its Directors will have pondered many different such scenarios as its asbestos legacy unfolded. We can only speculate as to how stakeholders interests would have been served had others been custodians of Cape's assets.

It can be argued that Cape got off lightly. It mined the most dangerous forms of asbestos fibre, and manufactured products – Asbestolux and Marinite - which, alongside sprayed asbestos-based composites, were some of the most harmful. Whilst it may have paid attention to the working conditions of its own factory employees in the UK, it did little for those who dealt with its products away from the factories. To its credit Cape lead the way in producing asbestos-free replacements. However, in South Africa the asbestos industry's record was egregious, even if symptomatic of the social and political climate in which it operated. Here Gencor came to the rescue in providing the bulk of compensation. At least Cape learnt one lesson – 'best in class' health and safety standards became the cornerstone of its emerging industrial services business.

For the shareholder, a holding of £50 worth of shares in 1953 would have been worth £265 at the time Cape was acquired in 2017[1]. The investor would have earned £403 in dividends[2] – a miserable return even before taking into account inflation over the period. So unless a shareholder was active in trading what was a particularly volatile share, there was no money to be made. The shareholder was, though, fortunate in having a share that had any value at all, given the fate of competitors. At a time, today, when Fund Managers are mindful of their investors wishes in terms of ethical and social responsibility, it is surprising that Cape was sustained to such a large degree by the institutions. If today's investment approach had been in place in the 1970's Cape would have struggled to attract shareholders or additional equity, and possibly not survived. It would most likely have been hidden in private equity, which is where, it could be argued, it now is. Shareholders leant support to Cape in responding to calls for additional funding through rights issues. These bailed it out on more than one occasion but did provide the funds for setting up the Scheme of Arrangement.

Over the period 1953 to 2017, the dividends amounted to a charge against profits of £203 million[2], falling well short of the amount provided for industrial disease compensation over the same period - £292 million[3]. Whilst it cannot be concluded that claimants have been served well, this amount is a bounty which might otherwise have not existed had Cape been liquidated at the time of the write-offs in 1985, or at the time of the initial South African settlement in 2002. It could have been more had Cape's management been less cavalier in its acquisition strategies. But overall the fact that Cape survived suggests that its leaders over the years managed the trade-offs between shareholders and claimants if not well, better than some others. Cape did serve its employees well in navigating its way beyond asbestos and creating a world class industrial services business. It served its retirees well too with a well-funded pension scheme. This was to an extent made possible by the protection afforded by the IDC legacy. The business might otherwise have been sold and dismembered.

The means of providing for industrial disease compensation was untidy and cumbersome. The Scheme of Arrangement, although well conceived, only covered short-term liabilities, with its ring fencing capped at £40 million. Whilst perceived as an independent fund the Scheme funds are held as an asset on the balance sheet of CIH/Altrad and, should any residual surplus arise, to them it would accrue. The method adopted, of setting aside profits as provisions was neither ring fenced nor cast in stone. 'Promissory note' provisions are a poor substitute, and the attitude to their release and disbursement by administrators can be different - as Cape learnt in handling Scheme funds. It would have been better had Cape set up a ring fenced independent compensation fund, earning definitive as opposed to notional interest, even if the sums afforded were less than the provisions set aside. Its reputation and that of its Directors would have been enhanced, and the situation avoided whereby it has left the translation into compensation of IDC provisions to others.

The case put forward by the Asbestos Victims Forum (AVSGF) for securing further funding for mesothelioma research has merit. Mesothelioma has the highest mortality rates of asbestos related diseases and this is expected to continue for many decades to come[5]. Total mesothelioma deaths in the UK from the late 1960's to 2050 are predicted to be about 90,000. Mesothelioma is particularly associated with exposure to amosite (brown) asbestos and Cape was by far the largest importer and user of the fibre in the UK. A great deal of asbestos remains in the infrastructure of the UK, increasing the risk of further mesothelioma deaths over the next thirty years. Productive research could have the effect of reducing the terminal effects of the disease in the future, and for CIH/Altrad thereby potentially reduce the need for Scheme based compensation. Additionally it could benefit those who have been exposed to the fibre in Cape's products still to be diagnosed but beyond the reach of the Scheme of Arrangement, and even those abandoned in South Africa.

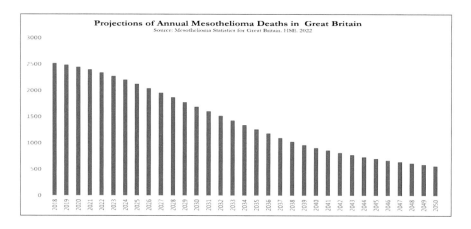

CIH/Altrad was left by Cape with substantial provisions to meet current and future claims. The definition surrounding the setting of these provisions in 2016 directed their use for 'all claims to be settled under the Scheme of Arrangement and will be '*sufficiently funded to include all other UK claims settled outside the Scheme of Arrangement*'. The definition therefore could embrace the proposed fund for Mesothelioma Research. Cape's provisions of £172 million in 2016 by 2022 had been reduced to £118 million, a portion of which was for allocation to the insurance settlement. For CIH/Altrad, which, since acquisition has maintained Cape's record of satisfying claims as and when they arise, it would be a means of de-risking the extent of future claims.

To those employees of Cape Industrial Services who generated the profits to provide for future disease liability it would be a fitting application of £10 million of the residual provision fund. They deserve the satisfaction of seeing that the fruit of their labours reach those who still remain as victims of Cape's asbestos legacy.

Bibliography
And Index

225

Bibliography

Individual Cape Annual Reports and Accounts and shareholders circulars are not referenced. Research covering asbestos related aspects of the narrative has been largely derived from secondary sources. Those interested in detailed research are directed towards the substantial collection of documents available at the University of Strathclyde Archives and Special Collections. This embraces the Cape Asbestos working papers assembled by investigative journalist Laurie Flynn and research of academics Geoffrey Tweedale and Nancy Tait. The history of asbestos mining in South Africa has been the subject of well researched publications by Jock McCulloch, providing much of the background to the earlier chapters.

Chapter 1

1. **Cape Asbestos 1893-1953. The Story of the Cape Asbestos Company Limited**. Hugh Barty King and Michael Newton. Harley Publishing Co., London. 1953. I am grateful to Michael's son, Christopher for giving me permission to reproduce illustrations included in Chapters 1 & 2 from this publication.
2. For an analysis and statistics covering the benefits of asbestos in fire protection in the USA see **Asbestos and Fire. Technological Trade-offs and the Body at Risk.** Rachel Maines. Rutgers University Press. 2005.
3. **Worldwide Asbestos Supply and Consumption Trends from 1900 through 2003.** Robert L Verta. US Dept of the Interior and Geological Survey. Circular 1298. 2006.
4. The early days of asbestos mining make for an interesting read in **Kaias & Cocopans. The Story of Mining in South Africa's Northern Cape**. Anthony Hocking. Hollards, Johannesburg. 1983.
5. **Minerals and Migrants. How the Mining Industry has Shaped South Africa.** Francis Wilson. MIT Press on behalf of American Academy of Art and Sciences. 2001.
6. See also **Asbestos Blues. Labour, Capital, Physicians and the State in South Africa.** Jock McCulloch. Indiana University Press. 2002. This is one of many illuminating publications by the same Author.
7. **Dust Storm**. Daily Telegraph Magazine feature. Oct. 6th 2007
8. There is a short history of the evolution of Rocksil and the Stirling plant to be found on the website of the company's successor Superglass Ltd.
9. **Magic Mineral to Killer Dust. Turner and Newall and the Asbestos Hazard.** Geoffrey Tweedale. Oxford University Press. 2000. Again an Author of many scholarly publications.
10. **Asbestos House. The Secret History of James Hardie Industries**. Gideon Haigh. Scribe Publications Pty Ltd. 2006.
11. **Asbestos Dynasties – The Eternit Multinationals**. 1 Eternit and the SAIAC Cartel. Bob Ruers. The International Ban Asbestos Secretariat Publication. 2012.
12. **Men Who Matter. Mr G F Newton.** Investors Chronicle. Jan. 27th 1961.
13. **Oxford Dictionary of National Biography.** See references in Lord Elton's books: **Among Others. Some pages of Autobiography.** (p.215). Lord Elton. Hutchinson. 1938. And **Imperial Commonwealth.** Lord Elton. Collins. 1945.
14. **Notes on Nationalism.** George Orwell. Polemic. October 1945.

15. A good account of the 1931 Regulations and aftermath is given in **The Way from Dusty Death. Turner and Newall and the Regulation of Occupational Health in the British Asbestos Industry.1890s-1970.** P.W.J Bartrip. The Athlone Press. 2001.
16. This was one of many considerations I picked up from the fascinating and erudite publication **Asbestos – the Last Modernist Object**. Arthur Rose. Edinburgh University Press. 2022.
17. Cape's decision not to provide warning labels on Marinite at this time was disclosed in later litigation (see Chapter 12).
18. **Women Mining Asbestos in South Africa. 1893-1980.** Jock McCulloch. Journal of South African Studies. June 2003.
19. **Death Still Stalks Former Asbestos-Mining Town.** The Star. November 12th 1997

Chapter 2

1. Ibid. **Kaias & Cocopans. The Story of Mining in South Africa's Northern Cape.** Ch. 1.4.
2. Ibid. **Minerals and Migrants**. Ch. 1.5.
3. See **Nat Capitalism and the South African Mining Industry.** G Fasulo. South African History Online.1955.
4. **Occupational, Domestic and Environmental Mesothelioma Risks in Britain.** RR696. HSE. 2009.
5. Capamianti and the Italy connection is well covered in **Cape Asbestos 1893-1953**. Ch. 1.1.
6. **History of Cape Contracts Ltd.** F.S. Page. Manuscript. 1981.
7. **Cape News** August 1994.
8. Ibid. **Asbestos Blues.** Ch. 1.6.
9. The outcome of this investigation did not materialise until 1973. **A Report on the Supply of Asbestos and Certain Asbestos Products**. HMSO. 1973.
10. Ibid. **The Way from Dusty Death** Ch 1.15.
11. Evidence disclosed arising from **Cape Intermediate Holdings v Dring**. **Appeal Judgement. 2019**. Documents are available through the Asbestos Victims Support Group's Forum. See also Chapter 12.
12. Ibid. **Asbestos Blues.** Ch. 1.6.
13. Quoted by Richard Meeran in the ITV Documentary **Real Life. You will know them by their trail of death, 2004,** relating to the South African litigation. See Chapter 7.

Chapter 3

1. See **British Resistance Archive.** Captain Rupert St George Riley.
2. For a good account of Section D and George Courtauld's role see **Section D for Destruction. Forerunner of the Special Operations Executive**. Malcolm Atkin. Pen and Sword Military. 2017.
3. Both the Kimberley and Rand Clubs have published interesting histories. **History of the Kimberley Club.** Constance Warner. 1965 and **The Story of the Rand Club.** Rene de Villiers and S Brooke- Norris. 1976.
4. See **Anglo American and the Rise of Modern South Africa**. Duncan Innes. Ravan Press Johannesburg. 1984.
5. Ibid. **1973 HMSO Report on the Supply of Asbestos.** Ch. 2.9
6. **Cape News.** August 1994.
7. Ibid. **Kaias & Cocopans. The Story of Mining in South Africa's Northern Cape.** Ch.1.4.

8. Ibid. **1973 HMSO Report on the Supply of Asbestos.** Ch.2.9.
9. See **South Africa's Gold Mines & The Politics of Silicosis.** Jock McCulloch. James Currey. 2012.
10. Refer **Proceedings of the Pneumoconiosis Conference held at the University of Witwatersrand.** February 1959. Also **The Way from Dusty Death** Ch.1.15 and **Magic Mineral to Killer Dust** Ch 1.9.
11. Revealed in **Cape v Lubbe CLC 1559 (CA).** and referenced in **Tort Litigation against Multinational Corporations for Violation of Human Rights. An Overview of the Situation outside The United States.** Richard Meeran. City University of Hong Kong Law Review. 2011.
12. **Asbestos Regulations 1969.** No. 690.
13. Ibid. **The Way from Dusty Death.** Ch.1.15.
14. Ibid. **Cape Intermediate Holdings v Dring. Appeal Judgement 2019.** Ch 2.11.
15. Ibid. **Occupational, Domestic and Environmental Mesothelioma Risks in Britain.** Ch.2.4.
16. Evidenced in **Lethal Work. A History of the Asbestos Tragedy in Scotland.** Ronald Johnston and Arthur McIvor. Tuckwell Press. 2000. See also **Clydebank, Asbestos the Unwanted Legacy.** Clydebank Asbestos Group. 2000.
17. **Control of the Asbestos Hazard.** The Lancet June 17 1967.
18. **The Times. Special Report on Asbestos.** November 28th 1967.

Chapter 4

1. As a means of seeking to demonstrate exercise of control by Charter over its subsidiary Cape Asbestos, details such as this were disclosed in the case of **Parker v Bell Asbestos Mines Ltd. et al. 607F. 1985.** District Court for the Eastern District of Pennsylvania.
2. Ibid. **US Geological Survey.** Circular 1298. 2006.Ch.1.3.
3. Ibid. **Kaias & Cocopans. The Story of Mining in South Africa's Northern Cape.** Ch.1.4
4. Ibid. **Anglo American and the Rise of Modern South Africa.** Ch.3.4
5. **Cape Review 1980.**
6. **Final Report of the Advisory Committee on Asbestos.** HMSO. 1979.
7. **International Convention on the Safety of Life at Sea. (Solas) 1974.** It was not until 2002 that asbestos was banned in ships.
8. For an insight into the character of laggers see **The Politics of Asbestos. Understandings of Risk, Disease and Protest.** Linda Waldman. Earthscan. 2011. Also by the same Author **Through no Fault of Your Own. Asbestos Diseases in South Africa and the UK.** Institute of Development Studies. 301. 2008.
9. See **Isle of Grain Power Station. Hansard. UK Parliament.** 14th April and 20th June 1976..
10. A comprehensive account of asbestos litigation in the U.S.A can be found in **Asbestos Litigation.** Rand Institute for Civil Justice. 2005.
11. A detailed account of this and other cases including the reference to Dr Richard Gaze can be found in **Outrageous Misconduct. The Asbestos Industry on Trial.** Paul Brodeur. Pantheon Books . New York. 1985.
12. Revealed in **Adams and Others v Cape Industries PLC and Another.** 1984 A. No. 2597. Court of Appeal. 1990.
13. Refer **The Social Context of Occupational Disease: Asbestos and South Africa.** J Myers International Journal of Health Services. Vol II. No.2 1981.

Chapter 5 & 6

1. Ibid. **Parker v Bell Asbestos Mines** Ch.4.1.
2. Ibid. **The Way from Dusty Death.** Ch.1.15.
3. **Proposed Capital Re-Organisation** including a Proposed Issue of 8.4% Cumulative Redeemable Preference Shares. March 18th 1985.
4. **Cape News.1980.**
5. **Alice – Fight for Life.** Yorkshire TV July 20th 1982.
6. Ibid. **Outrageous Misconduct.** Ch.4.11.
7. Ibid. **Asbestos and Fire..** Ch. 1.2.
8. Ibid. **Kaias & Cocopans. The Story of Mining in South Africa's Northern Cape.** Ch.1.4.
9. **Recommendation from the Scientific Committee on Occupational Exposure Limits for Man-Made Mineral Fibres (MMMF)**. European Commission. 2012.
10. Ibid. **Adams v Cape Industries PLC.** Ch. 4.12.
11. **The Observer** January 8th 1984.
12. **The Times** June 28th 1988.
13. Johns-Manville's litigation is well covered in **Dirty Business, Exploring Corporate Misconduct.** Maurice Punch. Sage Publications. 1996.
14. Annual Reports Charter PLC 1980-85 and Ibid. **Parker v Bell Asbestos Mines** Ch.4.1
15. Ibid. **Adams v Cape Industries PLC. (**1990) CH 433. Ch.4.12.

Chapter 7

Illustrations from 'Cape News' are reproduced by permission of the Successors of Key Communications, publishers.

1. Interviewed in '**UK Firms to face Judgement on Lethal Foreign Industries'.** The Observer August 23rd 1998.
2. **Lawyers Leigh Day: Troublemakers who are a Thorn in the side of Multinationals.** The Observer. August 2nd 2015.
3. **Sithole & Others v Thor Chemicals.** (1999).All ER (D) 102 (CA). A good account is given in the Royal Institute for International Affairs briefing paper No 4 dated May 2002. **Corporate Accountability in Search of a Treaty?** Halina Ward.
4. **Connelly v RTZ Corporation PLC.** HL 24 July 1997. This and the Cape PLC South African litigation are well covered in Richard Meeran's **Tort Litigation against Multinational Corporations for Violation of Human Rights.** Ch.3.11.
5. Ibid. **The Politics of Asbestos.** Ch.4.8.
6. **Lubbe v Cape PLC** (1998) CLC 1559 (CA). See Chapter 8.1.
7. See **Cape News** 1998.
8. Refer **Shell Tankers Ltd v Jeremson.** CA 2001.
9. **Guidance for the Assessment of General Damages in Personal Injury Cases.** First Edition 1992.

Chapter 8

1. **Schalk Willem Burger Lubbe (Suing as Administrator of the Estate of Rachel Jacoba Lubbe) and 4 Others and Cape Plc. and Related Appeals.** July 20th 2000 [House of Lords decision].

2. **'Dying with Every Breath They Take'.** Daily Express. November 15th 1999.
3. House of Commons **Cape PLC Early Day Motion 449** March 18th 1999.
4. See **Free Capital. How 12 Private Investors made Millions in the Stock Market.** Guy Thomas. Harriman House Ltd. 2000.
5. See Richard Meeran's **Tort Litigation against Multinational Corporations for Violation of Human Rights.** Ch.3.11.
6. House of Commons **Cape PLC Early Day Motion 661** January 15th 2002.
7. 'Cape pays the Price as Justice Prevails'. Richard Meeran. The Times. January 15th 2002.
8. **Proposed Disposal of the Manufacturing Division**. Circular to Shareholders August 22th 2002.
9. **The Story of the Asbestos Relief Trust.** J te Water Naude. Occupational Health Southern Africa. 2014 .20.1
10. **Dust, Disease and Labour at Havelock Asbestos Mine, Swaziland.** Jock McCulloch. Journal of South African Studies. Vol 31. 2005.
11. See articles in **The Financial Times Special Report - The Asbestos Crisis.** September 9th 2002.

Chapter 9

1. **The Times.** November 26th 1996.
2. **'What Killed My Dad'.** BBC2 November 4th 2004.
3. See Shareholders Circular **'Proposed Scheme of Arrangement in Respect of Asbestos Liabilities and Placing'** dated 16 June 2005.
4. The original case was **Fairchild v Glenhaven Funeral Services.** (2002) UKHL 22.
5. The case to which the ruling applied was **Rothwell v Chemical & Insulating Co. Ltd.** 2007. UKHL 39.
6. See Scheme Creditors Circular **'Proposals for a Scheme of Arrangement between PLC and the other Scheme Companies and their respective Scheme Creditors'** dated 15 March 2006.

Chapters 10-12

1. Ibid. **Scheme Creditors Circular** Ch. 9.6.
2. **David Brian Chandler v Cape PLC** (2012) EWCA Civ.325.
3   Judgement **Cape Intermediate Holdings Ltd v Dring**. 2019 UKSC 38. And High Court Judgement 2020 EWHC 1873 (QB).
    Refer also https://asbestosforum.org.uk/cape-case
4   **Cape Holdings and Asbestos Research**. Parliamentary Motion EDM 93 May 23 2022.
5   **Mesothelioma Statistics for Great Britain**. HSE. November 2022 and **Occupational, Domestic and Environmental Mesothelioma Risks in Britain.** Ch.2.4.

In Conclusion (Page 222)

1. It is assumed that the shareholder did not take advantage of the 1980, 2004 or 2007 rights issues or the offer of Convertible Preference Shares in 1985.
2. It is not always clear from the accounts whether, at certain times the dividend tax is included or netted out. Given the short periods involved any correction to the figure would not be material.

3. IDC Charges - the figure of £292 million, represents the cumulative declared charge to the Profit and Loss Account between the years of 1953 and 2016, together with the Scheme of Arrangement funding and is based on the following:

The Company began declaring the amounts being paid or reserved to cover IDC in 1973 when a provision was established. Prior to that date IDC sufferers were entitled to and were paid compensation for industrial disease both in the UK and South Africa. This was charged as a working cost and not quantified in the accounts. The inclusion of these costs would have the affect of increasing the total figure, particularly if at today's prices. In 1996, former Managing Director Geoffrey Higham, in a deposition arising from the USA litigation, stated that some £50 million of compensation had been dispensed within the previous twenty years. This figure compares with £21 million declared in the accounts and included in this analysis.

In 1979/80 the amount provided in the P&L account was based on the quantification of claims lodged and outstanding at the end of the financial year, any additional charge required being written off against trading profit. This was subsequently the basis on which future provisions were made. So additional charges subsequently made were not quantified. For example in the case of pleural plaque claims settled on a wrap up basis, the amount expended could well exceed the provision. But it is also possible that there could have been a write back of provisions if they proved more than required.

Provisions were made net of insurance recoveries; however it is possible that subsequent claim resolution involved some further insurance recovery.

Provisions were made net of tax relief. Long term provision figures charged against the P&L Account were discounted reflecting the time elapsing between the setting of the provision and the anticipated cash call. Adjustments were made annually reflecting changes in interest rates.

It is considered that taking all these factors into account the figure of £292 million is well supported on the basis described above. The amount expended against the total provided up to December 31st 2016 was £118 million, leaving a balance of £172 million to cover the insurance settlements and future IDC liabilities.

Index

Individual Cape entities are listed under 'Cape Companies', which may also contain country references. For asbestos and related references look to headings 'Asbestos' and 'Industrial Disease'.

Biographical Note

A graduate of Cambridge and Durham Universities, Peter Gartside's early career was spent with refrigeration engineers Hall-Thermotank International before joining Cape in 1977. In 1980 he was appointed Managing Director of Cape Contracts Overseas and was responsible for the development of the industrial services business in the Middle East, South East Asia and Australia. Assuming the position of Managing Director, International, this involved additional responsibility for the European businesses. During this period the company won the Queens Award for Export/Technology on two occasions. After attempting to retire twice he continued to work for the company in an executive and consultancy role. This book follows an earlier publication 'Millennium to Millennium. Kelshall – A History'. He lives near Cambridge and other interests include church restoration and music.